CREATING THE PROJECT OFFICE

CREATING THE PROJECT OFFICE

A Manager's Guide to Leading
Organizational Change

Randall L. Englund
Robert J. Graham
Paul C. Dinsmore

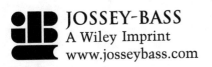

JOSSEY-BASS
A Wiley Imprint
www.josseybass.com

Published by Jossey-Bass
A Wiley Imprint
989 Market Street, San Francisco, CA 94103-1741   www.josseybass.com

Page 308 is a continuation of the copyright page.

Jossey-Bass books and products are available through most bookstores. To contact Jossey-Bass directly
call our Customer Care Department within the U.S. at 800-956-7739, outside the U.S. at 317-572-3986
or fax 317-572-4002.

Jossey-Bass also publishes its books in a variety of electronic formats. Some content that appears in print
may not be available in electronic books.

Library of Congress Cataloging-in-Publication Data

Englund, Randall L.
    Creating the project office : a manager's guide to leading
organizational change / by Randall L. Englund, Robert J. Graham, Paul C.
Dinsmore.
        p. cm.
Includes bibliographical references and index.
    ISBN 0-7879-6398-4
  1. Project management—Handbooks, manuals, etc. 2. Organizational
change—Handbooks, manuals, etc. I. Graham, Robert J., 1946- II.
Dinsmore, Paul C. III. Title.
    HD69.P75 E54 2003
    658.4'04—dc21

                                            2002152396

FIRST EDITION
HB Printing   10 9 8 7 6 5 4 3 2 1

THE JOSSEY-BASS BUSINESS & MANAGEMENT SERIES

CONTENTS

PREFACE

Faster, cheaper, better. Accidental project manager. In or out? Are you done yet? We're in a mess! Why can't we . . . ? If these challenges sound familiar within your organization, welcome aboard.

This is a book about improving organizational performance by implementing a project office system that develops project management as a core competency and thus adds value to the organization. A project office consists of a team dedicated to improving the practice of project management in the organization. The improvement in organizational performance is achieved by obtaining more value from projects, making project management a standard management practice, and then moving the organization toward the enterprise project management concept.

Enterprise project management is an organization-wide managerial philosophy. It is based on the idea that company goals are achievable through a web of simultaneous projects supported by a systemic approach that includes corporate strategy projects, operations improvement, and organizational transformation as well as traditional development projects. This means that companies view marketing programs, advertising campaigns, promotional events, new product launches, software development, change management, and continuous improvement, as well as traditional design and construction of new facilities, as *projects*, using project management approaches to bring them to completion. Virtually everything can be dealt with as a project under the enterprise project management concept.

The project office is the linchpin for implementing and maintaining a project approach across the organization. The project office is a gigantic building block for making enterprise project management become a reality in an organization. The project office adds value to the organization by ensuring that projects are performed within procedures, are in line with organizational strategies, and are completed in a way that adds economic value to the organization.

The audience for this book includes everyone involved in project management—project managers, team members, and middle and upper managers attempting to change their organizations into project-based enterprises. All projects involve change and thus every project manager and team member is involved in an organizational change process. Since the emphasis here is on improving the organization through better project management practices, this book will help project participants and managers at all levels make sense of the change processes they are experiencing.

Inexperience and ignorance about leading organizational change can be costly to the organization and the individual. We are not wont to disagree with an early reviewer who said, "This book can save careers." Another added, "This book can save organizations!"

The book began as a result of workshops on the topic of *Implementing the Project Office for Organizational Change,* sponsored by the Strategic Management Group and R. J. Graham and Associates. These workshops blended consultants and practitioners (most writers for this book participated, along with a few of their friends), who worked through the problems and processes of changing organizations to embrace the enterprise project management concept. This book reflects the material covered during those workshops as well as contributions from a constituency of consultants and practitioners through lifelong experiences. Contributors to the book include consultants Graham, Dinsmore, and Cohen, along with practitioners Storeygard, Bucero, and LaGassey. Englund plays a dual role, currently a consultant but drawing on many years as a practitioner and in an HP project office. Many other professionals also graciously shared their learning and worked their way into the collective knowledge compiled herein.

The design of the book is the result of suggestions from workshop participants. Other books on the project office acknowledge the importance of the office in facilitating change in the organization. Despite this acknowledgment, however, concepts on using a project office as a vehicle for organizational change are often left to the last chapter, almost an afterthought. Workshop participants who were currently working on implementing project offices agreed that this emphasis, although important, came too late. It is difficult to change the perception and function of any organizational entity after it has been established. Therefore, if the ultimate goal is to change the organization, then that should be the focus from the beginning. That is why we wrote this book.

The emphasis in this book is not on the day-to-day operation of the project office, although that topic is covered. Rather, the focus is the process of implementing a project office in an organization with the goal of bringing about organizational change that ultimately adds to the economic value of the organization.

Not every reader plans to go all the way to implement the *full Monty*—a strategic project office—and some may even get discouraged by the pitfalls we describe. However, we also include specific skill-building approaches and revised ways to think about things that offer value to these readers. The implications of power, operating across organizations, and project portfolio management processes are examples. These have wider applications than just a project office, but are even more potent when the PO leads the effort. We draw from a variety of fields and historical references in pursuit of our goal to cover the *why, what,* and *how* to lead the organizational change process.

PO of One

The term *project office* is not without baggage. For some people it means overhead and bureaucracy. They want a lean organization where competencies and action are dispersed across the organization, not in a central (expensive) unit. These same people may ask if they can establish POs of one, meaning that each project manager embodies all the traits, skills, and knowledge that we cover in this book.

We believe a PO of one is a worthy concept. We are talking about an organizational culture that supports the essence of a project office but not its structure. Individuals learning to unfreeze, change, and refreeze the people around them offer tremendous value. The steps along the path we describe can be taken by individual project managers. In fact, they may not have that title; they just happen to be doing projects or leading a change effort. They want the results they create through a set of activities to be great instead of average, and the outcome to contribute and fit with organizational goals instead of going on the shelf. The missing pieces that help make this happen are the process, experiences, and knowledge of best practices.

A PO of one may not be an established norm or term in usage, but it can live in the hearts and aspirations of devotees. We hope this book provides inspiration. We also hope that success then expands enterprise project management possibilities to higher levels of maturity.

Book Organization and Outline

Organizational change comes in three phases, so this book is organized in three parts to follow those phases. The first outlines ways to create the conditions for organizational change. The second covers operating the project office to make the changes themselves, and the third goes through consolidating the changes to embed them in organizational reality.

Part One consists of the first five chapters of the book. Chapter One covers the problems associated with organizational change processes and gives a step-by-step guide to the process of using a project office as organizational change vehicle. Chapter Two gives more detail on the first important step of that process, creating a sense of urgency for the change and making sure that the result of the change will ultimately add economic value to the organization. Any change process involves power and politics, so Chapter Three is a program manager's guide to organizational politics with an aim toward using that knowledge for creating a powerful coalition for change. Chapter Four covers many of the details concerning the functions and operations of a project office so that organizational change agents begin to develop a vision, strategy, and communications plan to let people know what the office is and what it does. Chapter Five is a case study showing how many of the concepts covered in the first four chapters were applied at 3M.

Chapter Six begins the second part of the book, covering the problems and processes of managing change when the project office begins to have first contact with members of the organization. Chapter Seven is a case study from HP Spain that shows how the manager of that project office managed its interface with the rest of the organization. Chapter Eight is another case study, from a U.S. Air Force Base in Italy, that describes implementing a project office in a very short time, under rapidly changing conditions, and in a highly bureaucratic organization. Chapter Nine calls on information from case studies as it covers the important topics of staffing and operating the project office.

Chapters Ten and Eleven cover the final part of the change process, that of consolidating the changes to make them an organizational reality. In these chapters we acknowledge that most change processes fail because they only develop surface changes and leave the basic assumptions of organization members untouched. Chapter Ten covers the steps necessary to change basic assumptions of organization members and thus integrate the new processes into the organizational culture. Chapter Eleven adds a few more important insights into the process, and discusses the action-planning templates in the Appendix, whose use will help make the changes stick.

We are aware that organizational change is a messy process and that few potential readers for this book will follow the seemingly smooth process outlined here. In fact, readers may find themselves at different points on the continuum of change that the book proposes. However, we believe there is potential value for all readers, regardless of where they are in the process.

For those just beginning to think about implementing a project office, the first two parts are most important. The ideas and case studies presented in these sections preview problems you will face, along with suggestions from those who have gone before you. If you have implemented a project office but find that progress has stalled, you will probably find Part One very helpful. People who experienced stalled implementations report that they did not spend enough time—or *any* time—creating the initial conditions for organizational change. Reviewing the first five chapters of this book may highlight important elements that were missed, elements that when put in place will move the implementation forward. Those readers who have a project office operating successfully will probably want to concentrate on Parts Two and Three so that they can prepare to consolidate the changes and finally make an effective and efficient project-based organization an organizational reality.

The path is arduous but worthy. We offer steps along the pathway and point out probable hurdles and roadblocks, based on experiences of others. The hero's journey includes options to push on, modify your approach, or stop. This book is designed to be your partner along the way.

January 2003

Randall L. Englund
Burlingame, California

Robert J. Graham
Mendocino, California

Paul C. Dinsmore
Rio de Janeiro, Brazil

To all the executives, project managers, and professionals
who contributed directly or indirectly to this work by providing
their experiences to be shared with the reading public.

THE AUTHORS AND CONTRIBUTORS

Authors

Randall L. Englund is an independent executive consultant, author, trainer, and speaker, serving to guide management and project teams through an organic approach to project management. His background was as a senior project manager at Hewlett-Packard Company (HP) in the Project Management Initiative, whose purpose, as a corporate project office, was to lead the continuous improvement of project management across the company.

During twenty-two years at HP, Englund consulted with product developers on cross-organizational projects, developed workshops, documented best practices, and assisted teams to conduct project start-up meetings, implement project management practices, and prioritize project portfolios. He was a program manager in computer system product development and a major account marketing engineer. He also worked in field service for General Electric Medical Systems.

He holds a B.S.E.E. from the University of California, Santa Barbara, an M.B.A. in management from San Francisco State University, and an honorary engineering and management degree from Cal Poly State University, San Luis Obispo, and attended Stanford University's Mastering the Project Portfolio Program. He is certified by the Product Development and Management Association as a New Product Development Professional and as a Certified Business Manager by the Association of Professionals in Business Management.

Englund and Graham joined forces, leveraging their practitioner, consulting, and executive education skills, to coauthor the book *Creating an Environment for Successful Projects: The Quest to Manage Project Management.* Both are frequent contributors to the Project Management Institute (PMI), as presenters, workshop facilitators, and authors.

You can reach Randall Englund at englundr@pacbell.net.

Robert J. Graham is an independent management consultant in project management and organizational change. Previously he was a senior staff member of The Management and Behavioral Sciences Center at The Wharton School, University of Pennsylvania. While at Wharton he taught in the MBA and Ph.D. programs and was a part of the Wharton Effective Executive program teaching project management to practicing executives.

Graham held visiting professor positions at the University of Bath and the University of the German Armed Forces. He was adjunct professor at the University of Pennsylvania and the Project Management Unit at Henley Management College in England. His first book was *Project Management as if People Mattered,* followed by *Creating an Environment for Successful Projects,* and then, with Dennis Cohen, *The Project Manager's MBA: How to Translate Project Decisions into Business Success.*

He developed a simulation, *The Complete Project Manager,* where participants make decisions and receive feedback around a number of behavioral issues in project management. The Strategic Management Group delivers a full multimedia version as a computer simulation called *Project Leadership.*

Graham has a B.S. in systems analysis from Miami University, as well as an M.B.A. and Ph.D. in operations research from the University of Cincinnati. He was a postdoctoral fellow at The Wharton School. In addition, he has an M.S. in cultural anthropology from the University of Pennsylvania. He earned Project Management Professional (PMP) certification from the Project Management Institute.

You can reach Robert Graham at otto@mcn.org.

Paul C. Dinsmore is president of Dinsmore Associates and a highly respected specialist in project management and organizational change. He received the Distinguished Contributions Award and Fellow from the Project Management Institute. He regularly consults and speaks in North America, South America, Europe, and Africa. He is the author or editor of numerous articles and several books, including *Winning in Business with Enterprise Project Management* and the *AMA Handbook of Project Management.* Dinsmore, a certified project management professional (PMP), writes the "Up & Down the Organization" column for the Project Management Institute's *PM Network* magazine.

Dinsmore has a B.S. in electrical engineering from Texas Tech University, a postgraduate degree in business administration from Getulio Vargas Foundation in São Paulo, Brazil, and attended the Advanced Management Program at Harvard Business School.

You can reach Paul Dinsmore at dinsmore@amcham.com.br.

Contributors

Alfonso Bucero, PMP, is now an independent project management consultant and speaker. He is operations manager of the International Institute for Learning (IIL) for Spain and Portugal. His background was as a project manager at Hewlett-Packard Consulting, where he developed and managed the PMO implementation whose purpose was the continuous improvement of project management discipline across the organization. He assisted in rolling out the PMO practices to a global project office.

During his thirteen years at HP he managed various customer, infrastructure, development, and change management projects. He spent the last two years at HP selling and implementing the project office; his case, presented in this book, explains the problems he had, the things he learned, and the way he contributed to organizational change through a PMO implementation. Bucero has a B.S. degree in computer science engineering, and he is a frequent contributor to international project management conferences and project office workshops.

Dennis J. Cohen is vice president and executive of the Project Management Practice area for the Strategic Management Group in Philadelphia, Pennsylvania. He works with clients to maximize project performance. He coauthored, with Robert Graham, the book *The Project Manager's MBA: How to Translate Project Decisions into Business Results.* He served the Wharton School as a research associate, senior fellow, and adjunct assistant professor of management, teaching courses in management and entrepreneurship and leading seminars in executive education programs. Cohen holds B.A. and M.A. degrees from the University of California, Berkeley, and an M.B.A. from the Wharton School of the University of Pennsylvania, as well as M.A. and Ph.D. degrees from the University of Wisconsin.

Colonel Gary C. LaGassey is program manager of Aviano 2000, the largest air base construction program in NATO and the U.S. Air Force. His Program Management

Office manages and integrates all aspects of the 264-project, $530 million upgrade of Aviano Air Base, Italy. He has been a deputy base commander and support group commander. Operational assignments include duty as a Minuteman launch officer. Staff assignments include duty as a major command inspector general team member, as a missile operations staff officer, and as a political military planner at the Pentagon.

He earned a B.A. degree in political science from the University of Maryland and an M.A. degree in public administration from the University of Northern Colorado. He is also a graduate of the U.S. Air Force Air War College and the NATO Defense College. Among his numerous military awards are the Legion of Merit and the NATO Medal for his role in the air combat campaigns in Bosnia (1995) and Kosovo (1999). LaGassey frequently presents at PMI Symposiums about his project office experiences.

Robert L. Storeygard, PMP, is an advanced project management specialist and is the 3M Traffic Control Materials Division (TCM) Project Office. He authored the extensive 3M Project Leadership Curriculum and teaches a number of project management-related classes at 3M. He is also the past chair and current international outreach chair of the 3M PMSIG, representing three thousand project managers and leaders throughout 3M worldwide. Storeygard works extensively in 3M's International environment, helping to deploy PM best practices throughout 3M's Latin American and Asian subsidiaries. In addition, he works with numerous St. Paul, Austin, and other plant sites, departments, and divisions to teach, consult, and help deploy PM in their business and technology areas.

He is a member of the Project Management Institute and a PMP Certification Instructor, served as the Minnesota vice president of professional development and the National PMI Education Specific Interest Group (SIG) co-chair. Storeygard speaks at many U.S. and international conferences on project and portfolio management, as well as the project office, and his work and writings have been published in numerous articles, presentations, and several books. Storeygard has B.A. degrees in education and attended postgraduate courses in project management.

He suggests, "If you need internal support for your PM efforts and project offices, you need to read Chapter Five, because without it you will be pushing rope uphill!"

CREATING THE PROJECT OFFICE

PART ONE

CREATING THE CONDITIONS FOR CHANGE

We write this book from the point of view of advising a small group of people, call them *change agents*, who are attempting to implement a project office to make the organization more project-friendly. Not all readers will be directly charged with implementing organizational change. However, since most readers are involved with project management, they will be involved with assisting in that change. People involved in change processes often find them chaotic and seemingly without logic. Understanding the entire change process from the point of view of the change agents directing it helps all participants better understand what is happening and why. Understanding the motives and logic of the leaders helps create better participants and followers. Each individual can also apply these steps to personal projects.

To move along the path of organizational change, we break the journey into three segments, comprising creating the conditions for change, making the change happen, and making change stick. The first one, creating the conditions for change, is covered in the next five chapters. Figure I.1 illustrates the complete journey.

Figure I.1 depicts a small group of people, the team of change agents, beginning a trek from the lower left corner. They are in a storm. Visions of a sunny paradise (upper right corner) feel like fantasy but still capture their imagination as something they want to achieve, something much better than their current reality. Not quite revealed to them yet is the complex journey they face. Each step along the twisted path is a chapter in this book.

FIGURE I.1. THE PATHWAY TO CHANGE.

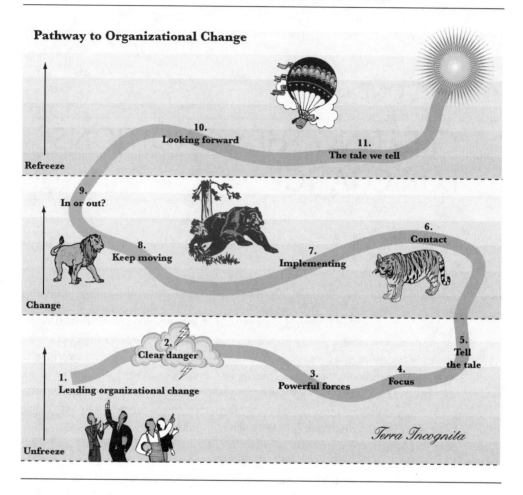

Pathway to Organizational Change

Refreeze

10.
Looking forward

11.
The tale we tell

9.
In or out?

6.
Contact

8.
Keep moving

7.
Implementing

Change

5.
Tell
the tale

2.
Clear danger

3.
Powerful forces

4.
Focus

1.
Leading organizational change

Terra Incognita

Unfreeze

Since the mission is to implement a project office as a vehicle for organizational change, the first step on the journey is to discover the processes necessary to lead an organization to change. Following the process outlined in Chapter One, the team identifies many clear dangers. Some of these dangers may lead to sidetracks or discontinuing the journey. To go onward the change agents need to create or identify a sense of urgency for the change among other members of the organization as well as determine how their efforts will add value to the organization. Once they figure this out, the team realizes it has little chance of success without developing some clout to deal with powerful political forces. The change agents understand that few people will listen to them just because they have a good idea. So the next step on the journey is to develop political acumen, a powerful sponsor, and a coalition of organization members that help guide them on their journey. With backing from that group, they proceed to focus on what functions the project office will perform, how those functions will add value to the organization, and how they expect those functions to expand and grow. This vision and strategy is put into a succinct plan and a language that others in the organization understand so that the team of change agents can tell their tale—harness internal support—to enlist the help of the entire organization.

This period spent creating the conditions that will enable change is critical to the success of the entire endeavor. Project managers recognize this time as akin to the preparation of a project plan, which indeed it is. It is also the honeymoon period for the project team, for during this time—while the project office is being discussed—it will not yet affect people's lives. That being the case, the project team can expect that serious opposition will not yet be formed. This is analogous to the "hundred days" that new U.S. presidents typically have before serious opposition mounts to their policies and programs. The change agent team can expect serious opposition to arise after this part of the journey is completed. Not known yet is what awaits them in the middle section of Figure I.1. Implementation usually requires invading new territories or jungles—other functional areas or businesses. Sensing invaders, the lions, tigers, and bears emerge from hiding places in the forest, ready to attack. For the change agent team to be ready for this opposition, they need to develop political acumen while time is available.

Since the first part of the journey is a planning period, the team can expect the usual problems associated with project planning. Some will say the planning is a waste of time. Some may press for quick results and eschew the entire idea of planning. Others may agitate to quicken the process and get into action sooner. But project and program managers know better. They know that planning is essential for success and can easily take 40 percent of the entire time allotted to a project. For those who insist on skipping this first phase and taking a shortcut, we offer two cautionary tales.

Cautionary Tales

Lands beyond the bounds of the known world tantalized the imaginations of ancient scholars, inspiring visions of a lush empire far to the south. Maps, drawn from supposition and mysticism, identified this area as *Terra Incognita*, the unknown land, newly discovered but not yet fully known. Only centuries later when brave sailors traveled south did they discover the world was much different. As we now know, the maps were incorrect, and their assumptions were false. However, what lies beyond boundaries is always mysterious and awaits discovery. The emptiness tantalizes us to explore and conquer this space.

Organizational change agents exploring the future of project management face similar challenges as the earlier explorers. Misconceptions abound about what is possible. Newly discovered fads drive managers to launch ill-conceived projects or initiatives. Modern explorers also face unknowns, resistance, and chaos.

More recently, in the spring of 1846, a group of immigrants set out from Illinois to make the two-thousand-mile journey to California. They planned to use the well-known Oregon Trail. One part of this group, the Donner party, was determined to reach California quickly and so decided to take a shortcut. They traveled with a larger group until reaching the Little Sandy River. At this point the larger party turned north, taking the longer route up through Oregon and then to California. The Donner party headed south, taking an untried route known as Hasting's Cutoff. Since no one, including Hastings himself, had ever tried this cutoff, they had little idea of what to expect. Their first barrier was the Great Salt Lake Desert, where they encountered conditions that they never imagined—searing heat by day and frigid winds at night. A more formidable barrier was encountered in the Sierras. After a severe snowstorm on October 31 blocked the trail, the party was forced to camp in makeshift cabins or tents just to the east of the pass that today bears their name. The majority of these unfortunates spent a starving, frozen winter—the worst ever recorded in the Sierras—trapped in the mountains. The few survivors of that camp, who wound up resorting to cannibalism to make it through the winter, reached California long after the other members of the original Illinois group—and in far worse spirits.

The first conclusion that can be drawn for the project office team is that many have gone before you with a journey of organizational change. Their collective experience forms the equivalent of the Oregon Trail, a process showing a known way to reach the desired goal. Although this path may seem long, ignore it at your own peril. Second, although the Oregon Trail was well known and well traveled, it was not necessarily easy. There were many difficulties along that trail and no doubt some people died even though they were on the known route. So taking the Oregon Trail is no guarantee of success—but it seems to greatly increase the chances. Finally, taking a shortcut leads into unknown territory like the Great Salt Lake Desert or *Terra Incognita*—the unknown land—as illustrated in Figure I.1. The route may look good on the map, but the map is not the territory. The best advice we give those considering a shortcut is from Virginia Reed, a Donner party survivor, who said, "Remember, never take no cutoffs and hurry along as fast as you can."

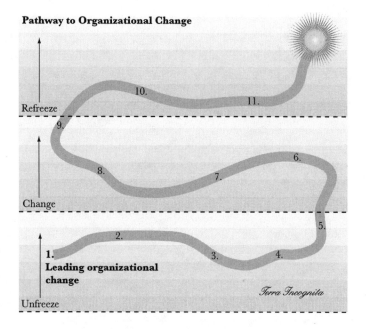

Pathway to Organizational Change

Refreeze

Change

1.
Leading organizational change

Unfreeze

Terra Incognita

This chapter begins by describing the project office concept and introducing the idea that the members of the project office need to think and act as organizational change agents. This is followed by a discussion of the idea of planned organizational change and the role of the change agents in that process. The change theme is then further developed by detailing the steps involved in implementing a project office aimed at leading the change process. The steps include establishing a sense of urgency, developing political acumen, creating a guiding coalition, developing a vision and strategy, communicating the change vision, developing short-term wins, developing broad-based action, consolidating the successes, and making the change stick. These steps will allow you to develop a project office that can lead the change to a project-based organization.

CHAPTER ONE

LEADING ORGANIZATIONAL CHANGE

Abandon despair all ye who enter here.

Dante's *Inferno* opens on the evening of Good Friday in the year 1300. Traveling through a dark wood, Dante Alighieri has lost his path and now wanders fearfully through the forest. The sun shines down on a mountain above him, and he attempts to climb up to it but finds his way blocked by three beasts—a leopard, a lion, and a she-wolf. Frightened and helpless, Dante returns to the dark wood. Here he encounters the ghost of Virgil, the great Roman poet, who has come to guide Dante back to his path and to the top of the mountain.

This book is your Virgil—a guide for all those involved with project management and the move toward project-based organizations. It depicts the journey or process of changing an organization to be more efficient and more profitable by developing an organization-wide project management system, often called enterprise project management.

The enterprise approach to managing projects is a managerial philosophy based on the principle that company goals are achievable through a web of simultaneous projects that calls for a systemic approach and includes corporate strategy projects, operational improvement, and organizational transformation, as well as traditional development projects. The concept is based on the idea that prosperity depends on adding value to business, and that value is added by systematically implementing projects of all types across the enterprise. If those projects are managed effectively, then the company's bottom line will be greatly enhanced.

Some readers may feel like Dante, facing an unknown ordeal to achieve success that can only be imagined. Many obstacles appear like beasts along the dark path. You, too, look for a guide and a way to reach the top of the mountain—and have found one here. Unlike Dante, however, you will need to enlist others to join you in the quest; no one can carry a project office alone.

Many organizations have attempted to improve their abilities and project management over the last decade. Much of this attempt met with limited success. People were sent out to be trained as project managers, only to find that when they returned to the organization they were not allowed to perform in the way they were trained. As people and organizations discovered that the individual training approach was not leading to improvements, there arose a movement where a person or group of people in the organization were charged with, or charged up about, systematically improving project management practice across the entire organization, thus helping the organization to change to an enterprise project management system.

This venturesome group has any number of names, including a Project Management Initiative or a Project Management Center of Excellence, with the umbrella name *project office* currently in vogue. As these groups became successful, they found that more of their effort was associated with organizational change than with the practice of project management itself. Thus these groups became primary change agents, either self-proclaimed or assigned, for the process of implementing enterprise project management.

Many participants in the project office movement were surprised to discover their role as change agents. Many lamented that to be effective in this role they should have initiated the office as an organizational change approach in the first place. This book takes just that approach and assumes that a project office, when properly implemented, will become a leading vehicle driving the organization toward project-based operations and thus enterprise project management. The book aims at helping develop this group of change agents so that their efforts will be enthusiastically applied throughout the organization, helping them bring about real change in the organization and avoid ending up as just another staff group.

This book is written by a combination of consultants and practitioners. As consultants, the primary authors extract general principles for implementing a project office and present these in chapters. There are also contributions from practitioners who are in the trenches, actually running project offices and applying many of the same general principles. This combination of general principles and real-life examples—theory with theory-in-practice—present an excellent road map for future practitioners to use.

The Developing Project Office Movement

Project management has its roots in the construction and engineering trade. Project management began outside the organization—the original project offices were in trailers parked out on construction sites. Introduction of PERT charts ushered project management into organizational settings. The real impetus to developing project management was its use in software projects and other new product development projects. Over time, and probably after a number of resounding failures, it became evident that project management was an important skill, one that should be developed in order to avoid future failures. Looking further into the future, some organizations began to see project management skill as a competitive advantage. Groups were formed to look into the situation and it was at this point, about the late 1980s and early 1990s, that we began to see project office groups emerge. This situation, at AT&T, is typical of the period:

> A small group of dedicated project managers, who had found each other in business meetings, conferences and classes, realized that they shared the same passion for project management. This group decided to band together to address the prevalent project management issues that existed at that time— constrained resources, lack of standard process or methodology, little or no training requirements and inconsistent project performance. They knew that most project managers in our company were operating within independent circles, without a consistent way of doing project management. Managers of project managers were using different criteria to determine what should be project managed. Very few project managers had much organizational support and fewer still were trained in project management. Most, when they did act as project managers, had it as a secondary job function [Schneidmuller and Balaban, 2000, p. 1].

Things were similar in other organizations that addressed project management problems. Most people became project manager by accident, and they were appointed to the task because they had time available, not because they had any particular project management skill. Projects were not run using any consistent methodology, if they were using any methodology at all. This lack of project management skill, methodology, and organizational support led to most projects' being late, over budget, and not done to customer satisfaction.

To combat this problem, groups arose such as the Project Management Initiative at HP, described in Chapter 9 of Graham and Englund (1997). This group was specific to the engineering function and concentrated mainly on new product development projects, so others arose in other divisions, such as the project office developed for HP Consulting, described here in Chapter Seven. In addition, more organization-wide groups emerged, such as the Project Management Special Interest Group (PMSIG) at 3M, described in Chapter Five, and the Project Management Center of Excellence at IBM, AT&T, and NCR, to name a few. This movement to develop project offices is also spreading worldwide. The Star Alliance, involving United and a dozen or so other airlines is one case, as is Embraer, a leading airliner manufacturer in Brazil.

Project office development is also happening across the organization, because the enterprise project management concept can be applied to a business unit, a department, or an entire corporation. It is useful to think of it in terms of levels and typical names:

Level 1	Project level	Project Control Office (PCO)
Level 2	Division or department level	Project or Program Office Project Management Center of Excellence (PMCOE)
Level 3	Corporate level	Strategic Project Office (SPO)

Thus as long as there is a multifunctional environment that requires the simultaneous management of numerous projects, the concept remains valid. This means that an IT department could well use such an approach and continue to interface with the rest of the functional organization even if the corporation did not undergo a full conversion to the concept. At the lowest level one can find project offices devoted to one large project or one program. These project office groups can also be designed to work in one department, for one division, or for one geographic location. At the highest level we find project office groups attempting to change management practices throughout the entire organization.

This highest-level group, the strategic project office, is the one that has the best chance for directing real organizational change. It is toward this group that this book ultimately aims. However, since project offices normally evolve toward that highest level rather than start there, we describe all types of offices and change processes involved in the evolution to the strategic or organization-wide project office. We also offer specific steps and skills that individual change agents can apply to improve personal effectiveness.

The roadblocks for moving an organization project-ward are invariably the stakeholders. Although lack of resources can also be an obstacle, people present the major challenges. Principal stakeholders for enterprise project management implementation are top management, project managers and team members, functional managers, internal change agents, and consulting support personnel (internal or external). If the initiative is top-down, starting with upper management, then the effort of getting buy-in from the rest of the organization must be taken on. If, on the other hand, the idea is filtering from the bottom upward, the sometimes monumental task of getting top management to provide support for the effort calls for skillful articulation and great persistence. In this book, we present a change process that begins at the bottom and concentrates on developing project management capabilities within one part of the organization, then later relying on a top-down approach to spread those capabilities organization-wide.

Failure in implementing a project office is generally triggered by a combination of factors such as lack of top management support, underestimating the scope of organizational change necessary, lack of methodology for managing projects, insufficient efforts for developing competent project professionals, bad timing, and inadequate management of the change process. Any one of these factors is enough to set askew an effort to implement the enterprise project management concept. However, people who have had difficulties with project office implementation usually say they should have taken a change management approach from the beginning. That is, they usually began by concentrating on the functions of the office itself rather than on the change process necessary to implement such an office. This book examines the implementation processes of successful offices and uses that approach to develop a general framework for success.

Organizational Life Cycles and Approaches to Planned Change

To understand the need for organizational change, it is instructive to look at a typical organization life cycle. To an outsider, an organization may look to be in a constant state of change. Much of the change in organizations can be seen as random shifts or reactions to competitor's product changes. Occasionally, however, organizations need planned change. The reasoning behind that suggestion is something like this. Organizations typically exploit new technology to help solve problems. As these organizations grow they institute policies and procedures that help them solve problems, both internal problems and problems of external customers they serve. If these policies, procedures, or general ways of doing things are successful, then the organization itself is successful and thrives. Over time, however, customers' problems change. For the organization to continue to thrive, it must change the solution procedures or search for customers who have the old problems that it can solve. At some point the pool of people with the old problems dries up. When that happens the organization will be forced to change its solution processes to solve the new problems or else cease to exist. And that is when the organization needs deliberate change processes. Many organizations find themselves in this position today as they move toward enterprise project management.

This need to change to more project-based procedures has recently emerged as a necessary change in the life cycles of many organizations because more of their work has become project work. As mentioned earlier, organizations began by instituting procedures to solve particular problems, normally repeated procedures aimed at producing standard products. Since these organizations have survived, we know that these procedures worked to solve the problems they faced. These procedures were later refined, enlarged, and taught to succeeding generations of workers so that the organization could enjoy the economies of scale. Procedures for developing new products or custom-made products were often haphazard as these products were usually considered to be one-offs and were a very small part of the organization's business. Over time, however, this changed dramatically for most organizations. The commercial life span of most standard products declined rapidly, giving rise to the need for project management in the new product development process. Custom-made products or systems solutions became the norm rather than the exception, giving rise to the need for project management in the product production process. This change was accompanied by the rise in the use of computers and the need for computer software and all aspects of organizational function, giving rise to the need for project management in the software development process. Changes in the environment, changes in customer expectations, and changes in the technology used in organizational processes have brought many organizations to the point where up to 80 percent of their work is project work rather than repeat process work. These organizations are at the point in their life cycles where they need planned organizational change to become project-based enterprises.

Planned organizational changes involve a conscious process with a specified leader, specified goals, and a time line. That is, it is itself a project, and the project manager should be the person in charge of implementing the project office. The overall goal of organizational change is to institute new processes and procedures that make enterprise project management the norm for the organization. The time line will depend on many factors including the age of the organization, how deeply ingrained its current procedures are, the degree of threat the organization faces, and the amount of support given by top management. In most large organizations this process can easily span three to five or even ten years.

Roles in the Change Process

Four key roles must be played effectively in implementing change fully and successfully:

- *Sponsors:* These are people who legitimize the change. They have the political and economic resources required to initiate and sustain a change project in an organization.
- *Change agents:* These people are responsible, with the sponsor's approval, for planning and executing the change project. Most of their activities focus on the targets of the change.
- *Targets:* These are the people who must alter the way they work as a result of the change. Targets are extremely important and active players in the implementation process.
- *Advocates:* These are the people who would like to see a change project idea happen but are not in a position to sponsor it. They, in effect, have a project and want to identify potential sponsors and persuade them to initiate it.

From our experience, the move toward enterprise project management normally begins with a group of advocates, a group of dedicated people in the organization who want to improve project management. On rarer occasions, the movement is initiated by an upper management sponsor. If the quest is begun by advocates, it quickly becomes imperative for them to find an upper management sponsor, someone with enough clout to bring about organizational change. The change agents are that small group of the most zealous advocates who become members of the original project office. This group often consists of practicing project managers who want to spread the good word of project management throughout the organization. The targets are usually other project managers, then project team members, and finally all members of the organization.

Organizational Change Versus Reorganization

Planned organizational change should not be confused with reorganization. When most people think of organizational change they think of the recurring "reorg," where departments are shuffled and lines redrawn on the organization chart. Participants in this seemingly annual ritual soon recognize that reorganization itself rarely results in real behavioral change. The usual result is that the same people sit in different seats but produce the same products by the same processes and for the same customers.

Reorganizations are wonderful for creating the illusion of progress while ensuring that nothing fundamentally changes. It is an attempt to get something for nothing—a feeling of the pleasure of progress without having to go through any of the pain associated with real change. Reorganizations are so closely associated with organizational change that those charged with such changes are tempted to reach for the organization chart first thing. In fact, a reorganization is probably the last step in any change process, a step taken to solidify changes already in place.

It is far more effective to eschew attacking the organization chart and instead begin by determining what needs to be done to develop real change in organizations. You can get any change process off to a good start by assembling a group of people who want to change, having them demonstrate how the change is good for the organization, and then working to have this change adopted throughout the organization. We call this the "Quaker" approach to organizational change (Englund and Graham, 2001). The successful movement to develop project offices will eventually lead to radical change in organization practices. As with any radical change process, those in the vanguard—the people implementing the offices—will often feel like missionaries introducing new practices into a hostile environment. Early missionaries found it difficult to get other people to change their ways, and some of them suffered mightily from the wrath of people they were trying to change. Legends tell us how quiet, nonthreatening Quakers found a better way.

Many missionaries used a heavy-handed, command-oriented approach. Proud native peoples rebelled and many missionaries were killed. The Quakers, however, set up farms and produced bountiful harvests. When hungry natives saw evidence of a rich harvest, they came to ask, "How do you produce such bounty?" Educating the indigenous peoples to new agricultural ways was much easier once the benefits were clear.

Business examples present similar stories: Dell Computer versus third-party retailers . . . Southwest Airlines' customer-oriented culture . . . eBay and person-to-person Web sales. These companies succeeded in demonstrating how a new concept can work.

Given the changes that a project office will cause in an organization, it is essential that the approach to developing the office be aligned with organizational culture. Much of the work of the project office can be seen as missionary work—trying to convince people they will be better off if they change to new ways. The metaphor of the Quakers' good-neighbor approach to organizational change is a valuable reference point to consider. It is one end of a continuum about how to implement a project office, shown in Figure 1.1.

The other end of the continuum is the old hierarchical, command-and-control, "Attila," do-what-I-say approach. Attila the Hun, as a leader, was able to get people to do what he commanded, mainly through his aggressive, ambitious, and arrogant nature. He was a savage conqueror who compelled those not destroyed by combat to serve in his armies. He delighted in war and became a prudent and successful general. He caused vast suffering and died, somewhat questionably, before his invasion plans could be carried out.

Many nineteenth-century industrialists built organizations designed to transmit orders from the top. This worked very well in its day, generating unprecedented prosperity across a broad spectrum of society, but has become less effective as the pace of change has increased in the modern world.

Change agents and their sponsors can determine their place on this continuum, usually by honoring the existing culture. Design a plan that lines up with the current position and then aim to shift direction over time. A hybrid strategy may be very effective—start with a grassroots small success that is comfortable for everyone concerned and then enlist upper management support to mandate its use across the organization. See Figure 1.2 for a more academic treatment of change initiatives.

FIGURE 1.1. A CONTINUUM OF CHANGE INITIATIVES TO CHOOSE FROM.

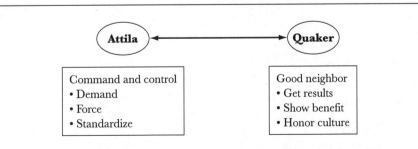

FIGURE 1.2. THEORY E AND THEORY O.

Beer and Nohria (2001) describe two basic types of change initiatives:

Theory E is the creation of economic value, often expressed as increased shareholder value. Steps of the change plan are crafted and monitored from above. Leaders focus on strategies, structures, and systems. Financial targets and incentives dominate the agenda.

Theory O maintains that creating sustainable competitive advantage is the best means of serving shareholders' long-term interests. The emphasis is on building organizational capability—a learning organization—and changing the culture that creates structures and systems.

Theory E approaches are top-down, centrally planned, and highly programmatic while Theory O is bottom-up and involves high levels of participation and emerging cultures.

Fundamental tensions exist between Theories E and O. The challenge is to combine the best of both.

Overall Organization Change Process

Much has been written on the process of organizational change. An important early model of organizational change was given by Kurt Lewin, who formulated a simple three-step process of unfreeze, change, and then refreeze. Lewin points out that the people in an organization may be frozen together with a set of assumptions and procedures that were successful in the past. It is very difficult to change anything that is frozen, so Lewin advises that before a change can take place in any organization, first take steps to "unfreeze" it. Combining this model with our own experience, we formed a three-phase approach:

- Creating conditions for change
- Making change happen
- Making change stick

Creating Conditions for Change

Changing behavior requires that organization members first stop doing what they are doing now. Many members of organizations find this unsettling. It often means they must abandon practices they have spent years developing. People will not readily do this unless they thoroughly understand why they are being asked to make the change and how they will be better off by making that change. The organizational change agent must be ready to lead the people through these trying times by showing why the changes are absolutely necessary and also showing people how they will be better off by adopting project management practices.

Experience and studies show the two most important factors in successful organizational change are first that it is supported by the very top of the organization and second that the people have a reason why they need to change. People are much more amenable to change when they understand why it is necessary. Thus this phase requires the change agents to create a sense of urgency by citing the clear danger of continuing on the current path, develop a coalition of powerful forces that will help to ensure the necessary support from the top, develop and communicate a vision of how the changed organization will function, and develop a strategy for using a project office to achieve that vision.

Making Change Happen

After creating the proper conditions, the change agents institute necessary changes throughout the entire organization. Here the concentration is on building widespread project management capacity. Much of this change will be accomplished by developing a set of standard project methodologies, training organization members on the use of these methodologies, and mentoring project managers and their sponsors. However, an equally important aspect of the change will be political. Changing practices and procedures will also result in a change in the power structure of the organization, so the change agent must be politically astute and understand the organizational power structure. During the process of change, one can expect organizational efficiency to decrease while people learn the new procedures. People in the old power structure will repeatedly call for a return to the old ways.

Making Change Stick

The final phase in any change process is to refreeze behavior in the new, desired pattern. This is where changing the organization structure will be most effective. By this point the increased organizational capacity has shown its value and enterprise project management should have the support necessary from the very top of the organization. Project management will become the way things are done. Experiences with large organizational change usually show that about a third of the members of the organization will find it almost impossible to make a change and will decide to leave the organization instead. This is not an undertaking for the faint of heart.

Implementing a Project Office as Organizational Change Process

When organizational change to a project-based organization is the final goal, people on the change agent team should think that way from the beginning. When they begin by thinking of the office in narrow terms, such as helping on one project or maybe in one department, they find it difficult to expand operations organization-wide. This is because the project office becomes associated with that one project or with that department, not the organization as a whole. In addition, they may have begun by concentrating on establishing standard procedures and acquired a reputation as another set of staffers getting in people's way. Here as always, first impressions are lasting. For example, the first task of a project office is often instituting standard procedures for project execution. When people in the organization first interact with the office, they may see it as forcing them to follow some restricting methodology. Once this idea gets into people's minds, it is difficult to convince them that project offices are really a way to institute desirable long-term, organization-wide change. These developments make it difficult to expand the operations of a project office. If you want to move the whole organization eventually, start out with that idea in mind.

Begin by seeing the entire movement of a project office as an organizational change process. Since that means the team in charge of implementing the project office must assume the role of change agent, some guidance here seems in order. View the process as a path with distinct steps along the way. Many options exist to continue, modify, or exit the path. We find suggestions by Kotter (1996) quite useful in thinking through the concept of implementing a project office as an organizational change process. The next three sections describe the action areas necessary for a successful change process. These areas are somewhat sequential, and often overlapping.

Phase 1: Creating Conditions for Change

The first step in creating the conditions for change in any organization is to establish a sense of urgency for the change, a central and compelling reason why this change must be done and must be done now. What you are proposing is a new order of things, a new and different set of processes. Learning new processes and doing things differently can pose difficult transition problems for many members of the organization. So before embarking upon the process it is natural for people to ask, "Why do we need to do this now?" With no clear danger, with no sense of urgency that this must be done, there is little chance that members of the organization will embrace the change. In fact, you can expect them to openly resist it. These are busy people with many things to do and little time to spare for participating in a change process unless they feel it is absolutely necessary. People do those things they feel are in their best interest. If you want people to change, first show them that it is in their best interest to do this and do it now. There is a management myth often forwarded that people naturally resist change. This is not really true; people do tend to resist change that they perceive is not in their best interest, but they are equally quick to embrace changes that they perceive as serving their best interest. Establishing a sense of urgency makes it clear that this change is beneficial and well worth supporting.

There are several ways to establish a sense of urgency. The simplest is to use the set of circumstances that led to the idea of establishing a project office in the first place. Often an overriding factor is a project failure, and usually a failure on a grand scale. When this is the case, you can establish a sense of urgency by showing that if a project office is not established then there will be more failures like the last one. This information can also be used in the future when people ask you, "Why did we establish this project office in the first place?" Keep reminding people you are there to prevent large project failures.

Another way to establish a sense of urgency is to compare what you are doing in project management to what the best companies are doing—often called benchmarking. Several tools are available, and using these tools often indicates that your organization is far behind the project management practices of other organizations. This can work well if the standard for judgment is organizations your upper managers admire. When you can show that the better organizations are implementing project office groups, you can use that to establish a sense of urgency. For example, the Chevron Corporation did a benchmarking study for project management and found that other organizations were much better than Chevron was at both selecting projects and executing them. They realized that if they did not improve their project selection and execution procedures, their profit levels would be much lower than those of other oil companies. This would negatively affect stock price and thus their ability to raise additional capital. Findings like that certainly establish a sense of urgency. As a result, a project office was established and the Chevron project development and execution process (CPDEP) was developed (Cohen and Kuehn, 1996). If you do not do a formal benchmarking study, then perhaps a word from outside the organization—from customers, suppliers, or stockholders—will work.

Another way to establish a sense of urgency is to establish a set of value propositions for the project office that indicate how the people in the organization, and the organization as a whole, will receive value from the work you propose. It also helps to paint a picture that describes the future organization that embraces enterprise project management. As people see the value and understand the enhanced capabilities of the future organization, they will determine that that is the way they want it to be. That desire for the future state can be bolstered by another picture of what could happen or the consequences if enterprise project management is not embraced.

These three methods, discussed in Chapter Two, are designed to establish a sense of urgency, a feeling within people in the organization that they had better do this and do it now. Directors of project offices who did not establish a sense of urgency report that they had difficulty gaining the attention of organization members. Oftentimes when they tried to advise members of what they were doing or trying to accomplish, they found everyone was otherwise engaged in what they felt were more pressing problems. We find most organizations generally biased for the immediate, preferring to solve a pressing problem rather than some vague, longer-term problem. We do not believe we will see change in this orientation in our lifetime, so it will always be necessary to establish a sense of urgency to get people's attention. Awareness of need is the first step in any change. But if you cannot get people's attention, you will not be able to develop that awareness. Thus the urgency for establishing a sense of urgency.

Develop Political Acumen. Change will alter the status quo, so it is a good idea for a change agent to spend time determining the lay of the land. By this we mean to determine such things as where power truly lies in the organization, who will benefit from the change, who will lose by it, and how deeply ingrained the organization's current practices are. Understanding where the power lies in the organization will be important, because the change process will soon need sponsors from upper management ranks and will certainly benefit if those sponsors bring some power and heft with them.

In any organization change, some people feel they will win in the change and be better off, and others feel they will lose and thus be worse off. Expect assistance from the first group and resistance from the second. It may be tempting to try to ignore or go around the second group, but you can expect that the result of such a move will probably just make the resistance stiffer. A better approach is to change resistance to assistance by showing people how they will benefit from the proposed change. History shows repeatedly that your biggest enemy can become your biggest ally when it is clear that support is in those parties' best interest. So it is important to determine what groups may resist your efforts and show them how they will come out ahead if they support you. We offer examples in this book about how enlightened program managers gained this support.

It is also important to try to get some idea of just how set the organization is in its ways. Over time, people in organizations develop processes for getting things done and for solving their problems. These processes are practiced, refined, and then passed on from generation to generation. Over time these practices begin to embody Truth in the organization and those who do not support them generally leave or are forced out. Like most groups, organizations embrace people who fit their pattern or grow into it and expel those who do not. This recently happened at Ford Motors. The CEO did not behave the "Ford way" and thus was replaced by a member of the Ford family. Those left in the organization are the true believers in the goodness and righteousness of the status quo. The older and the more successful the organization, the more deeply ingrained are its current behavior patterns. In general, older and larger organizations will be much more difficult to change and will take a much longer time to change than will younger and smaller organizations. For example, NCR reported that it took five years to get the "snowball effect" to propel project management into the forefront of its corporate thinking (Kennel, 1996, p. 1), and AT&T reports it is still in an infant stage after five years (Schneidmuller and Balaban, 2000).

Finally, learn from the past or be doomed to repeat it. Find out what happened to any failed change agents who came before you and determine what you can do differently.

Create a Guiding Coalition. Once a sense of urgency is established, develop a group of people across the organization who will help to define the changes needed and ultimately aid the implementation process. These people need position power and must be developed as a team. Develop a formal organization-wide group of people who are interested in a project office and will help guide the implementation process. A necessary part of this guiding coalition is an executive sponsor, a person in upper management of the organization with enough power, heft, and desire to champion change and spearhead the move to an enterprise project management system. Also develop or partner with others who have extensive persuasive and political skills. We present a behavioral process to accomplish this in Chapter Three.

People who study organizational change feel that if some change is important enough to the organization, a group of true believers who want that change will emerge within the organization. The project office movement is no different. Several organizations report that their guiding coalition began as a group of like-minded people interested in improving project management, who were able to band together based on that interest (as with the AT&T group discussed at the beginning of this chapter). Oftentimes these groups are formalized and even have names of their own, such as 3M's PMSIG, mentioned earlier (and discussed in more detail in Chapter Five). Other times a guiding coalition is developed from a collection of individuals who make themselves known to the head of the project office implementation team. Once these groups begin to form, it is important that they represent a broad spectrum of the organization. It may be necessary to recruit additional individuals so that all sections of the relevant organizational universe are represented.

Another method for creating a guiding coalition is to develop a cross-organization group such as a project management council. This is standard procedure in many organizations and has been reported in several successful implementations. For example, the Project Management Initiative at HP began with the formation of a project management council. The group responsible for implementation of a program management office at NCR reported that they found it useful to address multicultural issues by establishing global and regional project management councils. These councils included top practitioners from all major geographic areas along with representatives from other company organizations such as Human Resources, Sales and Marketing, Education and Organizational Development, Professional Services Management, and Strategic Planning (Kennel, 1996).

A most important factor in assembling this guiding coalition is the recruitment or appointment of an executive sponsor. It is common in any organizational endeavor for people to ask, "Who in top management is back of this?" Without someone at the top backing the endeavor, people will sense the lack of resolve at the top of the organization and will surmise, correctly, that the project office movement is doomed to failure. In fact, this is a self-fulfilling prophecy. If, however, a popular and powerful person at the top of the organization becomes the official executive sponsor of project office development and organization members understand that this is important, they will be much more willing, even eager, to help the process along. For example, implementation of the Project Management Initiative at HP was greatly facilitated by the executive sponsorship of Dean Morton, the chief operating officer. Likewise, the project office group at AT&T arose from the ranks but actively sought and acquired executive sponsorship with the rationale:

> Without an executive sponsor or champion, a council lacks the power or authority to implement its program plan. As a result, some project managers even resisted joining the council since it had no executive backing, viewing it as a waste of their time. The council is able to move quickly to obtain a sponsor. One of the existing council members had a vice president who shared the council's belief in project management and, when asked, willingly accepted the role and responsibilities. This was a significant turning point for the council. With an executive sponsor/champion, the council is able to accelerate progress and become a legitimate entity [Schneidmuller and Balaban, 2000, p. 1].

Develop a Vision and Strategy—Focus Your Thinking. The vision is a picture of the future, the strategy is a plan for developing a project office to get there. Once a guiding coalition is in place, there is now a group that can help to determine the vision of both the future organization and the strategy of the project office for achieving that vision. To begin, this group should work to refine the vision of a project-based organization, the vision that was developed as a part of creating a sense of urgency. From this vision they can begin to develop a list of what needs to be done to change the current organization to that new, project-based state. In a way, this becomes a to-do list for the project office. This list could include many functions and processes that the project office will eventually develop. Many of the possibilities for project office functioning will be covered in Chapter Four. The important point here is to develop that list and the overall vision with the aid of the guiding coalition. For example, NCR developed a vision "to be recognized as a leader in profitable multinational solution delivery in our core industries of finance, retail, and communications." They realized that to reach this vision several internal goals must be achieved so they developed an internal "end state" vision:

- All bids and proposals should fall within defined risk tolerances.
- Customer solution is our delivery in project form within a 5 percent variance from schedule and budget.
- Project teams are rewarded in terms of project success.
- Projects can be delivered seamlessly across functional areas.
- Project management can be delivered seamlessly across geographical areas.
- Project management in NCR is institutionalized.
- All projects are managed using the same processes.

With the vision and the to-do list in hand, develop a strategy for implementing the vision. Experience indicates that you will not be able to implement the entire list at once. It is just not possible, and the attempt would probably be overwhelming to the organization. It is a much better idea to start small, to choose one or two items from the list that you feel you can do and do well, show you can help people in the organization when you do those things, and then build on those successes. For example, the HP initiative began by organizing a project managers' conference as a way to help assess project management needs across the organization.

Many project management offices begin by building organizational capability, usually by developing standard project management practices for the organization. From this base they can develop more advanced functions such as project manager training and career development as well as training all members of the organization. They can move to the strategic office and develop capabilities for project selection and business skills for project managers, and finally develop venture project management, where the project is truly managed as a business venture. Vision includes change away from narrow measures of success to broader measures of business performance. The vision needs to be integrated with and support the corporate vision and strategy.

Communicate That Change Vision—Tell the Tale. Once the vision and strategy is developed, communicate it to all parts of the organization. Do not leave this task to e-mail. It is important that change agents go to divisions and departments personally and explain how the efforts will help solve local problems. This means that the vision and strategy statements include an assessment of how the efforts of the project office will help the organization increase shareholder value. Describing the lofty goal of increasing shareholder value will be necessary but not sufficient. Many people in organizations have only a vague notion of how their work affects shareholder value. They assume that if they do the work specified by upper managers, that work will be aimed at achieving strategy and increasing shareholder value. To have any real effect throughout the organization, communicate not only the overall vision but also how the implementation of that vision affects the way people do everyday work. Understand, at every level of the organization, the problems people face, the procedures they currently use to solve problems, and the ways in which the project office will help them solve their problems more easily, better, and faster. This is what people want to hear, and we do know that people are far better at hearing what they want to hear than at picking up unwelcome information.

Communicating a change vision can become almost a full-time occupation. To begin the process, build up your own level of enthusiasm about the need for the potential benefits of a project office. Your enthusiasm is important as a first step in generating enthusiasm in others. Enthusiasm is catching, moving from one person to another, but if it does not start with you, then there is little chance that it will generate spontaneously. Lack of enthusiasm is also catching. If you try to convince others of your change vision but you lack enthusiasm, they will sense your lack of resolve, and they will respond with their own lack of resolve. Once your enthusiasm is firmly in place, be ready to go to departmental meetings, coffee talks, or whatever organizational forum is appropriate to communicate the vision, how your efforts will help the organization, and how it will help the particular people you are addressing. Illustrations of successfully communicating visions appear in the case studies of Chapters Five and Seven.

Gear your communications program so that it will be memorable for those people listening. In most organizations, this means creating a "hero story" about how someone used good project management practice and saved the day. As with most organizational stories, this one should have some basis in truth but does not necessarily have to be completely factual. The typical hero story involves an individual up against seemingly insurmountable odds and in an impossible situation who somehow, at the last minute, seizes upon a unique solution and emerges victorious in the face of certain defeat. The typical organizational tale will go something like this:

You know Joe, over in Systems, his projects were always late and cost a bundle, and our customers were howling mad. Management was going to show him the door, but Joe asked for just one more chance. Well, at the same time, our sales force had gone out and sold the moon, promising one customer a new system in six months. The bosses figured there was no way to make that deadline so they gave the project to Joe, figuring they could blame him for the lousy job. Joe didn't stand a chance, but you know what, he used those new project management practices and got the job done right on time. He showed those bosses, didn't he, and got to keep his job to boot. Why, he might even get the boss's job.

Phase 2: Making Change Happen

Generate Short-Term Wins. By now the conditions for change have been set and it is time to contact the target population—it is time to implement the change. An important point here is to start where the pain is, solve some of the more painful organizational problems, and show solutions that demonstrate immediate uses of a project office. As project leader you support the overall vision and no doubt have a plan to get to that vision, and you may have some initial steps in mind that you think are best for the organization. However, you can probably get more immediate notice if you spend initial efforts on problems that seem to be most vexing to organization members at the current time. Perhaps it is a perceived sense of overwork to fill out forms, or sense of lack of procedures that are generating complaints from project teams. Maybe you feel it is more important to help the organization select the right projects, and in the long run this may be true. However, while you spend time implementing project selection procedures, project managers may continue to complain about lack of a shared strategy or project execution procedures. If they perceive no benefit from your project office, you will get the reputation of being just another staff function that adds no value. First impressions are lasting, and once this impression is in place, it is difficult to change. This is because of Graham's Third Law:

> IF YOU'RE NOT ADDING VALUE,
> THEY WON'T VALUE WHAT YOU'RE ADDING.

In addition, there will be someone in the organization who did not want the project office in the first place, and who will trumpet that first impression to prove they were right. Once that process starts, it is difficult to stop. So the recommended strategy is for you to determine where the pain is now, then attack the immediate problems and solve them to show that your operation really does add value to the organization. Work with a group that is already sold on the need for better project management. That will make it much easier for you to use best practices and show the best results. Then you will be in a much better position to proceed with the longer-term goals.

Develop Broad-Based Action. This is a step for you to diffuse action throughout the entire organization. The things you and your staff and the project office can do independently are not enough to bring about organizational change. The change happens in any organization when there is a critical mass of people who change their behavior to match the new vision. A critical mass is usually considered to be about two-thirds of the people in any given organization. One handy rule of thumb is that about one-third of the people in an organization will be ready and willing, waiting for the change, another third will be on the fence and only change when they experience the benefits of the new process, and the final third will resist the change until they are forced to make the change or they leave the organization. The strategy then is to use that one-third early adopters to demonstrate the benefits of your vision. Then use those successes to convince the fence-sitters to join the crowd.

For people to experience the benefits of the new procedures, the procedures must first be developed and then communicated. Most project office endeavors begin by developing a set of standard methodologies to be used on all future projects. This is usually followed by instituting a training program to train project managers, project team members, and finally all members of the organization in the use and benefits of the project methodologies.

John Kennel from NCR advises:

> Educate the project management community first in order to build immediate credibility. . . . It is absolutely necessary that every associate who functions in the capacity of a project manager receive a complete curriculum of project management training. . . . As you move toward a projectized company, you must also provide training for all members of your corporation. This training begins with project management awareness education leading to very advanced program and international program management techniques and disciplines [1996, p. 6].

For all this training to have any real effect, you need to generate a majority rather quickly. Organizations discover that the benefits of training fade quickly if the techniques that are learned are not used on the job. Therefore, to develop a broad and solid base for future action, dedicate a significant amount of the professional development budget to this endeavor. That powerful project sponsor will certainly be beneficial at this point, as will good political skills for the members of the project office team.

As the project office plan goes into implementation, conduct a start-up process. Get everyone together to share the vision, discuss concerns, refine the plan, and accept assignments. Work on enhancing the emotional intelligence of the group. Also help them embrace the chaos that will ensue through their attempts to manage complexity. These processes are discussed in Chapter Six.

Consolidate Gains and Produce More Change. This is a step for you to increase change in the organization by using the new processes and procedures. Build on small wins. Up to this point you have concentrated on helping the members of the organization change by increasing organizational capabilities. Now it is necessary to begin to eliminate the organizational barriers to change—often classified in terms of structures, skills, systems, and supervisors.

- *Structures.* The organizational structure is often a formidable barrier to change, encouraging silos rather than teamwork. Oftentimes, the formal structure makes it difficult to act across the organization, a condition that is absolutely necessary for good project manager practice. Therefore, this is probably a good time to consider a reorganization that elevates project management to the director level with the appointment of a chief project officer. At a minimum, you need to set conditions for teams, allocating time, space, leaders, and support.

- *Skills.* The training program by itself is not enough. The members of the project office must also develop a robust project management development program and career track. This requires the project office develop such services as mentoring, consulting, certification programs, and conferences. Shift training to leadership and behavioral skills, process skills, and business skills.

- *Systems.* The normal personnel and information systems make it difficult to act across the organization to develop the skills and structures necessary. There is immediate need to add a measure of teamwork in performance reviews, rewards for teamwork as well as individual work, and some proactive accounting that would treat each project as an entity in itself and not as an appendix of the department. Have representatives from the human resources and accounting functions on the guiding coalition.

- *Supervisors.* Massive organizational change will not happen without backing of upper management and department directors. Confront nonsupportive department directors and enlist their support. Get a focus on teamwork from the top down, maintain clarity and shared purpose, and keep energy levels up.

Illuminating the barriers to change will be a daunting task. Developing skills is the easiest part, so this is where most project offices concentrate their efforts. But we know that these newly developed skills soon fade without supporting changes in structures, systems, and supervisors. Changing structure is a political minefield, because it requires a shift in power with the creation of a chief project officer. Without a very strong sponsor and support of the other organization officers, change will be impossible. Changing systems is also difficult as much has been invested in current systems, and the people who run them probably favor the status quo. Finally, getting the support of department directors has been notoriously difficult over the history of the project management movement. It is here that many change processes fail. Even when procedures have proven to be effective and the necessary skills have been developed, the structures, systems, and supervisors do not yield to change, and the process fails.

For this reason we opened this chapter with the reference to Dante. The sign over the door to Hell warned him to "abandon hope." Yet we believe there is reason instead to "abandon despair"—there is a process and help to address the difficult issues.

Phase 3: Making Change Stick

By this point in the change process, the value of moving to enterprise project management has probably been proven many times over. Project managers have been well trained, mentored, and supported, and good project manager practice has become the norm. It may seem that the new practices have taken root and now define the way things are done in the organization. However, experience indicates that this is not necessarily true. Old habits die hard and the old culture lies just below the surface, constantly ready to reassert itself.

Kotter (1996, pp. 145–147) described an aerospace company where a five-year change process yielded an increase in revenues of 62 percent and an increase in net income of 76 percent. The driver of the change, the division general manager, retired—feeling that the changes had been made, the results impressive, and the work had been done. Very soon, many of the changes that were put in place began to unravel; many small adjustments were made, mostly imperceptible. Within twenty-four months, some practices had regressed to where they had been four years before. Shortly thereafter the first major performance problems began to emerge. Kotter argues that this happens because "some central precepts in the division's culture were incompatible with all the changes that had been made. As long as the division general manager and the transformation program worked day and night to reinforce the new practices, the total weight of these efforts overwhelmed the cultural differences. But when the division general manager left and the transformation program ended, the culture reasserted itself" (p. 146).

The teamwork and cross-organization cooperation necessary for enterprise project management are antithetical to the reality experienced in most organizations. For this reason it is a good bet that the changes necessary to implement enterprise project management will be quite incompatible with the organization's culture. Even if systemic changes are made in the organization, the old ways will still linger for many organizational generations.

Culture change is an extremely long and complicated process. It means changing the way people construct their reality. People must experience the connection between new action and performance improvement on many different occasions and over a sustained period. The changes must be passed on from one generation to another, and this will probably have to happen several times before the organizational culture adjusts to the new reality. Process cannot be said to be complete until the day when there is no one left in the organization who can remember doing things any other way.

By the beginning of the third phase of the change process, a strategic project office should have been established. The people in this office are in a unique position to lead this final phase of the change process. An important aspect will be their ability to follow a project from inception all the way until the end of the product that was produced by the project. In the past, the costs for the project were normally counted in one part of the organization, perhaps R&D, while the benefits of the project's product were counted in a different part of the organization, perhaps in Marketing. Projects were seen as an expense rather than as an investment, so the return on investment in the project was rarely calculated. With a changed accounting system and a strategic project office positioned high enough in the organization, the accounting for the project investment as well as the return on that investment now come together in one place. This information will help develop portfolio management and project selection procedures as well as pave the way for developing a venture project management program, where project managers feel responsibility beyond the completion of the project itself and throughout the life of the project's product.

With this final change, project management will be seen as much more than just a set of techniques to complete projects on time and on budget. Project management practices become totally intertwined with business management practices—project and business management will be seen as the same thing.

Chapters Ten and Eleven contain a discussion of the difficulties of cultural change, suggestions for implementing cultural change, a description of the changes that will be necessary for venture project management to become a reality, and suggestions for implementing those changes.

Summary

This chapter presents many concepts and ideas regarding planned organizational change, the three phases of that change, the role of the change agent during those phases, and the progression of project office development to support the entire change process. The box in Figure 1.3 presents a summary of these ideas in capsule form. This can be used as a one-page guide to the entire organizational change process. Details concerning the steps in this process are given in subsequent chapters.

FIGURE 1.3. CHANGE PROCESS FOR PROJECT-BASED ORGANIZATION.

Change Phase	Change Agent Processes	Project Office Development
Create conditions for change	Establish a sense of urgency.	Benchmarking (continual function). Organizational vision. Value proposition.
	Develop political acumen.	Stakeholder analysis.
	Create a guiding coalition.	PM council with organization-wide representation. Powerful executive sponsor.
	Develop a vision and strategy.	PM office vision, what it will do. Strategy, start small, expand with success.
	Communicate that change vision.	Meet with all organization constituents. Generate their enthusiasm.
Make change happen	Generate short-term wins.	Apply standard process to some immediate problem. Show value. Level 1–PCO.
	Develop broad-based action.	Develop constituency through training, mentoring, consulting, developing a career path. Level 2–PMCOE.
	Consolidate gains and produce more change.	Reorganization to establish a CPO. Level 3–strategic PO. Change reward system; develop portfolio management and venture project management.
Make change stick	Make project management the norm.	Change organization culture by providing leadership, training, means, and the motivation to make the change the new reality.

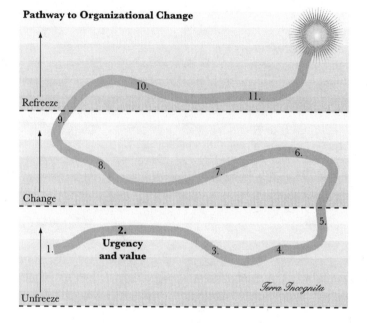

Pathway to Organizational Change

Refreeze

10.

11.

9.

Change

8.

7.

6.

5.

1.

2. Urgency and value

3.

4.

Terra Incognita

Unfreeze

Following the process outlined in Chapter One, the first step in implementing organizational change is creating a sense of urgency for that change. To implement a project office system that spans an entire organization requires creating a sense of urgency among many members of the organization. A short-term sense of urgency can be created by pointing to a clear danger, something that threatens the future of the organization. However, experience indicates that this urgency often does not last once the danger passes. In this chapter we give longer-lasting ways to create an organization-wide sense of urgency regarding the need to implement a project office. These consist of establishing that the office will add value to the organization, comparing your organization's project management practices to those considered the best, and describing a desired future of the organization that is based on developing project management as a core competency.

CHAPTER TWO

CLEAR DANGER: CREATING A SENSE OF URGENCY AND ECONOMIC VALUE

Brutus is an honorable man.
SHAKESPEARE

Chapter One describes how organizational change efforts seem destined to fail unless those directing the change can establish a sense of urgency for that change. Pointing to a clear danger is a useful technique for getting people's attention, but that attention often wanes once the immediate danger has passed. To build a longer-term sense of urgency we develop that step plus three additional actions for consideration in this chapter.

1. *Use the clear danger.* The first suggestion is to concentrate on the set of circumstances that brought forward the need to establish better project management in the first place, normally a project crisis or missed opportunity, and to show how establishing a project office will help to avert such crises in the future.
2. *Add value to the organization.* Once it is shown that future crises can be averted, the next step is to focus attention on the longer-term benefits of the project office to the organization. This is best done by developing a value proposition indicating how the office will make the organization better and more successful.
3. *Benchmark current organizational practices.* To demonstrate this added value, consider benchmarking the current practices of your organization against those of industry leaders who have already established a project office system. If the benchmarking shows that your organization is falling behind the industry leaders, a sense of urgency for better project management will increase quickly.

4. *Describe a desired organization.* To begin the focus on benefits of organizational change, it is useful to create a picture of the future organization, a description of what the organization could be like once the change process is completed and project management established as a core competency. When people see how that type of organization will function and what it can accomplish, they will want what they see, and there will be an urgency to start developing it immediately.

Developing a Clear Danger

Implementing a project office will require cooperation among many different parts of the organization, often among organizational entities that typically do not cooperate with each other. Developing a clear danger to the survival of the organization is one well-known way of fostering cooperation and even getting people to temporarily suspend long-held beliefs to work toward organizational survival. For example, in *Morality and Expediency*, Bailey (1977) describes a situation where professors agreed to fabricate enrollment in certain courses so they would not lose state funding. The author points out that one core value of the professor is to tell the truth, and indicated that any professor who published a paper with lies would be severely chastised. However, the group was willing to suspend that morality for the expediency of maintaining a higher level of state funding.

Similarly, the members of many university departments fight each other continually, downgrading the field of study in any department but their own. However, when the state funding agency appears with a mandate for interdepartmental cooperation, departmental members find themselves able to come together to give a unified front and present many plans for interdisciplinary research. Of course, those plans evaporate once the funding is secure and the usual interdepartmental animosities reemerge.

These examples show a typical pattern in response to threats. That is, people with a wide variety of often conflicting interests are able to unify and work together when there is a clear danger. Once the sense of danger has passed, however, old feuds and the old ways quickly reassert themselves. This response illustrates the type of unity of purpose that change agents would like to generate to initiate any change process. The groups of people to be convinced range far and wide across the organization, each with its own set of problems to solve and each with its own set of changes in mind. Your initial task as a change agent is to create a sense of urgency concerning the need for enterprise project management and a project office that is so strong that groups with diverse agendas would be willing to abandon, or at least temporarily suspend, their own change efforts in order to support yours.

Spinning Your Wheels

As noted earlier, the desire to increase project management ability often results from a series of project failures. In many organizations, the first response to these failures is to send a few engineers out for training in project management. The assumption here is that project management is a skill that can be easily learned and then practiced in the organization. The reality is that although project management skills can be learned easily enough, those skills are so antithetical to the way most organizations function that they are not easily applied. In fact, when engineers return to the organization, they find that their newfound skills are so strange to organizational beliefs that attempts to practice those skills are actually seen as career-limiting moves. For example, organization members may look askance when the engineers suggest time for project planning, they may walk out of meetings set up to agree on project goals, and will often bristle with indignation at any suggestion that people work full time on one project only. As a result of such responses, newly trained engineers either give up trying to practice project management or leave the organization. Either way, the organization experiences yet another failure in project management, this time with the additional pain of spending money for training and getting nothing in return.

At some point we would hope it becomes clear to upper managers that project management is more than just a set of skills; it is an approach to doing business that requires wholehearted organizational support. At this point the concept of a project office may be considered. Successive failures may warm people to the idea that there is a need for a concentrated and dedicated group of people to systematically develop a project management capability within the organization. This realization may come at the upper management level or may arise from a groundswell across the organization. The initial urgency will be to prevent future failures and stop spending all that money for nothing.

The causes of project failure are fairly well known: usually some combination of lack of a clear goal, lack of following a project management methodology, lack of top managers' support, lack of interaction with customers and end users, or lack of trained personnel to manage the project. The change agent needs to be ready to show how the project office addresses these deficiencies. Developing methodology, working to increase upper management support, interacting with customers and users, and training project managers are often introductory steps that many project office managers take in order to attack the most urgent organizational problems. In addition, these functions are known to be critical factors in project success (Dai, 2001). The change agent team could thus consider implementing these functions as a first step in their implementation plan.

Some Problems with Minimizing Cost as a Project Office Goal

A project office may be pushed to minimize costs on projects. Excessive cost might be considered part of the clear danger. Is this a viable strategy? While it may be helpful to get people's attention by concentrating on minimizing costs, this initial concentration could be detrimental for the long-term future of a project office and the organization. It will not help the project office to get a reputation of being a watchdog for management. Also, this concentration aligns the project office with an old perception of project management, one that will not serve the office well in the future.

In earlier days, project management was sold as a way to minimize cost. It was touted as a set of techniques that would enable project managers to deliver a specified outcome at a specified time and at a minimum cost. These are the *triple constraints*, the basis for early project management practice. Over time it has become apparent that the triple constraints are too constraining and that they often lead to poor decision making on projects. But since people in organizations continue to emphasize the need to minimize costs, project management techniques stay mired in the triple constraints. This is one reason why project management seldom concerns top managers in the organization. They see it as a set of techniques for minimizing cost, not as a way of operating projects to help them achieve strategy and add value to the organization.

This is an important issue in the framing of both the problem and the proposed solution. A project crisis is good for gaining attention, but framing the project office merely as a response to crisis will be detrimental in the long run. If the project office is seen as a watchdog group there to oversee project spending, it develops a negative image and there is little chance of getting cooperation from project managers and other organization members. There is also little chance that upper managers will associate the office with achieving strategy and change. In framing the function and purpose of the project office, first understand people's concerns with costs and indeed address that concern as a part of the purpose. Then move the function of the project office to adding economic value.

Costs are often a political football. Large construction projects such as a Channel Tunnel or the Boston "Big Dig" are often chastised for going as much as 500 percent over budget. However, the original budget figure is probably a lie, a figure used to get voter approval for the project. Once the project is under way, true costs emerge. However, since the project is already under way, voters usually approve spending the extra money. Politicians often feel that the people will not vote for the project if they knew how much it is really going to cost, and they may well be correct. And politicians are not the only ones who underestimate project costs in an effort to see a project initiated. It also happens in organizations. This indicates that preliminary cost estimates are an important first place to look when there is concern with cost control. This also indicates that an important additional function of a project office is to work to produce reliable and truthful estimates of project costs whenever projects are first being considered.

"Brutus is an honorable man" is Mark Antony's line in Shakespeare's *Julius Caesar*. He repeated it during his oration at Caesar's funeral. He used it to build rapport with the audience who believed in Brutus. However, Brutus murdered Caesar. By the end of the oration, the audience ran Brutus out of town.

For our purposes, Brutus is the budget, an emphasis on project costs. Proponents of a project office need to acknowledge that costs are important. Draw a lesson from Mark Antony's speech as a brilliant persuasive tool. Help people come to realize that emphasis on budget is shortsighted. Clear dangers are all around, and narrow focus on costs is a big one. The real honor is in creating value. *Do the right thing and the money will follow* is the first law of money.

People in organizations say they want to minimize cost, but do they really? Despite all the discussion about the cost of projects that failed, it is usually plain to see that cost would not be a factor had the projects succeeded. It seems a rule of life that for successful projects the costs cannot be remembered while for failed projects the costs cannot be forgotten. It is not the cost of the project that worries people, it is the cost of the failure. This is another indication that the emphasis of the project office should be on developing practices that minimize the chance of project failure rather than on framing rules to minimize project costs.

People in organizations say they want to minimize cost, but do they really? An easy retort to this idea is that it is easy to minimize project costs in any organization—just don't do any projects. With no projects, project costs are zero. This is quickly seen as folly; people want the benefits that the projects produce, and they would like the benefits to outweigh the costs. It is easy to argue that firms cannot succeed by minimizing cost, they succeed by adding value. The same is true of project management. It is not the cost of the project that is the real concern, it is the value added.

People in organizations say they want to minimize cost, but do they really? Many people assume that if project costs are minimized, then the value added will be maximized. However, cost must be incurred to create value and many times the more cost incurred the more value is created. A simple example of this is the cost of testing product ideas with potential customers. These potential customers often come up with the best ideas, the ones that really add value to the product. Of course, if costs are being minimized by not consulting potential customers, then the organization builds whatever the engineers say is best. There is a long history of product failures that followed this minimum cost route. The costs associated with testing ideas with potential customers are usually agreed to be well worth the investment, to ensure increased value. It is not the cost of the project that is the real concern, it is the ability to maximize the value added.

People in organizations say they want to minimize cost, but do they really? If you really want to know what concerns people, listen to the stories they tell. Most of what you hear will be of the hero story variety, where someone thinks up an ingenious idea or meets a customer expectation in a way to help save the organization. The hero story is about people overcoming enormous odds in order to help ensure organizational survival. The hero story is seldom, if ever, about the manager who minimized cost. If people were really concerned about minimizing cost, then that would be the story they tell. But they don't, so it seems that what they are really interested in is survival. It is not the cost of the project that is the real concern, it is the ability to maximize the value added and thereby ensure organizational survival.

The argument here is that it is difficult to create a sense of urgency for organizational change by arguing that the change will help minimize costs. This is not where people's interests really lie. The argument should be that instituting a project office will help ensure that future projects add maximum value to the organization. In addition, it would be a fatal mistake to identify the project office as a cost-cutting endeavor. Developing enterprise project management requires cooperation on many different levels and it is difficult to get cooperation if the project office is seen as a cost-cutting operation. Cutting costs does not move people's souls, but adding economic value to help ensure organizational survival does.

Adding Value to the Organization

The key to the value proposition is that the project office builds organizational capability in the crisp execution of projects and thus promotes maximum benefit from project outcomes. The ability to derive this benefit requires thinking beyond the traditional triple constraints in project management—thinking outside the traditional project management box of outcome, cost, and schedule. Thinking outside the box, as shown in Figure 2.1, means that project managers consider both how their decisions affect their projects and how those decisions affect the value of projects to the organization.

For example, decisions on outcome may affect customer satisfaction, which in turn may affect market share and thus the ultimate value of the project outcome to the organization. Similarly, decisions on project schedule may affect both market share and the duration of financing for the project, both of which would have an effect on the value of the project in the organization. So building the value

FIGURE 2.1. THINKING OUTSIDE THE BOX.

Success of Overall Organization

New Product Development Project

Outcome: product specification

Customer satisfaction

Cost: product development cost

Break even point

Cost: product manufacturing cost

Schedule: product development time

Profit per item sold

Market share

Capital required

Economic value of project

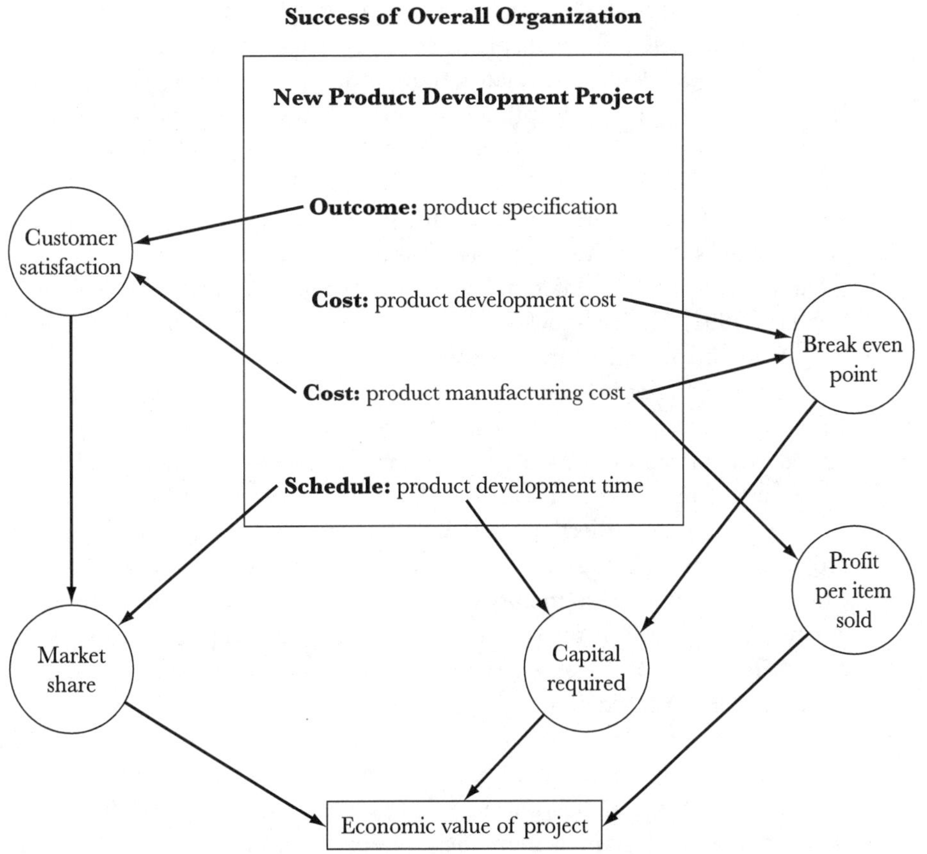

proposition requires thinking beyond what is normally assumed to be of value for the project manager and developing the project office and subsequent project management practices toward generating value for the general managers and the organization as a whole.

Projects as Investments, Not Costs

One of the first steps in creating value for the organization is for the project office to change the organization's mind-set so it sees projects as investments, not as costs. Adding economic value to organization is usually understood as getting a return on investment that is greater than the total cost of that investment, including the cost of the capital needed to finance that investment. Projects are not normally seen as investments because their costs are normally expensed. At first glance, that approach looks practical; after all, the majority of project costs are salaries, and those costs are normally expensed in the departments of people working on the project. Because the salaries are spread across many departments in the organization and the people work on several different things at a time, it is often difficult to calculate the total amount of money spent on any given project. In addition, the return—the profit generated by final project outcomes—usually accrues to totally different departments from those that had the expenses. For these reasons, it is difficult for organizations to determine any return on what they pay for projects. Thus the first step in linking projects to the concept of adding economic value is to begin to view projects as investments, not costs.

Presented here is a different way viewing projects, suggested by Cohen and Graham (2001). We begin by looking at the cash cycle of the firm, shown in Figure 2.2, to understand return on investment.

The cycle begins by financing a sum of money, then investing that sum to acquire an asset, then operating or selling that asset to generate cash, which is then returned to the organization. We can look at projects the same way, as in Figure 2.3.

A sum of money is financed when the project is selected. That sum of money is spent during the project execution. The money spent results in an asset, the project outcome. That asset is then operated over its life cycle to generate cash, which is then returned to the organization. If the amount of cash generated is greater than the cost of the project plus the cost of operating the asset plus the cost to finance the project, then there is a positive return on investment and value is added to the organization.

The cash cycle view changes the way projects look to an organization. Besides becoming investments rather than costs, projects have vastly longer lives; they are not over when their output is first produced, they last until the organization receives a return on its investment or abandons their output entirely. This

FIGURE 2.2. THE CASH CYCLE OF THE FIRM.

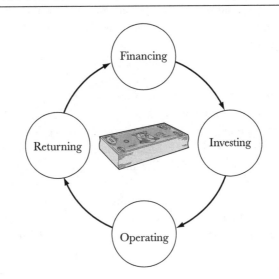

FIGURE 2.3. THE CASH CYCLE OF THE PROJECT.

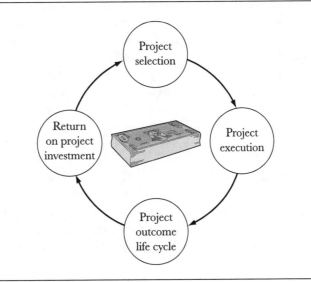

view also shows that the project should not be measured on the basis of simply producing a given product at a given cost at a given time. Rather than the traditional triple constraints, the project should be measured on the economic value added it generates.

The project office is in a unique position to show how projects add value to the organization by calculating both the investments and the return on investments in one place. For the first step, the project office can help in initial project selection, calculating both initial investment and potential returns. This service, often called *project portfolio management,* is one that is often offered in a mature project office. Second, the project office can be instrumental in helping with project execution to enhance potential returns. Training, mentoring, coaching, and consulting with project managers and project team members are services typically offered by a project office. Third, the project office can gather results from the project outcome life cycle, the cash flow that is generated as the project outcome operates. Finally, the project office, since it follows projects from beginning to end, is in a good position to calculate the return on investment and thus the economic value generated. Top managers understand the importance of adding economic value. Positioning a project office to perform this function aids in developing a sense of urgency for the endeavor.

Developing a Value Proposition

Concentrating on adding economic value for each project helps prevent future project disasters. However, this new emphasis will come at a cost, which is the investment to be made in the project office itself. In this section we concentrate on the value the project office adds in addition to helping individual projects. Level 1 project offices help the individual projects, whereas level 2 and level 3 offices help the organization as a whole. One of the most important arguments for a project office is the value proposition. The value proposition indicates how the organization will be better off by taking the recommended step. In essence, this is the core of the argument for why people should support the project office.

Achieving Strategy. There is a need to prove to upper managers that project management is an important aspect for implementing strategy and that a project office can add value to the corporation by helping the strategy implementation process. In many organizations this will be a very hard sell. Some general managers would find it a large stretch of the imagination to link project management to strategy implementation.

For many years the benefits of project management have been sold in operational and not strategic terms. Because of this, general managers often think of project management as helping in the operation of the business and not implementing strategy. However, strategy is implemented through projects. The current organization is the sum of past projects. Strategy implementation normally requires some combination of developing new products, entering new markets, creating a new image, streamlining production and distribution costs, and developing new marketing programs. All these elements are achieved through projects.

In addition to executing these projects, a strategic project office can be instrumental in helping to choose which projects to do to implement strategy. The ability of the project office to calculate a project economic value added will be instrumental in developing a portfolio process. Looking at which projects did well in the past is an indication of which projects to choose in the future. The entire process of linking projects to strategy and then executing those projects such that strategy is achieved can be attributed to the operations of a project office. This is an often overlooked value that the project office can add to the organization.

Increasing Return on Investment. Implementing an effective project management program adds significant value to information technology (IT) organizations, concluded a recent survey conducted by the Center for Business Practices (CBP), the research division of the project management consulting group PM Solutions. All of the forty-three senior-level project managers surveyed said that project management initiatives improved their organizations. According to the survey findings, effective project management programs yield an average 28 percent ROI and overall business improvements by an average of 21 percent. The survey evaluated the merit of project management according to twenty different IT metrics. The most significant improvements occurred in schedule estimation (42.1 percent) and alignment to strategic business goals (41 percent). Other major improvements were in the areas of customer satisfaction, assessing project costs per hour, product quality, and ability to meet project deadlines.

Building Competitive Advantage. Many organizations look on developing project management capability as a competitive advantage. This can be achieved through executing projects better so the organization is more efficient, makes better use of its resources, or can sell project management capability as a reason to use the organization. One aircraft maintenance company adopted better project management techniques and was able to significantly reduce lead time and thus service aircraft much faster than its competitors. This ability to execute projects crisply led to a competitive advantage. Whoever is in charge of implementing a project office should determine by talking with upper managers what it is that would lead to a competitive advantage for their organization. Then demonstrate how establishing a project office develops the desired competitive advantage through better execution of projects.

Creating New Products. One of the obvious uses for project management is in the process of creating more new products from a given workforce. For organizations that rely on new products for a large percentage of their income, the ability to create more new products with a given set of resources can add tremendous value.

Increasing Sales. Achieving sales sometimes requires a project begun in the customer's organization in order to fully utilize the products being sold. Your organization's capability in managing those projects in the customer's organization can be used to help make the deal.

Decreasing Costs. The project office can aid in decreasing project costs by creating repeatable elements that can be used in a variety of projects. For example, a project office could manage a software module reuse database. Those in charge of developing a project office should be ready to show just how much money can be saved when each new project does not have to reinvent the wheel. Learning from one project and applying that knowledge on the next project is an important function of a project office and one that can lead to tangible value in decreasing project execution costs.

Exploiting Unanticipated Capabilities. Building a project office may allow you to achieve things in the future that you cannot anticipate currently. The general idea is that once the office is established the organization will start to use the new capabilities in ways that may be invisible in the current environment. One example is given in Chapter Eight, where a project office established to construct housing was suddenly asked if it could reconstruct a runway in a short time frame. From that example the program manager states, "As the program team reviewed the original plan and assessed it against our PM methodology, we found hundreds of ways to accelerate the process to meet the timing deadline imposed upon us and ensure the quality desired by the customer." The successful program office was then asked to manage an upcoming special event—again, a far cry from building houses, but well within the scope of an effective project office.

Evolving Toward Self-Funding. Project management and the project office itself are often seen as additional overhead costs. Resistance is to be expected from those parts of the organization that feel they will be charged for the service and they will not use it. One way to mitigate this argument is to plan for the project office to evolve into a self-funding organization, one that charges for its services, normally an internal charge. In this way, costs for the services are borne by those who receive the benefits. More adventurous organizations may also consider selling the services of the project office to other organizations for profit.

What Happens If You Don't Do It

Crawford (2001, p. 19) cites the Gartner Group strategic planning assumptions. Their research shows establishing a project office is predictive of success in IT projects. The Gartner Group states that companies with a project office will experience half the delay and canceled projects encountered by companies without a project office. In addition, the lack of investment in a project office could mean continuation of the project disasters that have been experienced. Thus the clear danger becomes the negative consequences of not making the project office investment.

Benchmarking Your Organization's Project Management Practices

An additional tool for creating a sense of urgency is benchmarking your organization against others. Sometimes a word or two from the outside is worth a hundred internal memos. Experience shows that top managers pay attention when it is shown that their performance is lagging when compared to other organizations that they respect. The experience at Chevron is a good example:

> Between 1989 and 1992, Chevron benchmarked the performance of projects in both their upstream and downstream business. These benchmarking efforts found that, on average, the Chevron projects were taking longer and costing more than those of their competitors. In response to the state of the company, Chevron created processes for each of these business segments from early on which focused on capital projects. In 1993, the effort was undertaken to produce a generic process . . . the resulting process is the Chevron Project Development and Execution Process, CPDEP [Cohen and Kuehn, 1996, p. 5].

As a result of this benchmarking effort, Chevron developed a project office with the goal of developing this process and then implementing it throughout the organization. It is impressive how widely the process is known, implemented, and appreciated across the company. Obviously, implementation of this process represented a radical change in Chevron project managers' behavior. To complete this change, they enlisted the support of the CEO:

> To date, the implementation has been successful as demonstrated by the significant improvement in Chevron's project performance relative to its competitors. Chevron continues to seek new opportunities to improve their return to shareholders. The Company believes the CPDEP process will continue to provide improvements they are seeking [Cohen and Kuehn, 1996, p. 5].

Obviously, benchmarking can be an important tool in creating a sense of urgency for better project management. Several benchmarking organizations and surveys are available, including the Top 500 Project Management Benchmarking Forum, run by PM Solutions, (http://www.cbponline.com/benchmarkingforum. htm) and Human Systems Global Network (http://www.humansystems.net).

One such tool that was specifically designed to wake up upper managers is the Project Environment Assessment Tool (PEAT), based on Graham and Englund (1997) and administered by the Strategic Management Group (http://www. survey.e-perception.com/peatdemo). The PEAT questionnaire measures nine organizational factors that help create an environment that supports project success: strategic emphasis on projects, upper management support, project planning support, customer and end user input, project team development, project execution support, communications and information systems, overall organizational support, and adding economic value. The tool was administered to eight organizations that are well known as "best practice" models in project management. Organizations can compare how they rank by comparing their scores on each success factor to those of the models. People can use this data to get the attention of upper managers.

Describing a Desired Organization

The next suggestion to help create a sense of urgency is to describe an organization that would be very desirable, so desirable that people feel a sense of urgency to begin moving toward that state immediately. This provides a better idea of what the project office is ultimately aiming to achieve. It is difficult to say what the new organization will look like. However, we envision some sort of matrix structure, with one side being the general operations of the business and under the control of a chief operating officer (COO), the other side running the project operations and under control of a chief project officer (CPO). These concepts are discussed further in Chapter Four. More important than structure, however, is behavior. The behavior characteristics listed in this section are based on the discussions in Graham and Englund (1997) and Cohen and Graham (2001), which are also used in the PEAT questionnaire. The ultimate goal of a project office system should be to generate a desired future organization. We come back to these factors when "Looking Forward" in Chapter Ten.

Strategic Emphasis

The first characteristic is a strategic emphasis for projects, which indicates how well projects align with the strategy of the organization. Under normal departmental systems we find organizations typically attempting too many projects that have been begun independently of one another and often without knowledge of one another, perhaps supporting some departmental strategy, and with only a vague idea of the criteria for project success. Under a departmental system, the sum total of projects rarely represent a coherent whole aimed at implementing strategy of the organization.

Under the enterprise management system, all project participants will be fully aware of their company's business strategies and understand how projects always link to that strategy. Members of the project core teams participate in forming goal statements and understand how each project will add value to the organization. Members of project teams will understand how their project is linked to other projects and how the whole will help to implement the business strategy. The upper management of the organization will have acted as a team to select all the projects in the organization and will have developed clear measures for project success.

Upper Management Support

The next characteristic is a high level of upper management support for projects. Under a departmental structure upper managers tend to support projects in their own departments and give only lukewarm support for projects in other departments—or even oppose them. For the enterprise management system projects will no longer be associated with particular departments. Since the project will have been selected by an upper management team, all upper managers will fully support all projects in the organization.

To accomplish this, all upper managers will need to fully understand the project management process and to allow project team members to do their jobs without interference—measures they will be willing to adopt because they will be much more interested in project results than project control. Each project will have a project sponsor, a person in upper management who is responsible for the success of the project. Since the upper management team fully understands the project management process, they will avoid many current interference practices such as changing the project deadline when progress seems slower than expected, adding people to the project at the last minute, or pulling people off the core team during project execution.

Project Planning Support

A third desired characteristic is a high level of support for project planning. Managers in departmental structures often fail to appreciate the amount of planning necessary for projects, especially projects that require large interdisciplinary teams. Under an enterprise project management system, support for project planning and the project planning itself will be matters of routine. This means the project core team will develop a detailed project plan where both key products and services for the project and key project milestones will be identified and scheduled. Historical data from past projects will be used when developing those plans so that the team will believe the project really can be completed by the scheduled deadline.

Customer and End-User Input

The fourth characteristic for success is a high level of customer and end-user input in defining the final product of the project. Under departmental systems, department members may assume that they know best what customers want since they are expert in that particular area. An enterprise project management system makes no such assumption. Instead, end users of all project results will be clearly identified and representatives of the end users will be consulted early in the project planning process. Due to this early-and-often interaction, user expectations will be well known, and team members will know how the end users will use the final product as well as the problems the end users are trying to solve. And user representatives will consult with the team on a regular basis to the point where an end user will become a wider member of the project core team. Clear measures of customer satisfaction and quality plans will be a part of project planning.

Team Support

The fifth characteristic for success involves those practices that support the project team members and allow them to focus on the work of the project. Remember that the three keys to success in any project are focus, focus, and focus. Ideally, most team members will work full time on only one project. They will not feel they are working on too many projects, and their current project will be their top priority. A core team will be established to work on the project from beginning to end, and all project team members will feel responsible for the final success of the project. Upper managers will provide support for team-building activities to promote project success.

Performance Support

The sixth success factor is called project performance support. For this factor the project is fully staffed, the members are given time and space to work on the project, fermentation and creativity are encouraged so project team members can speak the truth to upper managers, and upper managers work as a team to help projects succeed. In addition, the organization has a formal project office with the job of improving project manager performance.

Information System

The seventh characteristic is a true project management information system, one that facilitates good communication among project team members on any given project and also among different project teams. In addition, a PMIS would ensure adequate information to all stakeholders and would help to facilitate a learning environment by containing project reviews and lessons learned from all projects in the organization. Real organizational learning takes place when the results of project reviews are also made available to other teams within the organization. Many organizations attempt this organizational learning feature, and a few are able to share the learning with people on project teams. However, the difficulty is usually in making these results available to other teams within the organization. This is an important role for the project office.

Organization Support

The eighth characteristic is an organization designed to fully support activities of project management. The reward system in place would be designed with project management in mind. Project managers will be appointed to projects based on their skill level and not just their availability. In addition, *project manager* will be a recognized job title the organization, and project managers will be adequately trained and will have a clear career development path.

Economic Value

For the ninth characteristic, project management will become much more businesslike and project managers' success will be measured by indices such as net present value, return on investment, and increasing shareholder value. This means the project manager will be responsible for more than just completion of the product. Responsibility will include how well the product achieves the goals of its strategy and increases economic value of the organization. The project office will play a large role in this transformation.

On the Other Hand

So far, we discussed the benefits for a project office. There is, however, another side to the story, and the change agent team should be aware of that side. Dinsmore (2002b) reported on a project office workshop held in Australia by the Human Systems Global Network. The group brainstormed a list of arguments both in favor of and opposed to the PO. Husky justifications do favor the PO—consistency of approach, a home for project management, economies of scale, learning from experience, common control and reporting procedures, ownership and accountability of data, reduction in the risk of failure, promotion of repeatability and reusability. The list goes on: greater consistency of outcomes, platform for improvement, review and maintenance of standards, consistent training, auditing criteria, development of priorities and strategies, alignment to business and corporate goals, links to best practices, maintenance of knowledge base, and quality tracking.

The Human Systems Global Network was biased toward the project office, since most participants (about seventy) hailed from some form of corporate project management office. Yet, when asked, they readily threw rocks at the concept and ultimately showed just cause for snuffing out any PO proposal. In spite of the favorable undercurrent, the negative arguments, once put on a flip chart and articulated to the group, were perceived as being strikingly real and thus demanding very respectful consideration.

- Can provide no hard evidence to prove that it improves project success
- Concentrates power in parts of the organization
- Hinders project managers' initiatives
- Increases overhead, so may not be worth the investment
- Stimulates bureaucracy
- Diffuses responsibility of project managers
- Dilutes the ability of project managers to direct activities
- Diverts good project staff from managing projects
- May multiply mistakes
- May cause distractions from delivery
- Tends to be process driven, not project driven
- Creates resentment among project managers
- Stimulates power struggles within the organization

Christine Dai (2001) supported the first argument above in her dissertation research. She compared results from organizations with and without project management offices, along with some with an in-between form, and concluded, "For advocates of PMOs, the findings must be rather unsettling—and surprising—given the uniformly positive tone about PMOs seen in the literature review. In essence, the random sample results do not show that reported project success is higher in organizations that have PMOs in comparison with those that do not."

The important other finding of the Dai research, however, was that reported project success was higher in organizations that were practicing the critical success factors. These are similar to factors mentioned by the Human Systems Global Network group. Some organizations used a project office to develop the use of the success factors, while others did not use such a vehicle. The important point to realize here is that how organizations developed the practices was not important. What was important was that they did develop the practices. Many organizations find it difficult to develop the practices without establishing a dedicated group. For these organizations, a project office becomes very important—they will not be able to develop the practices without it. For these organizations the Dai research should actually increase the sense of urgency for establishing a project office, because without it the critical success factors will never be developed.

Summary

In this chapter we develop a variety of methods for establishing a sense of urgency for developing a project office. Potential change agents are cautioned not to rely solely on a short-term danger because this often results in a short-term sense of urgency. In particular, we argue against establishing a project office with the goal of minimizing cost. Such an office could be seen as a watchdog for upper management and thus have difficulty in effecting a change to enterprise project management.

A more comprehensive goal is adding value to the organization. This goal aligns the members of the project office with the overall goal of the organization and thus enhances their effectiveness.

Various ways the project office could add value are presented, along with a description of how organizations would function if project management were developed as a core competency. To complete the picture, some possible negative aspects of a project office are listed to show why some members of the organization will not readily embrace the concept. Project office implementers should be ready to address these negative images as a part of the process for creating a sense of urgency.

The complete successful change agent

- Identifies the current pain in the organization
- Creates a picture of the new organization as so compelling and attractive that people want it, almost desperately
- Identifies clear dangers to avoid taking shortcuts that lead to disasters
- Is not tempted to explore new lands that offer more promise than they are capable of fulfilling

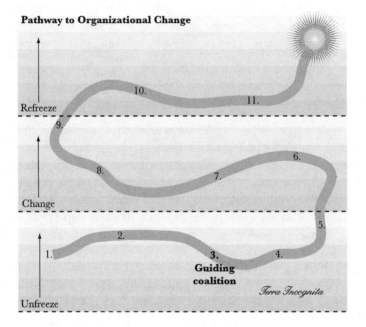

Pathway to Organizational Change

Refreeze

10.

11.

9.

Change

8.

7.

6.

5.

1.

2.

**3.
Guiding
coalition**

4.

Terra Incognita

Unfreeze

This chapter covers power and politics, stakeholder analysis, recruiting a powerful executive sponsor, developing the ability to speak truth to powerful people and a process for doing so, and developing a process for operating across organizations. The objective is to identify useful practices for recruiting and managing a powerful group of people as a guiding coalition for implementing a project office.

CHAPTER THREE

POWERFUL FORCES:
BUILDING A GUIDING COALITION

A common theme in the success or failure of any organizational initiative is building a guiding coalition—a group of sponsors and influential people who support the change. This support (or lack of support) represents a powerful force either toward or away from the goal. Gaining support means the difference between pushing on, modifying the approach, or exiting the path. Moderate success may be achieved without widespread support, but continuing long-term business impact requires alignment of power factors within the organization.

Consider an example of what can happen when a powerful force is not in place. A participant in a project office workshop passed along this series of correspondence:

Currently, I'm rolling out the methodology. I've reached about 140 end users in IT and there's still the business units. In a way, I am enjoying giving the overview/rollout because I get to meet new people, hear their concerns, and make lame jokes. So far, so good.

The next day:

The one thing I hate about training or conferences is that I get excited and come back to work rejuvenated; ready to share what I've learned. More often

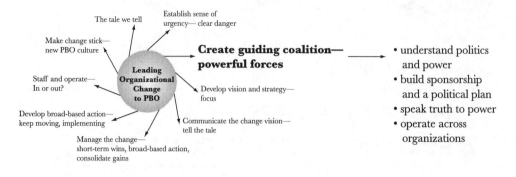

than not, my enthusiasm is met with apathy. Do you get these responses from others? Do they enjoy the training but then find they aren't allowed to practice what they've learned?

This is a common problem when the environment does not support project work, especially so when setting up a project office. Three days later, the participant found out what happens "when the bough breaks":

Well, before I could locate new and better employment, I was told to leave my company. Yes, either I resign or they'll fire me. Needless to say, it's been a stressful week. . . . The reason I was given for this sudden decision was that the CIO doesn't like me. That's what I get for using the "chain of command." Apparently, those who never speak are rewarded. I should know this by now but I'm still an idealist and I refuse to give that up. Somewhere out there is an employer who actually wants someone as upstanding, goal and ideal oriented, and caring as I am . . . someone whose agenda is for the good of the company and not myself.

Advice offered back to the person at that time:

I encourage you to hang on to your values. In fact, sometimes it seems that's all we have to hang on to, and if we're not strong in that regard, the going is rougher. As we look back on times like this, it's the right things we do that give us satisfaction.

This person advises others:

In retrospect, these are the lessons I learned:
    1. Get a commitment from an executive sponsor *and* check back frequently to make sure they haven't changed their mind about what the objec-

tives of the project office are. (In my case, I was not permitted to have contact with the sponsor—the CIO. When I went over my supervisor's head to the CIO to discuss if the objectives are consistent with when I was hired, the CIO found that insubordinate and believe it or not, ordered my firing. When my boss refused to fire me, he too was "laid off," thus eliminating our entire office.)

2. The project office director/officer/manager should be someone internal, if possible. If an outside resource is brought in, resentment from the "old curmudgeons" (those who don't feel they need a project office because it's fine as it is) will be felt and actively demonstrated.

3. Based on statement #2, if the resource is brought in from the outside, begin evangelizing the benefits of a project office immediately . . . bottom to top, top to bottom, it doesn't matter. A project office is viewed as overhead so you'll need to win proponents ASAP.

Too late, this person learned the power of a nonguiding coalition. Getting explicit commitments up front, the more public the better, is a key step to implementing the change. It also takes follow-through to maintain the commitment. But if commitment was not obtained initially, it is not possible to maintain throughout.

Another scenario is described in *Surviving the Rise and Fall of a Project Management Office* (McMahon and Busse, 2001). Many laudable steps occurred in the establishment of the project office. Among the challenges:

One of the early signs of trouble was the reluctance of the IS Director to educate the areas outside of IS [Information Systems] on the techniques and benefits of project management. This Director felt the IS Department needed to become experts before reaching out to other areas. This approach fostered an "us vs. them" attitude by several business users. They expressed concern that standards and a methodology were being imposed on them from the IS group without the benefit of any input or training. The PMO Manager attempted to provide some insight into the benefits of project management; however, this was met with firm resistance.

A crack in the foundation that led to the fall:

The groundwork had been laid for staff and management participation for an organized approach to project management. Then came disruption to the champions' participation in this initiative—the PMO Manager left the organization. On the heels of this departure, the PMO was dealt a heavy blow by the departure of the only upper management champion this cause ever had—the IS Director. Along with the arrival of a new IS Director came a new set of initiatives, which was to become the final blow for this PMO.

McMahon and Busse advise those working with project offices to build deep roots.

The importance of building coalitions, enterprise level placement of the PMO, and recurring staff education all contribute to building deep organizational roots that cannot be pulled out by a change in personnel, no matter the level. Obtain and expand sponsorship throughout your organization. This is how to build something that will last beyond the priorities of the person who initiated it. If your organization is considering a PMO and does not have this type of support, this is a major risk for which a mitigation strategy must be developed.

Politics

Politics happen in any and all organizations. Remarkably, power and politics are unpopular topics with many people, an attitude that makes it harder for them to become skilled and effective. Most organizations do not suffer from too much power; indeed, people generally feel there is too little power either being exercised to keep things moving or available to them. They often resort to a victim mode and feel powerless and therefore free of obligation to do anything.

However, this is an opportunity to exercise personal power. What we hear from participants in many programs is that the biggest pitfall is not allowing enough time to fully assess the environment—learning how to operate effectively in a political environment.

What is a political environment? A negative reaction to the word *political* could be a barrier to success. Being political is not a bad thing when trying to get good things done for the organization. The political environment is the power structure, formal and informal. It is how things get done in day-to-day processes as well as in a network of relationships. Power is the capacity each individual possesses to translate intention into reality and sustain it. Organizational politics is the exercise or use of power.

Understand the power structure in your organization. A view of earth from outer space would not show the lines that separate countries or organizations or functional areas or political boundaries. The lines are manmade figments that exist in our minds or on paper but not in physical reality.

Power is not imposed by boundaries. Power is earned, not demanded. Power can come from your position in the organization, from what you know, from the network of relationships you have, and possibly from the circumstances, meaning you could be placed in a situation that has a great deal of importance and focus in the organization.

One of the most reliable sources of power when working across organizations is the credibility you build through a network of relationships. It is necessary to have credibility before you can attract team members, especially the best people, who are usually busy and have many other things competing for their time. Credibility comes from relationship building in a political environment. Is there a credibility gap in your environment? Be aware of the lingering effects of organizational memory—people long remember what happened when. You can easily align with someone who has the power of knowledge credibility, but relationship credibility is something only you can build—or lose.

The following comments were offered by a participant in a workshop about a process for influencing without authority: "This course might be OK for people whose jobs are project management or leadership. It's tough to put up with, recognize, tend to, or pamper politically oriented people at my level—people who actually do measurable work. I don't have time to apply the law of reciprocity. I think that it would be better to teach a course to the politically minded on how to be less politically motivated."

This man reflected an ambivalence toward politics that is detrimental to his own success. He would probably agree with this anonymous definition we found on a Unix discussion group: "The word *politics* is derived from the word *poly*, meaning 'many,' and the word *ticks*, meaning 'blood-sucking parasites.'" Although this attitude is not uncommon, it stands in the way of adopting some meaningful aspects of the process.

Politics will be present whenever an attempt is made to turn a vision for change into reality. It is a fact of life, not a dirty word that should be stamped out. Consider using the following affirmation to counteract the negative attribution of a political environment: *Peak-performing people use potent processes, positive politics, and pragmatic power to achieve sufficient profit and keep organizations on a path toward a purpose.*

The challenge is to create an environment for positive politics. That is, one where people operate with a win-win attitude, and all actions are out in the open. This approach is the opposite of manipulation, which is a win-lose process, employing an underhanded or without-your-knowledge-of-what's-happening approach.

One's attitude toward political behavior becomes extremely important in the modern business environment. Dr. Jeffrey Pinto, in *Power and Politics in Project Management* (1996, pp. 75–76), says options are to be *naive*, to be a *shark* who uses aggressive manipulation to reach the top, or to be *politically sensible*. "Politically sensible individuals enter organizations with few illusions about how many decisions are made." They understand, either intuitively or through their own experience and mistakes, that politics is a facet of behavior that happens in all organizations. Political sensitives neither shun nor embrace predatory politics. "Politically sensible individuals use politics as a way of making contacts, cutting deals, and gaining power and resources for their departments or projects to further corporate, rather than entirely personal, ends."

It's Really a Power Thing

The power wielded by a project office spans the spectrum from a sometimes weak-kneed project support office to the powerful concept of the chief project officer (Dinsmore, 2001). Naturally, this ambiguous span of power raises questions in the minds of other stakeholders. This in turn sets off conscious or unconscious resistance. The PO, while seen as a savior by some, begins to look like a big bad wolf to others.

For that reason, project office efforts may get shot down before they get off the ground—even if concrete technical reasons buttress the well-intentioned movement. The causes that sabotage a PO's inception range from power plays to subtle undermining. Here are the players that can keep POs from taking hold or ultimately cause their demise:

- *Big-time steamrollers.* Top managers often have strong views about how to organize work, perhaps with a strong process stance or quality view. Although the PO approach is not inconsistent with other management tacks, the PO may be seen as unnecessary organizational baggage, under the assumption that projects should somehow work without PO support. The PO movement then is steamrolled under the pressure of other top management priorities.
- *Lateral roadblockers.* These players sit at the same level as the champions of the PO cause. Resistance comes from the flanks, sparked by lack of information, poor understanding of how other areas will be affected, and fear that the initiative will reduce the roadblockers' relative power base within the organization.
- *Oblique snipers.* Managers with diagonal relationships may take potshots at an attempt to restructure work using a project office tack. Their power base may be threatened or they may not know enough about the concept to support it.
- *Grassroots sandbaggers.* At the project level, professionals are unlikely to get enthused about dealing with an area that may exercise control or interfere with the status quo. Unless a real benefit is shown to project practitioners (what's in it for me?), then natural indifference and resistance will build and the PO effort is likely to be met with crossed arms and foot dragging.

A Rose Has Its Thorns

Although the PO may be seen as a sweet-smelling solution, it comes with thorny organizational power issues. Here are some of the reasons people may resist:

- *The ignorance factor.* Even highly intelligent people are ignorant (not knowledgeable) about certain topics. An engineer may be merrily unaware of the glories of marketing, and a psychologist may ignore the concepts of information technology. Managers and executives may not be schooled in the concepts of managing multiple projects. And they are all unlikely to support what they do not understand.
- *Poor pitching.* The concept must be appropriately pitched to the stakeholders. If conscious time and effort are not put into selling the idea to all those who will be affected, then backlash is a probable by-product.
- *No custom fit.* The proposed version of the PO will work only if it fits the company culture and the situation at hand. If there is no logical technical justification for implementing a PO, then resistance will be high.
- *Rowing upstream.* The political moment has to be right. Mergers may be in the wind, or major market shifts, any of which may move the project office out of the river—or over the edge of the waterfall. Or there may be an internal power battle that blacklists your proposal.

So Why Insist?

It is not smart to enter battles you cannot win. So why insist if people do not clap and cheer at your proposal for implementing or reinforcing a PO effort?

First, it is important to verify that a project office is viable and makes sense. A PO is not the universal cure for all organizational ailments and may not apply at all in certain situations. If, for example, people are trained and motivated, methodologies are in place, and tools, software, and hardware are readily available—and a healthy, thriving synergistic project atmosphere exists—then there may be no need for a project office. Or, if the company is primarily process-oriented and works in a stable, nonchanging environment, a PO would be an unnecessary luxury.

Yet if those conditions are lacking and the setting is fast paced and constantly changing, then the organization probably needs a projectized culture to meet market demands and generate desired results. One way to do this is through a project office. If the need indeed exists, then it is worth pushing ahead.

How to Deal With the Power Ploys

None of the players mentioned as potential opponents are bad guys, out to sabotage efforts to improve company productivity. They are well-intentioned professionals concerned with getting their work done, naturally resistant to anything that might interfere with their activities or seem unnecessary for the organization to produce results. So to overcome these barriers, develop a strategy to deal with power-related issues. Here are some hints:

- *Don't hurry the river.* Things take time. Develop a strategy for involving people and getting buy-in and implementation over time.
- *Show benefit to the organization and to the stakeholders.* Although logical technical benefit to the organization is basic, the stakeholders all have their own selfish reasons to support or reject such an effort. Benefit, from the standpoint of each individual, must be shown and understood.
- *Look for a champion.* Don't try to carry the flag by yourself. Develop strong support and avoid labeling the effort as "my idea." Look for support at a sponsor level and create a critical mass of support.

Sponsorship

Schwab established a project office that supported functional business units. A senior manager provided the backbone that led to perceived value that it was easier to do business better. Then he left the company. There was a nine-month gap before a successor was named. The project office was rudderless, and its value was not promoted or demonstrated across the organization. Lack of management prioritization led to too many people doing too many projects and making a lot of work for themselves. Then people in the PO were laid off or dispersed into business units.

Kent Harmon, director of R&D effectiveness at Texas Instruments, noticed a similar phenomenon: the time required to implement a project office often exceeds the tenure of its executive sponsor. "It would be interesting to do process control charts for supervisor tenure," he says. "It's like finding the longest pole in a tent and making it shorter. It's unbelievable but management often assumes zero productivity loss will be incurred by these actions. Plotting success rate versus size of the organization would probably show midsize organizations are more successful. Our salvation is to turn despair to humor." He predicts the cycle time for a typical project office implementation at five to seven years. The HP Project Management Initiative operated on a ten-year cycle.

The good news is that an executive sponsor helps make a PO successful. The bad news is that it is tough to keep your sponsor around. There are pros and cons about where in the organization you recruit this sponsor and how to make the choice. Someone high in the organization, say at the vice presidential level, should certainly have enough power and experience to be effective. But make sure you ask the key questions: Are they interested? Do they have enough time? Will they be positioned for the next five to seven years to see the implementation through? It is also desirable that a sponsor come from a powerful and important part of the organization. Such a paragon may not be available; it may be necessary to trade off some power and position for enthusiasm and time. It may only be possible to get someone from the departmental level. If this is the case, than it seems doubly important to ensure that your sponsor is from a powerful department that is central to the success of the organization.

The rise and fall of a project office appears as a common theme. This may be a natural sequence as needs of an organization change. Sometimes it becomes obvious from political maneuverings among individuals that the project office has outlived its usefulness or is antithetical to their needs. The Spectrum Program Management group at HP (described in Chapter Four) experienced this activity when functional managers disagreed with how the office was run. Additional examples in Chapters Seven and Eight show how useful it can be to put extraordinary efforts into cultivating and maintaining sponsor relationships.

Political Plan

The quest to implement a project office requires a political management plan. One key element is to conduct a stakeholder analysis (see Chapter Seven for one way to do this). You quickly realize that it is impossible to satisfy everyone and that the goal might become to keep everyone minimally annoyed and use a "weighted dissatisfaction" index (Pinto, 1996, pp. 41–42).

Analysis of common success factors indicates that project leaders need to pay attention to the needs of project stakeholders as well as those of project team members. Identifying stakeholders early on leads to better stakeholder management throughout the project. Use diagnostic tools to analyze project office stakeholders. A stakeholder is anyone who has a reason to care about the effort—sponsoring the change, or dependent upon, supplying, or executing it. Ask "Who could stop this effort?"

You can build a compass like the one shown in Figure 3.1 to identify these players. Write down names and get to know people in each area. What motivates them, how are they measured, what are their concerns?

One approach is to assess whether they support the effort or not and whether their organizational impact is high or low. With that assessment in hand, act accordingly:

- *High support, low impact.* Stakeholders who support the project but do not have a lot of power to change or defend it should be kept informed and nurtured. It is important to keep the support of these stakeholders—but not as important

FIGURE 3.1. USE COMPASS TO IDENTIFY STAKEHOLDERS.

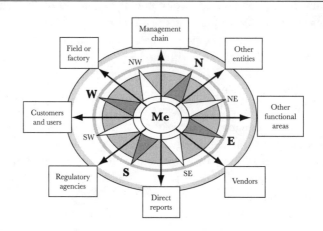

as it is to keep the support of stakeholders with both high support and high impact.

- *Low support, low impact.* Stakeholders who oppose the project and have little impact on it should not be ignored, but their comments and input into the project are not as important as are those of others. Keep these stakeholders informed of what is going on with the project. Try to make sure that these stakeholders do not inspire other, more influential stakeholders to oppose the project.
- *Low support, high impact.* Stakeholders who oppose the project office and have a lot of power over it should be watched carefully throughout the life of the project. These stakeholders should not be ignored. Communicate regularly with them and make attempts to determine how the project office can support their interests. Use change management and persuasion techniques to build support.
- *High support, high impact.* Nurture these stakeholders throughout the life of the project. Keep them informed of everything that is happening with the project office and leverage their support and impact to help gain support for the project from stakeholders with lower levels of support or counter opposition from those who actively oppose the project. They may be able to increase the impact of less powerful stakeholders who support the project.
- *Neutral.* Neutral stakeholders have the potential to go either way—either toward support for or opposition to the project office. Use influence techniques to gain their support. This is particularly important for neutral stakeholders who have high potential impact on the project.

Creating a Stakeholder Strategy

Berger and others (1994, 1998) describe useful sets of things to do and avoid when it comes to dealing differentially with stakeholder supporters and stakeholder resistors. For supporters, they recommend enrolling stakeholders in the change process, offering them ownership roles in it, and actively soliciting their opinions and listening to their ideas. Despite their initial support, it is unwise to expect them to manage or lead the change effort, and important not to dismiss or ignore their ideas—expect too much or too little of them, and you may lose them. For those who start out by opposing the idea, he recommends illustrating and reframing the change in terms of how it will benefit them personally, acknowledging the problems they identify and using them to determine if all options have been explored, and inviting them to voice their reluctance or resistance. It is crucial not to dismiss or ignore resistors in the hope that they will just go away, as they will continue to work for their own goals whether or not you watch them. Likewise, it is dangerous to assume that someone who resists one change will be a resistor for all changes—people have different priorities on different issues. It is easy to create opposition for yourself by expecting it instead of starting with an open door.

Another approach is to diagnose levels of trust and agreement with each stakeholder (see Figure 3.2). Based on the outcome of that diagnostic, modify your approach to getting their commitment.

Approach stakeholders in each area starting from the position of strength. For example, when trust is high but agreement about the change is low, start by reinforcing the effective working relationship that exists. Express desire that this bond will again help the two of you work through the differences. Only after establishing agreement on these objectives should you address the problem area.

FIGURE 3.2. DIAGNOSE STAKEHOLDERS.

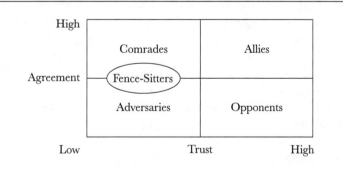

Source: Adapted from Block, 1991.

People often jump right into the problem. This prompts defensive behavior from the other person. Taking time to reestablish rapport first can prove far more effective in helping reach a mutually satisfying solution.

Another element of a political plan is positioning. Where the project office is located in an organization affects its power base. The concept of "centrality" says locate it in a position central and visible to other corporate members, where it is central to or important for organizational goals (Pinto, 1996, p. 57). The HP Project Management Initiative started in Corporate Engineering, a good place to be because HP was an engineering company. That put the initiative into the mainstream instead of in a peripheral organization where its effectiveness and exposure may be more limited. Likewise, a project office for the personal computer division reported through a section manager to the R&D functional manager. This again reflected centrality since R&D at that time drove product development efforts.

Most important decisions in organizations involve the allocation of scarce resources. Position and charter a project office with a key role in decision making that is bound to the prioritization and distribution of organizational resources. Be there to help, not make decisions. Put managers at ease and help them recognize that they are not losing decision-making power, they are gaining an ally to facilitate and implement decisions.

Implicit in creating a new order is the notion that conflict is inevitable. The use of power and politics becomes a mechanism for resolving conflict. Politics is a natural consequence of the interaction between organizational subsystems. A project office is best seen as a helping hand, there not to create conflict but to provide skilled facilitation leading to effective and efficient resolution. When people find that telling their problems to the program manager helps them get speedy resolution instead of recrimination, they feel they have a true friend, one they cannot do without.

A well-known political tactic is to demonstrate your legitimacy and expertise. Developing proficiency and constantly employing new best practices around program and project management, plus communicating and promoting the services and successes achieved, help the project office gain status in the organization. Combined with recruitment of sponsors and management of stakeholder relations, these measures often add up to an effective political plan. This factor is a recurring theme in all case studies in this book.

Pinto says, "Any action or change effort initiated by members of an organization that has the potential to alter the nature of current power relationships provides a tremendous impetus for political activity" (1996, p. 77). Such is the purview of a project office for organizational change.

Developing High-Level Commitment: A Business Case

This case is based on the American Productivity & Quality Center's report of a benchmarking study of Hewlett-Packard Consulting, detailing how HP became interested in developing a knowledge management system in 1995. Recognizing that sharing knowledge among projects, learning from others' successes and mistakes, and capturing reusable material from engagements was essential to success, HP management wondered why the sharing and leverage of knowledge was not occurring more often and more effectively. What needed to be done to make this behavioral change happen?

Customers expect innovation, rapid execution, and global consistency. They also want to tap into Hewlett-Packard's collective knowledge when they engage HP Consulting for their projects.

Obstacles existed primarily on an organizational level. Silo mentalities impeded knowledge sharing, which was neither measured nor rewarded. Providing slack time for employees to share knowledge was a challenge. Nonstandardized selling and implementing procedures for the same solution across the globe challenged the sharing of consistent solutions. Information was scattered all over the organization and not accessible. In the past, investment in managing knowledge was sporadic, bounded by organization structures, and focused on technology.

Overcoming Obstacles

The implementation team began by explicitly stating that knowledge was the currency of their business. The team emphasized that the organization's ability to grow would be directly affected by its ability to manage knowledge efficiently and effectively across all segments of the company.

The team realized it had to sell its business case to senior management and secure proper management sponsorship. The team knew that sponsorship could not come from a token head only but instead had to reflect involved, passionate sponsorship. It also had to include a senior-level manager who was willing to become intimately involved in building the initiative.

The team used a parable of the biblical figure Moses to engage sponsors in understanding their role and what was needed to make the initiative a success. In this story, a *committed and involved leader* (Moses) had a *vision* (leading his people out of bondage and into a land of milk and honey) and a *high-level sponsor* (God) who was *able to remove obstacles* (the Red Sea). Moses played a *direct role* in bringing the people to the promised land. (He took the lead in crossing the Red Sea into the desert and led them to the Promised Land instead of simply checking on the groups' progress on a quarterly basis!) At the end of this story, the newly appointed VP and general manager stepped forward and said, "I'll be Moses." This began a wave of support by the global leadership team that saw the initiative through its first couple of years. The actions that followed were in the footsteps of Moses. The general manager was highly involved in developing the initiative, gaining and sustaining support from the leadership team, communicating to the organization about the importance of knowledge management, and working closely with the team.

Right Makes Might?

The implementation team described in the preceding section was fortunate to encounter upper managers who would either initiate or support the project. More often, program managers encounter unrealistic schedule demands, too few resources, and too much to do. They find themselves between a rock and a hard place when they try to speak this truth back to those in power.

Some have asserted that science itself is not fundamentally driven by the search for truth. People who thought truth was an easy thing to discover often find how difficult it can be to pin a new idea down. To counter the belief that science is a clean, steady progression to a full understanding of all phenomena, Kuhn (1996) illustrates that it moves by jumps and starts, with periodic changes in the equilibrium of things.

Empirical research (Larson and King, 1996) has found that information is often distorted and manipulated in organizations. Subordinates want to send favorable information quickly and accurately to managers, but they generally prefer to distort or block unfavorable information. Similarly, managers want to accept information favorable to their self-image and beliefs and to reject or misinterpret negative or critical information.

The change agent team will be speaking to very powerful people and some of the news may not be to their liking. Being "right" may not always help.

Speaking Truth to Power

It is often difficult to get upper management properly involved in project management processes. The truth is that upper managers may need to change their ways to properly support and facilitate progress. It is even more difficult to give upper managers bad news, especially when some of the news may be due to their own lack of foresight and involvement. A key ingredient for prosperity that a project office can offer is the cooperative partnership established with management. This section explores ways that program managers can get the message through to people in power.

The key elements for change agents to speak truth to power are determining what is bad about the news, defining and delivering the truth, using your strengths, creating intent and motivation, and getting it done. Changes or projects that demonstrably help solve upper managers' problems while contributing to the overall welfare of the organizations have a much higher probability of receiving enthusiastic support. Speak that truth to the powers in your organization.

When constructing messages you expect people do not want to hear, first understand why that is the case. Sometimes the news is just too different from what they are used to; sometimes it means they might lose power or status. It may run counter to what they want from the world, or they may have what appear to be good reasons to avoid thinking about it, or it may simply seem overwhelming.

The news is different. The truth often goes against the grain, against the way people have learned what is true and thus the way they have ordered the world. For example, Galileo was labeled a heretic for proposing that the earth revolved around the sun. This idea, which was true, went against years believing and teaching that earth was at the center of the universe. Belief in the new order of the universe meant that many years of believing had to be abandoned, and this is difficult to do. Most people will not abandon such strongly held beliefs unless they are in real pain, unless there is good reason to do so.

People could lose power. In Galileo's case, the authorities knew that if they accepted the idea of the sun as center of the universe, going against what they had said for years, they would lose their long-held power to define the world. That would reduce their influence, which would be likely to reduce the resources available to them. Upper managers sense a loss of power to core teams. Functional managers lose power to project offices. Whenever news means a loss of power for someone in the organization, expect resistance to believing the news.

People want it another way. Many times people do not want to hear what you have to say because they want it another way. In Japan prior to 1858, people in power wanted to remain in isolation rather than trade with the United States. Those who stated an unpopular opinion were executed, perhaps in hope that if all new thinkers were gone then people could revert to the old ways. People may believe that one way to remain the same is to get rid of all people who want change.

The news may be overshadowed by other circumstances. The truth may not be heard because of tradition. For example, telling a sailing ship's captain he might be wrong in calculating longitude was considered insubordination and thus grounds for death, despite the truth of the message. It took the loss of four ships and thousands of sailors (sense of urgency) before England's Parliament (guiding coalition) commissioned the search for a reliable timepiece to determine longitude at sea (implement a change) and many years before it happened (making it stick). If people feel that time-honored traditions are being violated, that act may take on more importance than the news that is given.

The message may be too much work. Change is often hard work, and the change is not seen as worth the effort. If you tell upper management they have to become involved in order to help ensure project success, they may see it as an unwarranted demand. They want you to solve the problems, not use their time.

These examples illustrate that although a program manager may be "right" and know the "truth" of the situation, especially when grounded with solid evidence from the project management body of knowledge, that does not ensure that others in the organization will listen to or heed those words of wisdom. Apparently, right does not make might—it takes more persuasive skills and actions to be effective.

Defining the Truth

To speak truth to power, first clearly articulate the message that you want to convey. What is your message? If you have a message that needs to get through, then obviously it has not gotten through before, so ask yourself why. Review the list of obstacles to determine what parts of the message are most uncomfortable, or which of the reasons for resistance you can expect to meet. Knowing the source of resistance is half the battle, for then it will not be a surprise.

Collect facts and data about the situation. Use a systematic process that demonstrates thoroughness in the approach. Put everything together in a clear, compelling message that describes the current pain and paints a picture of an improved, desirable state.

Other truths become evident to the competent program manager: the triple constraints of scope, schedule, and resources must balance or trade off with each other; the organization can not deal with too many projects under way at the same time; each project should be clearly linked with strategic objectives for the organization; the planning process takes time; and the deadlines have to match up with data from the project planning process. A firm belief in these truths provides the energy, passion, and courage that it takes to negotiate with management about them.

Delivering the Truth

Once the message is clear and you know your resistance, decide how to deliver the message. You may have to become a revolutionary as part of delivering the message. Some effective delivery techniques include use of inside/outsiders or of true outside consultants, trying out the ideas as though in jest, or presenting data from outside sources. If all else fails, you can take the revolutionary road and simply try to implement the change yourself.

Use an inside/outsider. An inside/outsider is a person who works inside the company but is outside the particular part of the organization that needs to change, perhaps residing in the project office. These facilitators are skilled in processes for getting people to talk about problem areas. The inside/outsider is important for placing the problems in a company perspective. At HP, a member of the Project Management Initiative corporate project office often served that purpose.

Hire a consultant. Another approach is to bring in a credible outsider who can take the first bullets. The consultant can talk about how certain problems are commonplace in other organizations, thereby taking direct heat off the upper managers. The consultant can also give examples of how other organizations solved similar problems. Project office consultants may fulfill this role, especially if they stay connected with other professionals in the industry.

Work like a court jester. One of the functions of court jesters was to tell bad news to the king but hide it as a part of a jest. One way to work like a court jester is to develop a list of common problems, a list so pathetic it causes laughter. Present the list to upper managers as examples of things that happen in other organizations. Then encourage the group to discuss the list, a process that is likely to lead them to determine that these problems may indeed be happening in your organization. Using this process you never really say that your organization has these problems, you allow people to discover them for themselves.

Develop objective data from some other source. Let other people or sources identify the problems. Employee surveys often serve that purpose at HP. The Strategic Management Group offers PEAT (Project Environment Assessment Tool) based around work of the authors. The Human Systems Knowledge Network has an enterprise project management profile service that provides clients with a comprehensive assessment of how their enterprise-wide project management practices compare with those of other members of the network. Using such surveys allows people to see how their organization compares to others and recognize that it may be suffering from problems they had not noticed, whereupon you are there to help with a solution—without having been the one to point to the problem and thus become the bearer of bad news.

Do it yourself—become a revolutionary. The basic problems with being a revolutionary are that you are usually alone, there is little organizational support for your ideas, few see the need for your revolution, and you are disturbing the status quo. If the revolution is not successful, you get shot. However, a revolution may be what the organization needs, whether it is a sweeping change toward project-based operations, setting up a project office for a big deal, or simply embarking on a

significant program. Enlist the help of others both inside and outside your organization through building a guiding coalition. Overcome fear with courage.

Implementing the Speak Truth Process

A project manager at HP sensed that the organization had serious trouble. There
was no process in place to manage the hundreds of problem issues that had been
identified. For example, there were big gaps in the new computer architecture,
problems so significant that new product development was being delayed. If the
problems were not resolved rationally, immediate decisions would have to be made
that might compromise or severely limit future options for the product line. Architects argued for the purity and integrity of the architecture. Implementers wanted
pragmatic solutions that leveraged the work completed to date. She was one
among dozens of project managers depending on the new architecture. She had
no more authority than anyone else. But she did have one difference—she was
willing to speak truth to power.

Fortunately, she had already completed a number of projects quite successfully. She was technically competent and could understand the difficult nature of
the problems being encountered. She knew action was necessary.

She identified the functional managers whose business was suffering because
of the problems and asked them to get together for a discussion. She put together
a presentation that clearly stated the nature of the problems and their impact on
the businesses. She proposed that each business ante up key engineers to meet in
study groups that would research the options and propose solutions. People in all
project areas needed to review the proposals and agree to adopt them. This work
would have to take place concurrently with development efforts under way. The
upper managers were clearly frustrated by the problems and concerned about getting their projects completed on time. They had no spare resources to resolve
problems that they believed other people should be working on.

Her ability to articulate the current reality clearly and her passion in describing a future state that was quite different made the difference. She pointed
out the pain that could be felt by each person, she had the ability to design a
process that could lead to changes, and she linked the pain and change efforts to
needs of the business. She created a compelling picture of what needed to be
done, how to do it, and what the results would be. This council of upper managers, now on board as a guiding coalition, asked her to lead the new program.

Believing in the program, she agreed to get it going. She became the leader, the
source of the guiding vision, and the workhorse. She also planned to go out of business as a revolutionary as soon as she could. She went to the program management
department and requested a project manager. One of the authors (Englund) came

on board and gradually took over as chairman of the Architecture Control Group. After we successfully completed the tumultuous first phase, albeit behind schedule and over budget, she guided us through the retrospective analysis, saw that we were on the right path, went back to managing her project full time, and got promoted. We became quite competent on the new process and alleviated much management anxiety. The computer architecture is at the heart of the huge success being enjoyed by HP in the computer business. The woman who initiated the process continues taking on new development efforts within the company.

Another situation sprang from the results of an open line employee survey. A group doing projects for the field organization scored low on empowerment. Employees reported that they had little power to make decisions. They were concerned about overmanagement, conflict, mistrust, low levels of openness, and excessive control.

One of the project managers seized the initiative. Lacking both authority and the answers, she nevertheless looked around for help. She contacted the project office—the corporate Project Management Initiative. Armed with data from the survey, a solid proposal developed with help from the initiative, a proposed forum that provided the opportunity for open sharing, and her willingness to make a difference, she got upper management to commit to funding an offsite meeting for managers and key contributors. She persuaded her peers and upper managers to participate.

Englund arranged to bring in Graham as an outside expert. Graham described the Ten Sins of Empowerment (actually he listed only nine . . . and left one to the groups' own imaginations, as in Figure 3.3). Drawing on humorous examples, he succeeded in getting managers to laugh at their foibles. He played a dual role—the consultant and the court jester. A manager at the meeting was heard to say, "Certainly we cannot be as bad as the examples portrayed, or are we? At least we exhibit only some, not all, of the problems."

An exercise followed the presentation: break into smaller groups, pick one of the sins to study, conduct a force field analysis, and present your findings to the large group. The force field analysis consists of the following steps:

1. Describe the current situation.
2. Describe the ideal scenario.
3. Describe a worse scenario.
4. Identify factors that inhibit reaching the ideal.
5. Identify factors that prevent succumbing to the worse.

The first intriguing factor about the break-out discussions was what sins they would pick. Would they pick the same ones or all different ones? Well, there was a small mixture. Among the five groups, several different topics were picked. A

FIGURE 3.3. SINS OF EMPOWERMENT.

Questions to ask:

- Want control or *results?*
- Focus on technique or *goal?*
- Measure input or *output?*
- Must team do what you say? (*no*)
- Are mistakes punished or *supported?*

Not acting on the *preferred answers* leads to committing these sins:

1. No focus on strategy
2. Setting arbitrary deadlines
3. Not allowing time for planning
4. Pulling people off the core team
5. Changing specifications due to anxiety
6. Adding people late in the project
7. Low focus on customer and end user requirements
8. Team set in reactive mode
9. Not a learning organization
10. . . .

later discussion about action items resulted in pinpointing two areas for attention: get to know customers better and develop a shared vision.

The general manager was pleased with the session. The truth he received was how deeply everyone felt about the issues and the uniformity of concerns that were shared. All involved encountered a safe environment for discussion, the meeting was facilitated by someone outside the immediate business but still from within the company, and ideas from external experts were presented as healthy models for consideration. The focus on getting to a small list of action items plus the intensity of the shared discussions furnished motivation for change. The offsite meeting provided the opportunity for managers and engineers alike to discover the issues themselves and then propose action. This approach has much more staying power than having a new process imposed by management.

Lessons Learned

A business case can be made that changes are often necessary within organizations that set out to conquer new territory through projects and project teams, guided by a project office. The role of upper managers may need to change to support these new efforts. However, it takes concerted effort, often on the part of project managers who are closest to the work, to speak the truth to upper managers who have the authority and power to do something about what needs to happen (see the summary chart in Figure 3.4). The change may be revolutionary and require specific skills and process steps to be effective. In the examples given in this chapter, change agents sought the truth beneath their frustrations and successfully navigated the political minefields by exercising these techniques:

- Act from personal strengths, such as expert, visionary, or process owner.
- Develop a clear, convincing, and compelling message and make it visible to others.
- Use passion that comes from your deep values and beliefs about the work (if these are not present, then find a different program to work on).
- Be accountable for success of the organization and ask others to do the same.
- Get explicit commitments from people to support the goals of the program—then they are more likely to follow through.
- Take action, first to articulate the needs, then to help others understand the change, and finally to get the job done.
- Tap the energy that comes from the courage of your convictions . . . and from the preparation steps outlined above.

Recruiting and Managing a Guiding Coalition: Operating Across Organizations

The new leadership challenge is to sense and actualize emerging opportunities. Real power comes from recognizing patterns of change. One is the role of interdependence among complex interactions and highly distributed organizations. By sensing and recognizing emerging patterns in the chaos (see discussion in Chapter Six), managers become part of a large generative force that can reshape the organization.

Think of operating across organizations as a behavioral process, with action steps leading to greater cooperation among diverse partners. A political plan would not be complete without a process to influence without authority across functional areas, businesses, and geography. Inevitably, implementing a new order of things goes against the status quo and engenders political resistance unless people are involved in its development. Establish a guiding coalition by systematically applying persuasion and influence tactics. Sensing behavioral patterns and responding to them are essential skills for a program manager.

This process evolved from a number of project office implementations. As HP gained momentum in the computer business, it needed a phase review process that linked senior management concerns with product development progress. A

FIGURE 3.4. SUMMARY OF THE SPEAK TRUTH PROCESS.

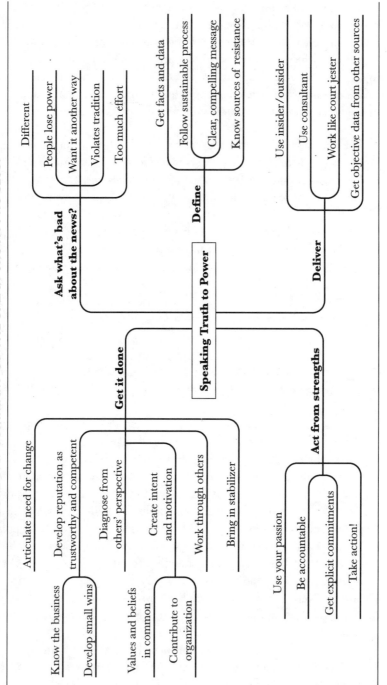

manager was chartered to develop a process that would function across the entire computer business. He researched what other companies did, formulated a plan, and then went on a campaign to solicit inputs from affected department managers. The thoroughness of the approach resulted in getting widespread support to implement the review process. It eventually helped resolve issues that led to HP's sustainable success in the minicomputer market.

A similar scenario occurred in the Sales Center. HP wanted to bid on a custom large-scale automation project, something drastically different from the direct sales off-the-shelf marketing approach. The Sales Center program manager conducted interviews with key managers who would typically oppose nonstandard business practices. His approach led to a successful order that opened up a new professional services business model. A similar approach was adopted for subsequent big deals and evolved into HP Consulting, now a significant revenue and profit generator for the company.

Englund observed these activities and applied them repeatedly within program management offices—developing cross-organization support for a hardware system product life cycle, establishing study teams to resolve computer architectural issues, and setting up a cross-functional SWAT team to identify ownership for hardware and software defect issues reported during personal computer product development. Later, at the corporate Project Management Initiative, the results were codified into a seventeen-step process that was then presented across the company.

Since the following process steps come from experiences in the corporate environment and from extensive sharing of practices in workshops and engagements with proven success, it is reasonable to assume the process can work for others and make a big difference for everyone. Greater success comes, not from applying one piece or another, but from applying effort to all steps in the process (see Figure 3.5).

Prepare for Relationship Building

The dynamics of any program are aggravated by the separation of organizational boundaries or geography. Proactive leaders recognize that people make things happen, and that getting to know their needs is vital to changing their behavior. Success in this environment requires extra effort to develop relationships, first to get the support of key people and second to get commitment to the program from each team member.

Starting with a premise that people have discretionary choice over what they work on next, continually ask, *"How do I get people to work with me on this program?"* There are many answers, and the answers vary by individual. Take the initiative to pursue answers to this question with vigor, for it provides the competitive advantage that achieves higher cooperation for your programs.

FIGURE 3.5. A BEHAVIORAL PROCESS
FOR OPERATING ACROSS ORGANIZATIONS.

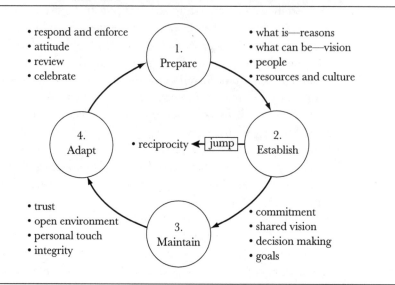

The initial step in preparation is to understand why the program is cross-organizational and why specific partners need to be involved. Ask questions of sponsors and do research. This understanding helps explain the program to others when seeking their support, thereby increasing credibility.

Clarify the program mission (what problem are we solving?) and develop a personal vision for a future state that is different from present reality. The theme for the 2002 Winter Olympics in Salt Lake City was "light the fire within." This is a good start, but for an enterprise project office to be successful, you also have to light the fire within other people. Tap the pain of current problems and paint a picture of something better. This vision becomes an energy source. It releases passion that turns into contagious energy. Make the vision visible and you will inspire other people to wish to participate because they clearly understand and come to believe in a similar vision. Practice your elevator speech—your ability to describe the program to any stakeholder during a short elevator ride in terms so concise, clear, convincing, and compelling that the person responds with "Wow, that's great! How can I help?"

Identify all people who will be stakeholders in your program. In each organization, recognize the influential people, ones who have position power or control resources, those who are sensitive, articulate, competent, and socially adept. Network with these stakeholders and influential people in accordance with the *law of reciprocity:* people expect a return (now or in the future) for what they give. Get support from others to extend your contacts.

Reap the synergy and productivity that comes from direct contact with people when traveling. Estimate the additional costs to operate across organizations, including travel and time. Develop a plan for implementing a cross-organizational program based on actual commitments received. This is also a good time to determine if costs exceed benefits. In that case, seek to contain the program.

Understand cultural differences (organizational, international, or functional) because people's actions, priorities, perceptions of reality, and style are highly dependent on cultural values. Diversity is both the greatest asset and the greatest liability of remote teamwork.

Establish Relationships

Establish relationship with cross-organization partners as soon as the need is recognized. Find or develop a program sponsor. Turn stakeholders and influential people into supporters by contacting all of them directly, describing opportunities, and sharing knowledge of the program (see Figure 3.6). Solicit their hopes

FIGURE 3.6. GAINING COMMITMENT.

A division general manager once requested development of an updated product life cycle linked to the corporate phase review process. The Systems Technology Group consisted of five R&D managers in one division with marketing, support, and manufacturing in separate divisions. The manager was well aware that the R&D managers "did not typically agree on anything," resulting in lengthy debates to implement something new.

A task force of experienced product developers put together a draft of a new life cycle. The leader conducted one-on-one interviews with each manager, soliciting concerns and objections. He took those inputs back to the task force and incorporated them into a new design. At an R&D Council meeting, he presented each of the concerns, verified the intent, and presented the solutions. At the end of the meeting, he asked for and received support for using the new process on all programs.

The next step was to go back to the general manager's staff meeting to introduce and schedule rollout for the new process. The manager was amazed that agreement had been reached, so he went around the room polling each manager for their support. Each manager nodded agreement. They further committed to training sessions for each of their departments.

Many years later both the life cycle and the process used to gain support for its implementation are still effective.

and suggestions. Write down their objections—these are gifts: the clues they offer about what you need to do to elicit their support. Follow through with changes. Get explicit commitments from everyone involved with the program—people are more inclined to do something once they commit to do so.

Assume everyone who needs to be influenced is a potential ally or can become one. Determine their goals, style, and needs. Imagine yourself in their position. Many interpersonal currencies can be exchanged, based on people's needs: exposure to new technology, information, response time, recognition, gratitude, resources. Diagnose your relationship using the stakeholder map and plan an approach tailored to each person's concerns.

Get all participants together face-to-face when beginning the program. Develop relationships and trust by doing team-building exercises. When reasons for the cross-organizational program are explained and concerns shared, participants come to accept one another and validate their roles. Recognize differences and seek consensus on values. A shared vision provides the intellectual cohesion that keeps cross-organizational partners focused.

Align priorities and establish a decision priority list based on the relative importance of schedule, scope, and resources. Define a process to raise and resolve issues quickly, including an escalation path. Separate technical from organizational issues; keep engineers working on technical issues and escalate organizational or business issues to a business or program team that will make the tough decisions. Empower decision making at the lowest reasonable level. Let everybody know how decisions are made. Document assumptions. Set up a specification change management process that not only helps to sustain decisions and foster stability but also permits flexibility.

Develop working goals and due dates. Because fuzzy goals become even fuzzier over distance, document specific goals for each partner that are clear, visible, and understood by everyone. Reduce interdependencies as much as possible. Document interface definitions and agreements that match deliverables with dependencies. Structure work so teams operate separately but in unison. Get conspicuous buy-in for accountability and results.

Maintain Relationships

Be aware that weak relationships are a dominant failure factor when operating across organizations. Trust is the foundation for effective teamwork. Maintain an open environment. Express genuine interest in other people and what is happening in their organizations. Be visible, approachable, positive, and supportive. Avoid favoritism. Regularly assess morale and relationships via two-way communications. Add a personal touch to communications. Be authentic and maintain integrity in all dealings.

Having good plans, especially current and realistic schedules and thorough communications, may reduce conflicts. Nurture constructive tension. Focus energy on common objectives. Make decisions based on objective criteria.

Be the leader who facilitates communications. Do this by designing easier and more effective ways to meet information needs of all stakeholders. Meet regularly with teams and individuals (also rotate the site) to keep focused and track progress. Be effective in managing meetings. Publish decisions and action items. Keep objectives visible in summary reports and distribute them widely. Get updated program documents to all sites or use a Web-based information system. Remote team members thrive on information about the program and a connection with the team. Even though travel budgets are usually tight, there is no substitute for meeting face-to-face at least once a year to prevent or resolve major differences and to celebrate milestones and other successes.

Adapt to Changes

Quickly respond to changes or variances. Rebuild teamwork by training new people together with people who need a refresher. Conduct just-in-time training when new challenges arise.

Approach other organizations with an attitude that no one site necessarily has the right answer. It is good management to adopt successful informal practices into formal procedures. Be sensitive to the ebb and flow of group dynamics; back off when the natural energy of the team is at work, and push back when they go off on tangents. By being flexible, by learning and adapting to situations as they arise, and by working to have decisions turn out right, you may exercise more influence and achieve greater success than by trying to drive people rigidly.

Involve the complete team and make corrections based on project reviews. Capture information from persons leaving the program. Document their expertise and processes so transitions are smooth.

Upon completion of the program, conduct similar celebrations at each remote site. When relationships change, express appreciation for the opportunity to work together toward a common goal and for the cooperation displayed during the program. Each program and each relationship should have a clear closure. No matter how problematic any relationship has been, try not to burn the bridges behind you when you part company—you may well have to work together again in the future.

Summary

Recognize that organizations are political. A commitment to positive politics is an essential attitude that creates a healthy, functional organization. Create relationships that are win-win (all parties gain), actual intentions are out in the open (not hidden or distorted), and trust is the basis for ethical transactions. Determining what people want and need and providing value to recipients are currencies of exchange. Increased influence comes from forming clear, convincing, and compelling arguments and communicating them through all appropriate means. Effective program managers embrace the notion that they are salespersons, politicians, and negotiators. Take the time to learn the skills of these professions and apply them daily.

Position the project office within the power base of the organization. There is no one right answer to where the PO should report. Seek an energetic, enthusiastic, politically effective sponsor and stakeholder to champion and support the effort.

Conduct a stakeholder analysis to determine supporters and resistors. Approach them differently based on the results of that analysis.

Returning to the question about getting people to work with you, you can bring people on board by showing them that the program provides means to meet organizational needs; participants have more fun; the experience is stimulating; you help them more than others; they get constructive feedback; they are excited by the vision; they learn more from you and this program; their professional needs are met; they travel and meet people; it's good for their careers; together we'll accomplish more than separately; this is neat. . . .

This chapter covers several techniques for building a guiding coalition. The extent that these powerful organizational forces are on board (or not) now enables you to go ahead in a big way, modify or downscale the effort, or quit and move on to something easier.

The complete successful change agent

- Becomes politically sensitive
- Identifies the sources and roles of power in the organization
- Recruits an executive sponsor
- Senses behavioral patterns and develops skills to address them
- Develops a political plan
- Manages all stakeholders
- Effectively speaks truth to power
- Applies a systematic process to operate across organizations

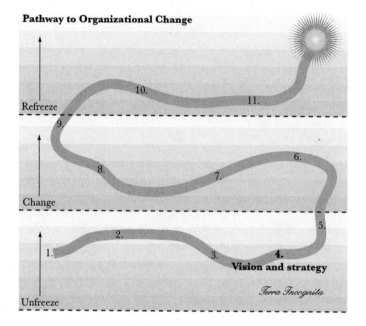

Pathway to Organizational Change

Refreeze

Change

Unfreeze

10.

11.

9.

8.

7.

6.

2.

1.

3.

5.

4.
Vision and strategy

Terra Incognita

This chapter describes the formulation of a project office and provides input for the change agents tasked with implementing one, especially when managing multiple projects is at issue. The responsibility of a change agent includes forming a detailed statement about what will be different in the organization and what it will look like. This chapter provides a range of alternatives and trade-offs to select from. It also offers a framework of process steps and questions to answer as a guideline for designing the best organizational approach and selecting the appropriate scope for the context of the existing organization.

The purpose of this chapter is to help potential change agents focus on a vision to be achieved, select an appropriate structure, and begin communicating a strategy to achieve the vision.

CHAPTER FOUR

FOCUS: DEVELOPING AND COMMUNICATING THE PROJECT OFFICE VISION AND STRATEGY

Project offices come in various sizes and shapes. They can be almost nonexistent, in virtual form, or they may be formal groups that exert powerful influence across an organization. Project offices are sometimes limited to a support role in planning and controlling a specific project; at the other extreme, they may be charged with full responsibility for implementing a multitude of strategic projects.

So the term *project office* covers a span of options almost as broad as the word *vehicle*. Just as vehicles range from tricycles to eighteen-wheelers, project offices cover an equally wide group of options, from virtual approaches to substantial and robust formal groups. The titles tacked onto the project office concept illustrate the variety of approaches.

The Titles

A project office is not always called a project office—the names span from the straightforward "Project Office" to sundry acronym-generators that mean different things in different settings. Here are some variations:

- Program Office
- Project Management Initiative

- Program Management Office
- Project Management Office
- Product Management Office
- Program Support Office
- Project Support Office
- Product Support Office
- Business Support Initiative
- Project Support Group
- Project Control
- Project Management Support Office
- Organization Support Project Office
- Virtual Program Management Office
- Program Support
- Project Support
- Group Program Office
- Divisional Program Office
- Project Management Center of Excellence
- Project Management Competency Center

The range of titles suggests that each project office is unique—so you could define an infinite number of PO types. But although it is true that an individual PO is "one and only" in some way, each can be grouped with other similar offices—for instance, the soft-treading support PSO on one hand, and on the other, the PO power-packed with authority.

Project Offices: From Low-Key to Omnipotent

Since the project office is designed to provide a systemic approach to managing projects—to ensure they are supported within the organization from the viewpoint of methodology, best practices, and information flow—the PO is vital for an organization to reach goals and implement strategies. While a PO provides benefits to the organization through advocating and supporting project management, the question about how that is done raises eyebrows, internal jealousies, and sometimes the tempers of stakeholders. This happens because expectations vary widely regarding PO scope definition and how to structure the initiative.

Basic questions require definition. For instance, should the PO be constituted as a staff or line function? Should it simply provide support for methodologies and project processes, or should it have full authority to make things happen on projects across the organization? Here are some classic approaches, starting with the staff functions:

Project Support Office. One classic variation of the PO is the project support office, which provides these types of services or internal consulting:

- Planning and scheduling
- Tracking
- Contract preparation and administration
- Administrative and financial services
- Scope change administration
- Project management tools
- Project metrics
- Document management
- Asset tracking
- Status audits

These services are either provided from a centralized pool or brought into the project team by project office staff members temporarily farmed out for the purpose.

Project Management Center of Excellence. Another slant on the project office calls for those capabilities to be developed within each project, with the project office standing in the background as the champion for boosting excellence in project management. Organizations such as IBM call this approach the "Project Management Center of Excellence." A PMCOE focuses on these activities:

- Training
- Process standardization
- Internal consulting
- Competency enhancement
- Identification of best practices
- Project prioritization
- Tool definition and standardization

- Enterprise or portfolio reporting
- Advocacy of the project management cause
- State-of-the-art benchmarking

The PMCOE differs from the usual PO, being less aimed at providing operational support and more concerned with getting up-to-date methodologies and competencies in place. The term "program office" is also sometimes used to describe the same scope of work. Figure 4.1 shows the PMCOE's external focus in search of project management excellence.

Can these two concepts (support and excellence) be joined under one roof? In other words, can the aims of the Project Support Office be joined with those of the Project Management Center of Excellence? Although a sizable difference in thrust exists between the two types of project office (the PSO's internal-operational objective versus the PMCOE's strategically focused goals), they can be combined under special circumstances where the project office leader has the profile to maintain a dual focus (operational and strategic). Joining the support and strategic functions,

FIGURE 4.1. PROJECT MANAGEMENT CENTER OF EXCELLENCE.

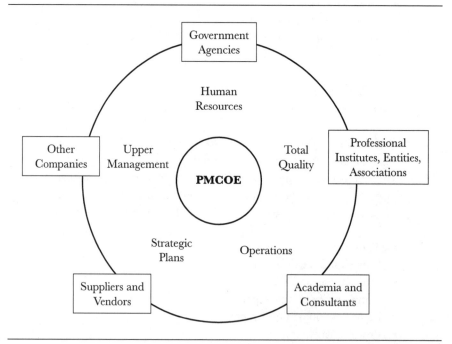

however, presents the following challenges: it is difficult to maintain balance between operational and strategic needs, and it is usually necessary to provide multiple support offices whereas one center of excellence is sufficient in most companies.

Is the project office as a staff function adequate to meet an organization's needs, or is a line role with formal project authority a better option? Both situations are addressed in the literature and are practiced in hundreds of organizations. The next two sections describe line variations of the project office concept.

Program Management Office. The program management office (PMO) version puts the project office in charge of projects, giving it responsibility for resource assignment, recruiting, developing project managers, project selection and prioritization, alignment with business strategies, portfolio reporting, methodology and project management processes, accountability for programs or projects, human process change management, and coordination of project managers.

As discussed in Chapter Three, a PMO requires a solid political base. The PMO must be part of the organization's power structure if it is to be effective, so it is important to assess what impact the PMO will have on existing functional manager responsibilities. Fixing priorities is also part of the PMO's responsibilities as some projects are handled by the PMO, others by third parties and yet others at a unit level. Regardless of who does the work, the PMO assumes responsibilities for success on projects and manages the project managers.

Chief Project Officer. The chief project officer (CPO) concept takes the project office to the top of the organization and provides central authority over strategic projects. This position is similar to the operational, financial, and information-management roles of the COO, CFO, and CIO. Responsibilities of the CPO include involvement in business decisions that result in new projects, strategic project planning, setting priorities and negotiating resources for projects, oversight of strategic project implementation, responsibility for an enterprise-wide project management system development of project management awareness and capability throughout the organization, periodic project review, including decision to discontinue projects, and top level stakeholder management, facilitation, and mentoring. Figure 4.2 shows the CPO's range of responsibilities.

Few organizations have CPOs at this time, but the job's formulation is a natural extension of the visioning process. The CPO population should increase as organizations achieve higher levels on the project management maturity curve. Many of the job's functions will evolve as individuals and organizations find what works and does not and then adapt.

These groupings of POs are not particularly new. With the exception of the CPO (a more recent concept), they were recognized as appropriate groupings in

FIGURE 4.2. CHIEF PROJECT OFFICER.

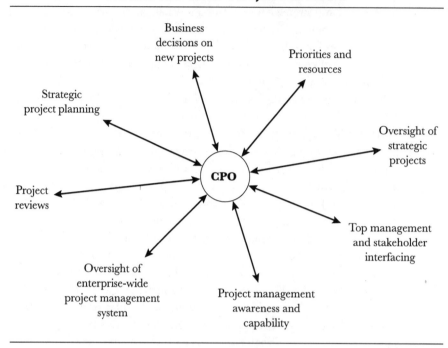

a working session of the Top 500 Project Management Benchmarking Forum held in Milwaukee, Wisconsin, in 1996 (Toney, 2002). (The benchmarking forums are held two to four times a year under the coordination of Frank Toney, director of the Executive Initiative Institute, Scottsdale, Arizona. The sessions serve to gather information on best practices and stimulate an exchange of ideas on the practice of project management.) After considerable debate the thirty representatives who met in Milwaukee came to consensus that the basic project office types are indeed the PSO, PMCOE, and PMO.

Variations

Although the PSO, PMCOE, and PMO groupings are helpful for discussion purposes, in practice POs are rarely just alike—even if they are part of the same category. The functions described separately may fuse together into different forms. For instance, the staff functions of the PSO and the PMCOE might merge, even though the PSO is inwardly targeted, and the PMCOE is aimed at scanning the outside environment to continuously improve methodologies and PM approaches. If those differing thrusts can be combined under the guidance of one group, then that hybrid form is perfectly feasible. Other possibilities include incorporating staff support functions with a PMO. Another variation couples the PMCOE with the CPO.

A Vision and a Strategy for the Project Office

To focus on the right concept and properly design a project office, consider several angles, since no one-size-fits-all PO can accommodate the characteristics of every organization. Here are questions designed to raise fundamental issues prior to initiating design of the organization:

- *What is the size of the organization that the project office is to serve?* Is it global or otherwise geographically widespread? Or is it local and concentrated? Or is the target audience only a part of the entire organization?
- *What are the desired outputs of the project office?* Information for management? Support and internal consulting for projects? Standardization of methodologies? Implementation of cutting-edge technologies? Stakeholder articulation?
- *What are the probable roadblocks to implementing the concept in the organization?* Lack of upper management support? Strong resistance from the grass roots? Underestimating of change management necessary to implement the concept?
- *What is peculiar about the organization that will facilitate or hinder the PO concept?* Is the company project-driven by nature (construction, software development) or is it product-driven (soap, furniture)?

These fundamental questions set the backdrop for the project office design process covered in this chapter. Once the underlying issues have been addressed, a detailed approach is called for. This means analyzing the dozens of variables that affect project office design and the subsequent performance of the PO. Figure 4.3 lists the possible variables.

After the project office design parameters are pinned down, the next step is to formally define them. This may be conventionally registered in the form of written documents:

- Charter
- Internal organization and external interfaces
- Policies and procedures
- Roles, responsibilities, and position descriptions
- Competency and training requirements

FIGURE 4.3. FOUR CLASSES OF PO DESIGN VARIABLES.

Class	Variables	Options
1. *Context*	The need for a PO	Market-driven? Internally driven?
	The articulators	Top management? Specific area? Cross-functional?
	Company background	Project-driven? Functional? Other?
	Implementation intent	Revolutionary or evolutionary?
	Intended scope of PO	Purely for implementation? Tied to business strategy?
2. *Organization and People*	Management Premise	Line or staff function?
	Direct authority	CEO? Department head? Committee?
	Scope of projects	All projects? Major projects? Area project?
	People for projects	Recruits? Trainees? Allocates? Supports?
	Size	Large group? Mostly virtual?
3. *Support Functions*	Methodologies	Develop? Implement? Monitor?
	Tools	Select? Adapt? Train?
	Records maintained	For all projects? Priority projects?
	Type of support?	Proactive? Support when asked?
4. *Project Execution*	Tracking and reporting	All-inclusive for management? Project by project?
	Auditing	Support function to PMs? For management control?
	Planning and scheduling	Support to projects? Hands on on-site assignments?
	Communications	On enterprise basis? Single project support?
	Change management	Proactive management? Supply procedures?

Just as in the case of any other project implementation, starting up a project office requires a logical sequence of actions. The project involves not only technical issues but challenges of a behavioral and political nature. Here is the sequence:

1. *Assessment and conceptual design.* Assess current project management practices and develop a concept that will be coherent with company needs.
2. *Detailed design and solution development.* Develop each part of the solution, including methodology and processes, software and system requirements, and organizational aspects.
3. *Pilot testing.* Test the proposed solutions on a specific project to obtain buy-in and improve the solutions.
4. *Implementation.* Initiate use of the solutions on a broader scale. This phase includes the behavioral side of change management as well as technical implementation.
5. *Maintenance.* Manage the processes implemented to ensure optimum performance and maintain training to develop full engagement.

Indeed, the project office is an enterprise-wide solution for tracking multiple projects and for maintaining focus on company strategies, yet designing a PO presents sizable challenges because of the number of variables involved. The PO function varies in scope from purely strategic to operational support to full line responsibility for completed projects. The PO's physical size may range from minuscule to grandiose, and the operating philosophy may often be more virtual than real.

Consider also the norms in the organization around terms used to describe activities. One implementation struggled when its designers rolled out a *pilot* version, thinking of it as a prototype that would help get feedback about the design. The problem was that most of the participants expected a pilot to be almost ready to go, the first implementation of the final product, so they were horrified about its weaknesses. A different iteration of a project office got a better reception when it used the term *experiment,* which had few existing expectations in the organization, to describe a trial run. New terms may help avoid the baggage associated with existing vocabulary.

The success of the final design is measured by the degree to which the PO shines a powerful spotlight on project management in the organization and ensures that projects perform within procedures and in line with organizational strategies. Meeting that goal requires customization based on the design questions and parameters outlined. Unquestionably, custom tailoring is the way to go, since in the case of the project office, one size does not fit all!

After the Giant Step:
Communication and Building Commitment

Mapping out the vision and strategy for the project office, using the variables and options just described, is a giant step in the right direction; it makes implementing a productive project office much more likely. Yet it is not enough to actually make it happen. Although coming up with the right PO concept is indeed a critical success factor, the way the view is communicated and sold to the rest of the organization is equally important.

Whereas formulating the concept of a project office function is primarily an intellectual process, communicating and selling the idea resides in the behavioral field. It involves factors like reaction to change, human ego, turf struggles, and allowance for time to absorb new concepts. So once the PO concept has been hatched (PSO, PMCOE, PMO, CPO or one of the sundry other variants), then careful planning goes into how to garner the needed support to make the idea come to life.

To implement any new concept—especially one as complex as a PO—it is useful to start by putting in place a process for understanding, acceptance, and buy-in with the principal stakeholders: the project managers, vice presidents, functional managers, and support staff. To develop understanding, people have to be exposed to the idea and then process it over a period of time, all in their own personal style. This may involve listening to a talk on the topic, participating in a workshop, surfing the Web for more details, reading about it in the literature, and discussing it in detail with colleagues. The process will take weeks for some people and months for others, just to understand what the PO is supposed to do.

To get people to accept the concept involves dealing with other issues. Here stakeholders struggle with these questions:

- How will the PO affect my present status?
- What's in it for me?
- Will someone be trying to control what I do?
- What risks will I run by supporting the proposed PO?
- Who else is in favor of the idea?
- How does the PO affect internal politics?

Once again, it takes time for people to find answers and move on to full acceptance.

Buy-in for the PO means that stakeholders understand and accept the concept and are ready to put it into practice. For this to happen, a number of prerequisites are needed: genuine motivation, detailed planning, implementation, and persistent follow-up.

In practice this means that the implementation of a project office should follow a carefully crafted pathway to ensure that full commitment to the cause is achieved. Steps that facilitate buy-in to the PO concept include

1. *Information campaign to generate understanding of concept:* series of lectures, information on intranet, distribution of literature, discussion with consultants
2. *Forums for stimulating acceptance:* intranet discussions, seminars, workshops
3. *Special events for creating commitment:* start-up workshops or team integration seminars to ensure all project office stakeholders are working toward the same goals

So the implementation of a successful PO depends not only on developing the right concept for the organization but on how the idea is communicated to primary stakeholders and the rest of the organization. That communication is even more important, and it is highly sensitive to the need for people involved to initially understand the PO concept, then to accept it after a process of internal questioning, and finally to buy into the idea and fully support it.

Surveys

More information is becoming available about project offices. Aside from articles and papers published by organizations like the Project Management Institute, other information is generated in informal and formal benchmarking forums held in local and global settings. Academia also produces studies and information on this relatively recent solution for supporting multiple projects. This information may provide additional guidance to compare and select among alternatives based upon what other organizations have learned.

From Down Under

Summary results of a questionnaire about the project office were presented in Sydney, Australia, in October 2001, at a workshop of the Human Systems Knowledge Networks, Pacific Rim. Lynn Crawford of Pacific Rim Networks summarized a survey of thirty-three member companies, including Ericsson, Sydney Water Corporation, Road and Traffic Authority of New South Wales, Goodman Fielder, Optus, Telstra, CS Energy, Lucent, and Resitech.

The survey, which generically referred to project offices as PSOs, covered companies that use different titles for the PO as suggested in the beginning of this chapter. Some observations from that study:

Most of the companies surveyed (82 percent) had more than a thousand employees. Nine percent had less than three hundred employees and the remainder were in range between these levels. Nongovernment companies represented 55 percent of the sample, so the survey included substantial input from government organizations. The PSOs surveyed supported different quantities of projects: 73 percent supported more than forty-one projects, 12 percent supported ten projects or less, while 15 percent supported between eleven and forty projects. Most PSOs were physical (85 percent) while 15 percent were virtual. Over two-thirds of the PSOs (71 percent) had line authority, while 29 percent were classified as staff functions.

Levels of the PSO function in the organizations also varied widely. Eighteen of the organizations surveyed had the PSO at the enterprise-wide level, while sixteen were positioned at divisions or business units. The eighteen enterprise-wide PSOs comprised two dedicated steering committees, two enterprise-level steering committees, eleven functional line managers, and three "others."

Seventeen companies considered the level simply as project office or program office, while ten organizations classified their PSOs as "portfolio offices." Two organizations had what they called "client project/program offices."

Funding of the PSOs fell into three categories: overhead is charged in 50 percent of the cases and PSO costs are charged to projects in 16 percent of the cases; in the remaining 34 percent, costs are shared between overhead and projects.

In terms of accountability, 21 percent of the organizations held the PSO accountable for project management results. The remaining 79 percent structured the PSOs as purely support functions.

The functions carried out by the PSOs were divided into the following major categories:

- Planning and control support
- PM methodology
- PM career development
- Reporting
- PM tools
- Lessons learned
- Communications
- Linking projects to strategic goals
- Audits or reviews
- Purchasing and contract administration
- Resources management

In a further breakdown, the survey classified detailed activities by "sets" according to the frequency in which they appeared.

Top Set of Activities

- Maintain PM methodology
- Provide templates
- Provide or arrange training on PM tools
- Provide policies and procedures
- Provide technical expertise on tools
- Develop policies and procedures for use of PM tools
- Develop PM methodology
- Disseminate best practices
- Select PM tools
- Set standards
- Gather project status information
- Liaise with and between functions, divisions, business units
- Provide project management benchmarking
- Work toward continuous improvement on projects
- Capture best practices
- Provide, arrange, schedule, and conduct training
- Enforce PM methodology, standards, and procedures
- Conduct periodic project performance reviews

Second Set of Activities

- Assist in development of project plans
- Identify best practices
- Provide support for troubled projects
- Assist with project report preparation
- Conduct and facilitate risk assessment and planning
- Foster PM community of practice
- Maintain repository of project data
- Provide project start-up support
- Develop and maintain PM Web pages
- Establish PM competence and skills assessment
- Conduct enterprise project and program reporting
- Produce internal newsletters
- Provide and arrange coaching
- Conduct postimplementation reviews
- Provide cost and time estimating consultation
- Regulate use of PM tools

Third Set of Activities

- Provide and arrange mentoring
- Conduct trend analysis

- Conduct team meetings and events
- Introduce project management
- Prepare exception reports
- Prepare program reports
- Prepare and maintain quality assurance and control plans
- Conduct resource planning
- Provide project portfolio management
- Develop and maintain internal PM accreditation process
- Establish and maintain issues logs
- Prepare and update project budgets
- Prepare and update project schedules
- Develop and maintain project classification system
- Assist with development of business case for projects and programs
- Promote projects
- Maintain skills data base
- Prepare project portfolio reports

Fourth Set of Activities

- Initiate and facilitate team building (development)
- Conduct client satisfaction reviews
- Prepare project reports
- Maintain change control log and follow-up
- Establish projects selection criteria
- Recommend cross-project resource allocation
- Validate timesheet entries and follow up on questionable items
- Enforce use of project selection criteria
- Review business benefits
- Deploy resources to projects at all locations
- Recommend and assist with strategic project termination and harvesting of benefits
- Establish and maintain risk logs
- Maintain and disseminate technical specifications
- Provide value management
- Conduct performance reviews
- Conduct function and product audits
- Manage project extensions
- Manage contract closeout
- Track changes
- Manage purchasing
- Initiate contract changes

From the United States

Another survey on POs was published in *PM Network* in August 2001. Authors Block and Frame observed that little information existed on the implementation and configuration of project offices, although the concept has been around for about ten years. Most POs were established in the late 1990s for specific purposes such as dealing with the Y2K conversion, the Euro currency changeover, and enterprise resource planning projects.

The study was based on responses from participants in seminars conducted by the authors, comprising seventy-four project office workers, 40 percent of whom came from the IT field and the rest from varied industries. Most respondents (81 percent) came from organizations having more than a thousand employees, while 8 percent worked in medium-sized companies with more than three hundred employees, and 11 percent were employed in smaller enterprises (one to three hundred employees).

These were the primary PO functions as indicated by the respondents (multiple responses were allowed):

- Establishing methods and standards, 79 percent
- Consulting, 64 percent
- Mentoring, 58 percent
- Training, 58 percent
- Project tracking, 53 percent

"Maintaining a stable of project managers" was indicated by only 28 percent of the respondents, reflecting the fact that many PMs are fully dedicated to their projects or operate in separate business units.

The study confirmed that POs generally tend to be small. Sixty-eight percent of the respondents indicated POs of five or fewer people. Only 3 percent had more than twenty people, with 22 percent having between six and ten and 8 percent between eleven and twenty people.

In response to the question, "Why was your PO established?" the participants provided multiple answers:

- Lack of repeatable methods and standards (66 percent)
- Senior management directed (60 percent)
- Project delays (53 percent)
- Poor project planning (53 percent)
- Poor project performance (39 percent)
- Cost overruns (38 percent)

The question "What was the greatest contribution to your project office success?" resulted in the responses: "competent project office professional staff" (55 percent), and "senior management support" (51 percent).

Where is it all heading? What is the future for project offices? Authors Block and Frame say, "Project offices will continue to proliferate in organizations, as more and more adopt project management practices and find that they must institutionalize the project management effort in order to implement these practices effectively" (2001).

Block and Frame observe that outsourcing is one of the options raised in the research. David Griffith, senior partner with Solutions Integration and the founding chair of PMI's Project Management Office Special Interest Group, has seen a substantial increase in outsourcing for many project-based services. While some project office functions have been outsourced, organizations are tending to bring this core management competency close to home.

From the University

In the doctoral dissertation "The Role of Project Management Office in Achieving Project Success" (2001), researcher Xiaoyi Christine Dai of George Washington University stated that no major empirical research study had been conducted on the title theme or on any aspect of PMOs. She noted that existing information was based on anecdotes, personal experiences, consulting experiences, and analyses based on limited research efforts.

The acronym PMO was adopted in the research project even though authorities in the field often use the terms *project office, project management office,* and others such as *systems program office* synonymously. In the study a project office is assumed to be for managing one project and a project or program management office exists to provide supporting and facilitating services to multiple projects; it manages no projects directly.

The survey results were obtained through two approaches. First a thousand letters were sent randomly to selected Project Management Institute (PMI) members. The response rate was 23.4 percent. Additional results were obtained through a combination of e-mail and letters to 470 selected potential PMO-related candidates, which resulted in a response rate of 20.4 percent.

The research yielded significant information on the nature of PMOs and related current practices. Here is a sampling of the findings, all of which are statistically justified in the dissertation.

- *Trend in PMOs.* A distinct trend involving increasing numbers of PMOs emerged in the mid-1990s. Based on the growth patterns that resulted from the survey, the author concluded that PMOs will continue to increase in number at least for the next several years.

- *Management level for PMO establishment approval.* In the survey, an overwhelming proportion of PMO establishments were approved at an upper management level (85 percent). This supports the theory that upper management is at least somewhat involved and interested in their respective organizations' approach to project management and particularly in the PMO approach.
- *Frequency of full-time staffing for an organization's PMO.* In over 90 percent of the cases studied, full-time staffing of a PMO was the preferred model. The research did not yield accurate information on ranges and averages of staffing. It is likely that such numbers will depend on the nature and variety of the roles assigned to a PMO and its position within an organization.
- *Major functions and services of PMOs.* Although the range of services indicated by the respondents was broad, the findings can be summarized as follows:

  All ninety-six PMO respondents from the targeted sample reported a major function as performing "PM standards and methods."

  The next most frequently reported item was "consulting and mentoring."

  The following functions were also mentioned frequently, though at lesser levels: providing administrative support, providing and arranging PM training, and maintaining historical archives.
- *Survey conclusion.* The survey concluded that additional research is required to yield conclusive evidence regarding the effectiveness of the PMO concept, yet the author allowed that the research hypothesis, that the PMO presence index has a linear influence on reported project success, "could be largely accepted."

Project Offices: Some Real-Life Cases

A few cases that illustrate the wide range of POs are shown in this chapter (other detailed cases are woven throughout the book). Settings for the POs featured here include a multinational telecommunications company, a U.S. government-sponsored research program, and a major IT manufacturer and service company.

Part of a Global Organization—Ericsson Australia

The project office effort in Ericsson Australia started in 1997 with the establishment of the Center of Excellence, which lasted about twelve months and had a staff of one. Shortly thereafter, a formal project office was located in the major business unit, Australian Services, yet the PO maintained cross-organization responsibility.

For the first year, the PO aimed primarily at increasing the competency level of project management. That increased competence was designed to influence project performance, which in turn was to increase the probability of successful project completion. At that point the PO was acting primarily as a project support office or PSO. The roles and responsibilities for the project office in this stage of the Ericsson development include

- Owning the PM process
- Setting standards and benchmarks
- Developing PM competence
- Owning the profession
- Achieving certification
- Justifying position in organization

Thereafter, the PO was tasked with organizational responsibilities, including reporting on the project portfolio so the executive team could receive the information necessary to manage the project organization. This process included the meetings and structure to report and provide opportunity for intervention and escalation. This meant that the PO was beginning to act as an organization support project office, where the scope of work transcends project management processes and methodologies. The role includes active interfacing with the rest of the organization and an emphasis on the management of multiple projects. The roles and responsibilities of an organization support PO include everything listed for project support office, plus

- Drive adherence to process through reviews and other measures
- Establish management of projects
- Performance manage the project managers
- Manage forecast load
- Serve as capability owner for project management
- Continue to justify position in organization

The organization support PO therefore covers both project management competence and organization competence. This PO is designed to boost not only project competence and performance but organization competence and performance as well.

In mid-2001, during a reorganization, the project office staff proposed the adoption of a "business delivery model," with project office project managers sharing responsibility for business-related results, including an agreed margin. The roles and responsibilities of a business delivery PO include everything listed for project management support office, plus

- Support presales activities
- Be accountable for estimating process
- Manage order desk and end-to-end delivery process
- Provide business support, such as risk analysis for technical, commercial, and project definitions
- Drive project management performance
- Be accountable for delivering the agreed margin

The organization changes caused by the transition from manufacturing-based company to global supply chain resulted in a dramatic increase in the percentage of income directly generated by projects. Throughout the implementation of the project office concept, upper management was supportive and helped maintain the momentum. During 2001, with the slowdown in the telecommunications industry, major downsizing took place and this slowed the implementation of the business model PO, which is still under way at this writing.

Challenges faced in implementing and operating the project office concept stemmed in part from two other business units, Marketing & Sales and Services, which were responsible for delivering the contracted requirements. Establishment of the PO and associated processes made project performance more visible to the organization as a whole. Consequently, considerable friction appeared between various sectors of the organization.

Is Ericsson in Australia a more productive company due to implementation of project offices? According to Chris Cartwright, project management competence manager of Ericsson Australia's project office, "This is almost impossible to measure with all the major changes internally and externally within the industry and the company. What it has done is to raise the whole issue of project performance and provided the framework to manage this." He also notes that the increasingly project-based culture at Ericsson is reflected in the monthly leadership forums, where the CEO opens the session with traditional financial results and immediately thereafter presents project performance results.

A Pioneering PMO

In 1977, the Pacific Northwest Laboratory (PNL), which is operated for the U.S. Department of Energy by Battelle Memorial Institute in Richland, Washington, embarked on a program to improve project performance. The projects were largely aimed at developing new energy sources, improving existing energy sources, and examining methods for containing and disposing of nuclear waste generated from power reactors. To improve project performance, the lab decided to use a centralized approach to manage research projects that ran the gamut from early stages of research to beginning stages of development. Lee R. Lambert, now a consultant, was hired to lead the project management enhancement program.

An initial question generated discussion among principal stakeholders: should the project management office be structured as a control function with its costs allocated to organization overhead, or should it be perceived as a value-added function and be obliged to pay its own way. The charge-to-overhead approach would constitute a service tax assessed to all projects, whether the project managers wanted the service or not. Under the second premise, the PMO would provide recognized value, and R&D scientists would be willing to pay for the service from their research budgets. The value-added philosophy assumed that once the value of the support was demonstrated, every project manager would want to take advantage of the project management support. They selected the value-added alternative.

Process structure, procedures, discipline, and consistency in approach to managing PNL's projects were initially lacking, and these project management competencies would be a part of the new organization's charter. But, because the fear of being controlled (interpreted as stifling creativity by the scientists) in an R&D environment was substantial, PNL chose a nonthreatening name for this new organization: Management Information and Support (MIS).

The consistently demonstrated success of the service was almost immediate, according to Lambert; projects that used it got better results, were faster and more cost effective, and had better communications, and research project managers quickly grasped the potential return on their investment for using the concept. The feedback cited better work definition, more realistic schedules, much more effective use of resources among multiple projects, and ability to separate the truly important issues from the unimportant—all leading to timely and informed decisions and satisfied customers.

The demand for project support exceeded the supply of qualified project management staff available in MIS. Recruiting became aggressive. The focus was internal as the MIS group sought to enlist staff from the technical disciplines to which they would eventually be providing project management support. Many of PNL's qualified technical people opted to change career paths to join this new service group. In about three years the organization grew from one to nineteen people—all fully funded by the research projects they supported.

Several factors were key to achieving successful implementation of the PMO philosophy. First, it was handled using the principles of project management, with a focus on planning for success using the value-added component as the benefit hook. And constant assessment and evaluation of the perception of benefit from MIS services to the users allowed the PMO to concentrate on achieving consistency and discipline without reducing the project managers' ability to deliver innovative, creative, and high-quality R&D products.

After three years of operation, senior management reportedly considered eliminating the MIS organization, which would require the R&D groups to provide their own project support resources. In response to this proposal, the R&D scientific community rallied in support of maintaining MIS as established, thus providing testimony to the success of the value-added approach.

Through stakeholders transferred to other projects, the MIS story eventually trickled up to corporate level at Battelle Memorial Institute. In 1981, Battelle established the ultimate PMO—the Battelle Project Management Division, which eventually grew to more than three hundred employees devoted exclusively to the management of large, complex, R&D-driven projects. Substantial effort was made early on to establish and integrate enterprise-wide information systems including accounting, procurement, quality, policies and procedures, and training and staff development for the fully dedicated project management division.

Four years later, BPMD was formally recognized for its solid processes when it became the first nonmilitary R&D organization to receive a U.S. government Validation Certificate for its project management system. To this day, Battelle continues using its PMO approach for managing R&D projects.

A Complex Setting: HP's Spectrum Program

Program Management in Hewlett-Packard's Information Technology Group (ITG) evolved from the need for coordination of a major priority project—the Spectrum family of Reduced Instruction Set Computing (RISC) architecture-based computer systems, later known as HP-PA, Hewlett-Packard Precision Architecture. These activities occurred in the 1986–1990 time frame, when the new product platform was developed and became the basis for a prolonged, successful product family. The objective of ITG Spectrum Program Management was to provide systemwide, multidivisional product-oriented information for tracking product development and focusing management attention on high-leverage items in a highly matrixed organization.

The need for establishing a program management initiative for the Spectrum program became apparent after a number of dysfunctions in communications between technical professionals. For instance, engineers writing software did not get answers to questions or found that their code no longer worked with an enhanced version subsequently developed by another lab. Also, functional-level managers were called upon to do strategic planning but also had to meet deliverables and handle day-to-day decisions. Additionally, skepticism became prevalent—people no longer trusted each other to communicate changes that might adversely affect another lab. Although programs were clearly in place, the corresponding processes for managing the programs were lacking.

Peak ITG PM group full-time head count reached about twenty people, drawn from a variety of technical, professional positions. Temporary coordinators were sometimes brought in full time for a month or two around major milestones. The group was physically located in Cupertino, California. Remote members of the group came to the Cupertino headquarters periodically for meetings and specific tasks. The only virtual activities during this phase were conducted via e-mail. ITG PM was assigned a conference room (called the "war room") where core teams met weekly and schedules were posted on the walls.

The political situation, especially around the manager's Type A approach and a reporting relationship directly to the group manager, eventually led to splitting the group into separate hardware and software program management groups with new managers for each area. In early 1988, the groups were physically moved into different buildings to be closer to their development teams. Although an attempt was made to stay unified and share experiences, in practice the groups became more independent. Later the work diffused into the divisions.

The ITG Program Management group focused on key elements to ensure project performance. This was the main thrust of ITG PM's efforts:

- Form a multidisciplinary program or "core" team to oversee progress. This team works together from start to finish of the program and meets weekly.
- Develop a consolidated systemwide schedule and define individual milestones. An accompanying document is the Definition of Milestones.
- Publish a System Specification. This document lists all high-level committed features of the system.
- Be an independent organization to facilitate the development process and resolve issues. This means setting agendas for program team or ad hoc meetings, taking minutes, summarizing and recording agreements, determining ownership and due dates for action items, writing status memos for upper management, and keeping teams on track.
- Operate a document control center. This library has all the documents— External Specifications, Investigation Reports, System Requirements Definitions—and plans from all projects in the Spectrum Program.
- Manage prototype hardware. Where divisions used to make only a handful of products, even through pilot run, the Spectrum Program required hundreds of both lab and production prototypes.

- Assist other areas. ITG Program Management was also called upon by the System Architecture Lab to facilitate an issue resolution process.

Phase Reviews. A process called "phase reviews" emerged as a viable means to achieve consensus among all suppliers on a system for a customer. It also provided corporate management with visibility into major programs. The objectives of the phase review process are to define the computer product implementation review and control process when multiple HP development entities are involved, and to assure that complementary functional (matrix organization) activities are staffed and under way during the product life cycle, so that all pieces are in place when products are announced, sold, and shipped to customers.

Each phase review meeting must answer the question, "Should this system or project continue?" Each review stage has a template defining objectives and material to be included and providing space to record responses and commitments. The program management office assisted in preparation and running of phase review meetings.

These are the phases:

Title		*Exit Objective*
Phase 0	Product Planning	Objectives and strategy
Phase 1	Study	Commit to product objectives
Phase 2	Design	Commit to functionality, cost, performance, schedule
Phase 3	Develop	Start beta test
Phase 4	Qualify and Produce	Ship
Phase 5	Verify and Audit	Assure satisfaction; define enhancements, new marketing strategies, or program termination

The Process. The Program Management group at ITG perceived its role as implementers of a process to ensure that things happen, and subsequently as facilitators for carrying out the necessary follow-up to produce results. In this facilitation process, three common questions reflect the group's working philosophy: What is the issue? Who has ownership? When is it due? All three questions required full responses, documentation, and resolution.

The ad hoc small team concept also worked well when methodology was not clear about metrics on subjects such as system performance. In situations requiring special efforts, engineers and managers from labs and marketing were pulled together as a "tiger team" (a tiger is loose in the woods and this team is assembled with the one task of slaying the tiger). ITG Program Management typically determined the participants, arranged the time and conference rooms, planned the agenda and objectives, ran the meeting, and summarized the conclusions.

The Program Management group found that success on projects came from leading efforts through the internal process: the customer (Marketing) provides a system requirements definition; the suppliers (R&D) respond with a system specification; and the changes are requested, reviewed, approved, and distributed through a change control process. That process served to keep track of changes to the product, make sure the right changes were made, and communicate when changes were made.

The Program Management group at ITG did not replace functions of line managers. It was designed to complement line activities by looking for cracks or chasms in the projects and helping build bridges leading toward resolution.

Summary

Project offices cover a lot of ground. They range from the slightly supportive at one extreme to the all-powerful at the other. The names vary greatly, reflecting the myriad versions that exist. To focus on an appropriate vision and strategy for a project office, go through an analytical process involving variables and options related to the context, the organization and people, the support functions, and the project execution responsibility. Once the right concept is hatched, then involve stakeholders in the movement through a carefully thought-out communications plan, taking into account the need for all to understand the concept, accept it, and finally buy into it.

Surveys are few in number and probably not fully representative of what is going on in terms of project offices. Yet they offer insight and provide a basis for comparison. Specific case summaries confirm the wide range of project office styles in three distinct organizations. They show the variability in design and shifting roles over time, depending on organizational context. All implementations reflect a common commitment to achieving greater consistency and success through a coordinated focus on project management. Subsequent chapters in this book reinforce the need to ground the vision and strategy to the culture of the organization, then seek to extend and change the approach toward enterprise project management.

A complete successful change agent

- Formulates a compelling vision of a future, desirable state much improved over the present

- Understands the current organizational context as a basis for making changes
- Researches project office alternatives both within and outside the current organization
- Begins planning an implementation strategy
- Thinks big but starts small, developing small wins that build confidence to continue
- Develops a communications plan
- Brings a focus on achieving results through project management
- Knows that one size does not fit all

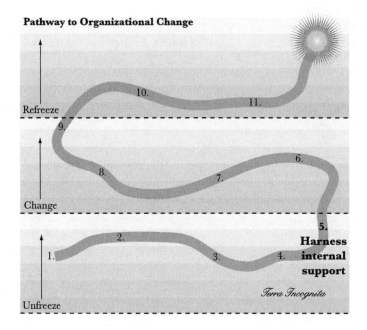

Pathway to Organizational Change

Refreeze

10.

11.

9.

Change

8.

7.

6.

5.
**Harness
internal
support**

2.

1.

3.

4.

Terra Incognita

Unfreeze

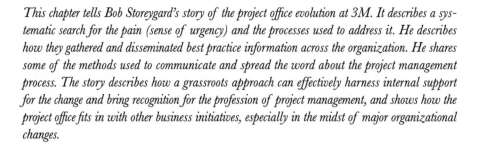

This chapter tells Bob Storeygard's story of the project office evolution at 3M. It describes a systematic search for the pain (sense of urgency) and the processes used to address it. He describes how they gathered and disseminated best practice information across the organization. He shares some of the methods used to communicate and spread the word about the project management process. The story describes how a grassroots approach can effectively harness internal support for the change and bring recognition for the profession of project management, and shows how the project office fits in with other business initiatives, especially in the midst of major organizational changes.

CHAPTER FIVE

TELL THE TALE: HARNESSING INTERNAL SUPPORT

Robert Storeygard, 3M

W̲e hope by now you believe project management is a discipline that has tremendous merit and bottom-line impact for organizations. You may have even come to the conclusion that a project office or similar PM function may be a good idea for your organization to embrace in order to shepherd and sustain the introduction and practice of this discipline. But unless the function is tied to the very lifeblood of the organization, it will be short-lived at best.

Finding Out Where It Hurts

How did Bob Storeygard tie the project office functions to the lifeblood of the organization at 3M? First of all, by knowing the starting point. As a number of areas at 3M were beginning to put together efforts to launch project office initiatives, they first collectively needed to address two questions:

- Do we have sufficient value to offer the organization in terms of project and portfolio management skills and techniques that would merit establishment of physical entities to deploy and sustain them?
- Is there enough identified and focused pain in the organization that people recognize the need for such help?

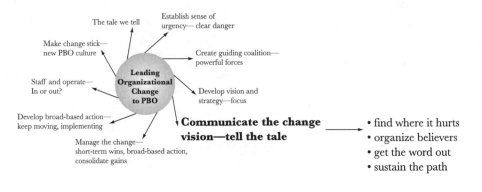

If the answer was no to the first question, they were not ready to approach the organization with the idea. Opening a project office prematurely can be devastating. They needed to have their own act together first before marketing themselves and the project office concept to others.

If the answer to the first question was yes and the second question was no, then their job changed, because the organization was not ready to hear what they had to offer . . . yet. They found they needed to intelligently bide their time and help the organization get in touch with its own pain. To do this, they created some initial "organizational pre-assessments" that would help organizations get consensus on identifying where they currently were in terms of markets, competition, internal issues, and skill sets. They approached this, of course, with a PM mind-set, but they did not limit or significantly steer the pre-assessments toward PM solutions to their issues. They let the chips fall where they might. Most organizations were just grateful to have someone independently work with them to help them clarify their own business situation. Sometimes it just takes someone with an outside business perspective to help a group see things more objectively and clearly.

Here are a few questions (and examples) that they used at 3M to guide organizations through the recognition process:

- What are the biggest or most aggravating business pains in your organization? (Identification: products fail to commercialize, loss of customers.)
- Does your intuition tell you that these pains could be from PM-related sources? (Relationships: lack of methodology, poor communications, or lack of stakeholder management.)
- Are your conclusions just your opinion, or do others who have observed or experienced the pain share them? (Validation: the pain is only seen in this organization, it's rampant across my area or in other areas.)
- Who else in the larger organization is experiencing similar pains? (Corroboration: another similar division experiencing same problems, industry groups formed to deal with it.)

If the answers to the two stem questions were both yes, then they realized that they had passed the first major project office gauntlet and were ready to proceed. But before moving on, they made sure to document their findings thoroughly from the pre-assessment activity. That was an essential step because such findings, in most cases, form the ideal basis for an initial offering of project office services to be introduced later.

Much of this early pre-assessment work with organizations at 3M began with concentrated efforts staffed through IT Education and Consulting groups. Similar but more product-focused versions of this effort were also being done in the Engineering and Product Commercialization areas. These efforts extended not only to IT-related groups domestically (within the United States) but also to international operations in Latin America, the Pacific Rim, and Europe.

Although these individual efforts netted some early success in helping organizations identify their business pain and situations, they were not always coordinated with or designed to enhance one another. Some of the key learnings and value came from helping organizations examine their business issues as well as their project and resource allocations and where that money was going. In some cases it confirmed good methods and techniques already in place, and in others it pointed up the lack of them.

These efforts helped various organizations within 3M identify their strengths and weaknesses, their position in their marketplaces, and suggested how the judicious application of project and portfolio management techniques might further their efforts.

So now the change agents knew they had something of value to offer and that the organization at large looked ripe to hear what they had to say and how they proposed to help. The next major question they addressed was, "What do we do about it?"

Early Attempts at Pain Relief

They realized that it would be premature to go straight for the implementation of a formal project office. A full-blown office is rarely the first or the wisest step to take in providing immediate relief to the organization. Using semimilitary parlance, they needed some preliminary efforts:

- *Triage:* Identify the more needy situations and help stem the bleeding (get some basic charters, plans, and communication mechanisms in place).
- *Stealth Missions:* Dive into serious pain situations (with permission, of course) and remove—in some cases, bomb—the pain to get it out of the way quickly and efficiently (get a sponsor in place for a project, remove a troublesome or non-functioning team member, help retain a customer through communication).

- *Reindoctrination:* Reeducation is sometimes needed to help people understand how to operate in a new environment where project management can be a major weapon. (Caution—beware the "sheep-dip approach" to training. That is, don't try to put everybody in the organization through the same training at the same time, regardless of whether they are ready to apply it or not.) As Storeygard notes, "effective training still needs to be done in the context of real work and done in a timely fashion."

Beyond these first steps, they needed to begin to build momentum at 3M toward change by finding other victims of similar business pain, commiserating with them, and beginning to provide opportunity for them to gather, share frustrations, vent, and eventually exchange best practices and ways to deal with the pain. At 3M, this began in the late 1980s with the formation of the Project Management Special Interest Group (PMSIG). This is a group that began with a half-dozen "believers" from various disciplines across the company, and today stands at over three thousand managers, project leaders, and team members in 3M worldwide.

The original organizing members of the PMSIG, convinced of the power of PM and possessed of a passion for the discipline (vitally important), began identifying and coalescing project leaders, managers, and others tasked with various forms of project leadership throughout 3M. They came together at first in a loose-knit confederation, but soon they gathered executive sponsorship and formed the PMSIG Steering Committee, which guided a number of years of unprecedented growth through means such as monthly presentations, a well-done but short newsletter, and a series of mini-conferences. Their executive sponsorship group and the PMSIG Steering Committee were the "guiding coalition" (discussed in Chapter Three) for many years and became the PM champions that were and are the vanguard of 3M's PM deployment efforts today. Storeygard says, "An important lesson learned was to seek these champions in various areas of the organization so as to spread the message quicker and more efficiently."

Concrete Second Steps to Deal with PM Pain

These early attempts at pain relief began to focus the organization to allow them to take more definitive steps in moving the effort forward. Here are additional steps taken to further build the foundation for eventual project offices:

1. Continued to document the business pain discovered, identified the sources, and began to develop organizational and individual PM assessment tools based on the pre-assessment questions. The results allowed them to immediately pro-

vide help to the organization as well as put the business case together for eventual project offices.

2. Continued to find or create PM champions, locating or working with someone in a position of influence, usually a middle or top manager, who got it—who could both see and articulate what PM could do for their organization. They helped lead the charge.

3. Continued coalescing the believers (others who knew PM could make a difference in their organizations) into the PMSIG support group and encouraging champions to lead and leverage this group.

4. Seriously approached developing a PM curriculum, not as a silver bullet but as a knowledge and personnel development mechanism for sponsors, project leaders, and team members. This was spearheaded at 3M by Storeygard through the IT Education area, but was soon broadened and contributed to by a number of areas through the PMSIG. It is still in active usage through the 3M Learning Center.

5. Created or obtained models of what success looks like. For example, they developed the Project Leader Competency Model (see Chapter Nine) and the PM Maturity Model (see Figure 5.1) and began a corporate dialog about them. The PM Maturity Model was created by Bob Storeygard and Jesus Diaz deLeon to help people understand and physically observe the maturation of their organizations as they began to practice the PM discipline more deeply. They viewed this as the "Stairway to PM Maturity" and encouraged organizations to keep the path visible as a reminder of how to move their organizations toward fuller maturity in the discipline.

6. Documented processes of how projects should ideally be run and cross-checked them with current methods in their shop, if any (add, replace, change).

7. Documented processes of how work actually gets into and out of the pipeline. This was the beginning of their portfolio management assessment.

8. Further developed the concept, knowledge, and reality of sponsorship for projects and programs. This was based on earlier work with developing PM champions.

Getting the Word Out

Once these concrete steps were under way, the group needed to get the word out that this was not some new corporate fad, it was—and is—a new way of doing business, and it is here to stay. This next set of ideas involved employing their best communications and selling skills (core to a good project leader, by the way) to get the organization's attention. They tried these ideas to get the word out:

FIGURE 5.1. THE PROJECT MANAGEMENT MATURITY MODEL AT 3M.

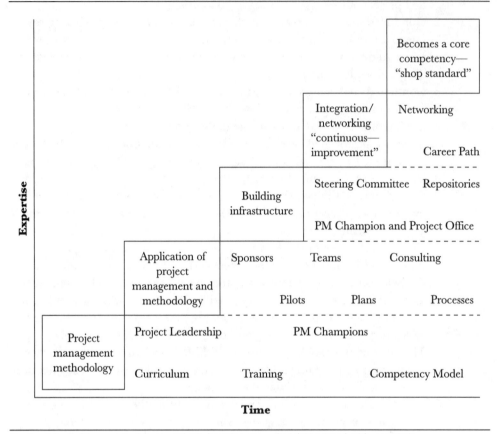

Source: Adapted from material copyright Robert Storeygard and 3M. Used with permission.

They got their newly formed PM coalition (the PMSIG) in the way of some serious corporate business pain, put their techniques to work, and helped the sufferers out. This quickly gained tremendous credibility for the PMSIG. The 3M PMSIG, through several events and meetings, got the entire corporation at least talking about PM and what it could do to help people get organized better and get products out faster. The PMSIG leaders then lent aid to a number of organizations that wished to seriously deploy PM, producing somewhat of a domino effect in the company—which continues to this day.

As the PMSIG continued to raise general PM awareness throughout the company, many organizations were curious to see if this new way of doing things would be good for their business. As with any new initiative, some early adopters led the way in deploying PM methods, techniques, and tools in their organizations, with the expertise and help of some of the PMSIG leaders. Soon, their organizations began to emerge as ones with a much better feel for their business issues and competitive position, as well as increased productivity and success rates in their project efforts. More organizations then requested this help as well, knowing full well that it was going to be a significant effort in terms of time and resources to make the shift.

They made PM education and networking opportunities readily available and visible. The 3M Project Leadership Curriculum is regularly available internally, along with the Project Leader Competency Model. The company's Education Web site provides the delivery mechanism, along with ready access to contacts, advice, and help, provided mostly by the 3M Learning Center and their involvement with the Minnesota PMI Chapter. PMSIG and PMI-related events are well publicized to the corporate population.

They started gathering and disseminating PM best practices that really made a difference in their organizations and the industry at large. This requires good communications planning, information repository sites, and technology, as well as the discipline and volunteer personnel (since most PMSIG involvement is voluntary) to keep the information up to date. This effort has sometimes suffered as time pressures to deliver products into the marketplace compromise infrastructure improvement (a continual balancing act).

They began coalescing project leaders into a definable group with its own identity. They also pushed for the emergence of project leader and project manager job titles and descriptions, as well as bona fide career paths. It is a cultural change for many organizations to begin thinking about project management as career ladder, but such ladders are rapidly developing across the industry. The combined project leader and project manager position calls for a unique mix of technical and managerial skills that does not precisely fit in either traditional career ladder. They are making headway at 3M, but it is still a struggle to change long-held views of the world.

They sought out potential pilot projects. The goal was to find programs that were in the midst of serious pain, engage them, and use PM skills and techniques to help them get better results.

They continued to build core knowledge and practitioners of good sponsorship through presentations and peer-to-peer networks. Sometimes a PM industry messenger of some reputation can help move an organization forward, even though the messenger probably conveys the same message told from the inside. It may be irritating to contemplate an outsider's effectiveness if you've been trying to spread the same word to deaf ears, but get over it . . . use whatever works to move forward.

They periodically take stock of PM penetration into larger organizations to see how well and deeply PM has been deployed. This is a key item for project office preparation—if there is enough critical mass to make a group receptive to a sustaining PM presence (the foundation for deploying project offices), it's time to move. If they pull the trigger too early and try to create a project office before the critical mass is there, they run the risk of firing a dud!

The key model created at 3M to assess PM penetration is shown in Figure 5.2. It has become known affectionately as "The PM Temple" (no religious affil-

FIGURE 5.2. THE PROJECT MANAGEMENT TEMPLE AT 3M.

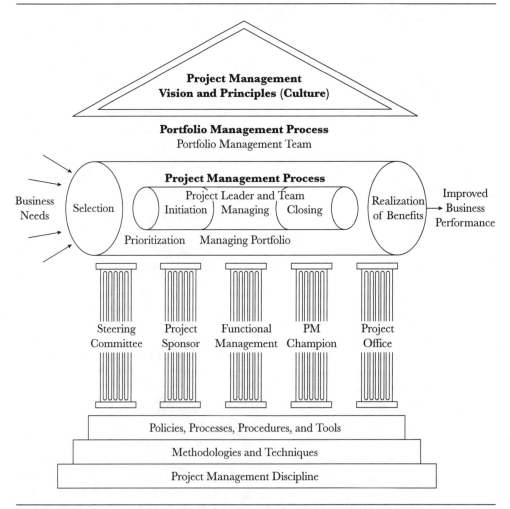

Source: Adapted from material copyright Robert Storeygard and 3M. Used with permission.

iation intended) and is intended to show what the components of a comprehensive, helpful, and healthful PM environment look like.

This model came out of work with international subsidiaries that, as they began the training and deployment for PM methods, techniques, and tools, asked for a one-page summary of the whole PM environment for executive management. The PM Temple eventually became a standard tool for illustrating what the major components of the environment should be. It can also be used as a visual checklist during an organizational PM assessment to see what components are in place, or not. Some organizations have gotten even more creative in color-coding parts of the diagram to indicate strengths, weaknesses, or in-process components. In other words, the PM Temple can be used as a barometer to gauge how well (or poorly) an organization is performing in creating a healthful, helpful PM environment. For more explanation of the diagram and 3M's use of it, refer to Storeygard (2001).

Sustaining the Path

Once they had momentum going in PM rollouts in various organizations, they had to find a way to keep the momentum going, and to periodically reinvent the movement to keep it fresh, relevant, and visible.

One of the critical things they found at 3M is that the creation, implementation, and continued improvement of both personal and organizational PM assessment tools (whether purchased or home-grown) provide an essential entrée into helping the business groups. These tools typically assess the situation against the models mentioned earlier to help organizations realize where they are starting from in their rollout of PM. The models paint the picture of what a successful environment looks like, and the assessment tools then provide ways to inquire about, quantify, and qualify where an organization is now so PM staff can be more prescriptive in helping people move forward.

After the assessments are complete, specific rollout plans are made to begin the distribution, training, and implementation of various PM techniques, tools, and methods. Some assessments result in the immediate realization that people either wish to or need to establish a project office–type function to handle the rollout of PM. Alternatively, many organizations move somewhat slower and want to see proof first that the PM rollout can indeed bring the sort of organizational improvements that are desired before they make any permanent investment of personnel. In this case, at a minimum, besides the PM rollout team or individuals, Storeygard highly recommends the formation of a PM task team, comprising key managers and project leaders within the target organization who can help oversee and assist with the initial PM rollout.

Once the organization begins to regularly embrace and practice solid PM techniques and methods, the foundation is laid for further consideration or creation of a project office. The office serves as a sustenance mechanism to keep the organization on track and moving forward as it continues to embrace PM ever more deeply.

The formation of a corporate support group for PM does much to awaken the whole organization to the need for PM and to enable the sharing of best practices. However, over time, organizations tend to become stagnant if not reinvented or challenged. There are also ongoing changes and business pressures that cause stress in terms of participating in this type of group; people lose interest if they discover their participation is not reflected in performance appraisals, or if they get no relief from other time pressures. As the 3M PMSIG has prepared fertile ground for PM and planted seeds all over the corporation, many new PM entities have sprung up to reflect the current business challenges and conditions and facilitate the migration of PM best practices within the corporation.

For example, as more project offices are formed, the PMSIG developed a subgroup called the POF (Project Office Forum), made up of the heads of many of the smaller (and larger) project offices throughout the company. POF meetings are similar to the larger meetings of the PMSIG but differ in scope and content. Several of the larger divisions also formed smaller focused groups of project leaders and team members, such as the Project Management Professional Association within Corporate IT Applications, and the Project Leader Forum in Traffic Control Materials.

These support groups also need to be careful to reexamine and reinvent themselves periodically so that they stay in touch with the true pain of the organization and do not just become part of the corporate bureaucracy.

Several other ideas are currently in use to keep the PM support movement alive at 3M:

- Continue to encourage and provide opportunities for project leadership career growth, including such things as formal career paths, external or internal certification, greater program and project visibility, and recognition.
- Encourage the maintenance of flexible methodology frameworks that can provide standardization at a higher level but enable substantial discretion and flexibility at the detail level—in other words, they do not want to standardize themselves into a corner! People will run the opposite way if too much rigor is imposed on them.
- Continue to review, update, amend, and enhance the models (competency and environment) that guide the project and portfolio management environment.
- Provide a framework and implementation assistance for the establishment of new project offices.

At 3M they developed an internal document called the Project Office Implementation Kit, which helps new offices get going. The POIK, as it is affectionately known, is a compilation, synthesis, and distillation of many PM industry books and articles that have been written about project offices. It is an attempt to boil all available information down to the essence of what future (and current, for that matter) project leaders need to know to get their offices defined and implemented. It also serves as a reference to help them sustain their efforts. The ongoing update of this document is also handled through the Project Office Forum so it always stays in touch with what is currently needed. Here are a few examples of what the POIK contains and how it is being used:

The first section simply tries to clarify what a project office is (or could be) and how it can benefit the organization. It also points out that not all POs are created equal—they can exist at a number of levels in the organization and can scale their services across a wide range of activities. Many people at 3M use this section to introduce the PO concept to their organizations, and if they cannot get their basic understanding and buy-in from this, then they realize that they are not ready to launch a PO yet.

The second and third sections explore the range of functions and services a PO could provide and how these services manifest themselves. Organizations have used these two sections in various ways, for example, as a service check against what they do now to see if they are providing an adequate level of service for the kind of office they are, or to help in defining the services their new office will try to provide. The critical thing these sections offer, in addition, is to clarify what roles are appropriate for the PO to play, as opposed to the actual project leaders and managers in the organization. It is important to note that at 3M, in most areas, project leaders do not reside in the project office itself, they remain in their functional areas.

The fourth and fifth sections of the POIK deal with how to plan, design, and implement a chosen level of project office. These are the newest and least proven sections of the document. Many offices have enough baseline information to proceed with their own plans after applying the first several sections of the POIK. These sections have been very helpful for offices that want more detailed support about doing needs analysis, determining levels of readiness, and actually laying out office plans.

This document is still a work in progress; it will change as the prevailing business environment changes. The next edition will focus more on the sustaining mechanisms and metrics existing offices can use to report on their impact to the organization in which they reside.

Futures for PM Converts

As more people and organizations come into the PM fold, Storeygard offers some words of advice he thinks will take the movement to new heights: "The more that project offices and project leaders can prove that their efforts contribute not only to the bottom-line profits of an organization but also to the top line in the way that efforts are selected and managed, the more respect and positional power they will have. This will require much better metrics and reporting on paybacks for PM investments to sustain and promote further PM rollouts in the future."

At 3M, people are beginning to see increased creation and use of project dashboards that inform organizations of their project and program progress. Many 3M project offices are now actively involved in helping divisions set up balanced scorecards, to monitor their organizations. However, Storeygard advises, "One man's metric is another man's chaff. Your metrics are *your* metrics, so determine what is critical to the success of your business and focus there!" Enterprise PM tools are now also getting much more consideration and use at 3M than in the past, despite their substantial cost.

Part of the challenge for project offices and PM rollouts in organizations remains, however, to find more and varied ways to engage middle and top level management, not only in supporting PM efforts but in helping these managers walk the talk themselves as the very future of their discipline moves more toward project and program realms. Storeygard predicts that management's ability to not only support PM but also practice it will be key to future business success. Many of 3M's more successful business unit leaders are now seeing their roles much more in terms of being project portfolio managers. They also are beginning to realize that if PM is perceived as "only good for the troops under them," then their success will be limited. Good PM needs to be practiced up and down the entire organization to be truly successful.

As project offices mature, they must also recognize the need to acquire new skills themselves to remain relevant. And one of the best ways to do that is to get involved with benchmarking and collegial relationships with other companies and associations actively involved in the furtherance of the discipline of PM (PMI, PDMA, IEEE, to name a few). The minute a project office feels it has its act together and knows all it needs to know, stagnation sets in.

As with most innovative organizations, the 3M groups need to be continually infused with new ideas and be informed by current and critical business needs and issues to remain relevant. They have tried several organizational models designed to accomplish this. In the case where the project office is in the line organization and does not have project leaders within the office, but distributed out in their functional areas, the project leaders themselves bring real-world cutting-edge perspectives. The other prevalent model used within corporate staff environments is to periodically circulate project office personnel out into the line organizations for projects or even short to mid-term assignments (anywhere from six months to between three and five years) to get line experience that can then be brought back into the staff organization. Both these models enable the project office perspective to remain fresh and aligned to current business needs.

Bob Storeygard is currently on one of those line assignments in Traffic Control Materials. He says, "Once we proved the worth of project management, I'm getting an avalanche of business, firing on all cylinders!"

Epilogue: How Does the Project Office Fit In with Major Organizational Change?

Finally, a few thoughts on how the project office movement can contribute to the company in the midst of major organizational change. Organizations face many initiatives that come about as a result of business circumstances, such as quality programs, regulatory requirements, and industry issues.

The introduction and institutionalization of Six Sigma at 3M is one example. Six Sigma has been infused at 3M on a grand scale and has brought many solid quality and measurement techniques and tools more into the forefront than ever before. Although the movement does contain noticeable aspects of project management, it focuses more on the hard side of PM—tools, deliverables including charters and control plans, and technical road maps—than it does on the soft side topics of team formation, conflict resolution, reporting, and communication. This is where the project office helps supplement and strengthen Six Sigma projects, as well as helping existing PM components to be more robust. Six Sigma is an initiative that is not going to go away. It is now a part of daily and ongoing corporate life at 3M, so the PM infrastructure will need to continue to help foster, sustain, and enhance its adoption.

As new corporate initiatives are implemented in response to changing business climates and economic times, a committed PM environment will continue to support those initiatives by espousing and following a few commonsense practices:

- Take a lesson from Robert Greenleaf's Web site (http://www.greenleaf.org) and exhibit a "servant leadership" attitude. This seeming oxymoron, in a PM context, means to 3M that project offices should always be prepared to help and equip someone else to shine, whether a manager, project leader, or other colleague.
- The efforts of the project office must be additive, not obstructionist. PO staff take the good ideas they find as they work with organizations and help augment those ideas with solid PM practices, rather than imposing a set of regulations on the groups they are supposed to be assisting.
- The adept project office is always ready to meet a new challenge by being flexible and ready, but not directive. People look to project offices for skillful help as well as connections and networking, and the PO staff need to be prepared to offer both.

- Cooperate with those seeking the project office's help, especially if they are making a good-faith effort to learn and adopt new practices. Eventually this will develop the kind of reputation that will encourage others to seek the project office out for help.

By following this sort of road map to establish and harness PM support within the 3M organization, project offices will continue to have an undeniable and lasting positive effect on the company.

Author Comments

The 3M case is an example of a bottom-up, internal group implementation effort where many suggestions from the first four chapters were applied. The clear danger was the identified and focused pain in the organization. The PM advocates began to add value by focusing first on current problem areas and providing specific help to solve them using PM-related techniques. Internal assessments created even more clarity—people could finally see the real causes behind many of their organizational woes. A powerful guiding coalition was seen in the executive sponsorship group and the Project Management Special Interest Group Steering Committee. To help the team stay focused they prepared a model of what success would look like, the PM Maturity Model.

They were able to start small, helping people apply tools such as methodologies and project charters, then move to project manager training. They created a groundswell of PM practitioners throughout 3M by getting them to rally to the PMSIG as a group that could actually effect change. Later they developed project management sponsors, encouraged a project manager career path, and began portfolio assessment services.

Communications were effective. PMSIG members had some successes and others began to ask for assistance. It was helpful to set up Web sites and publish their competency model and PM curriculum. In addition, the Project Management Temple works well as a one-page executive summary on the components of a good project environment.

A good example of consolidating wins to promote more change appeared in the distribution of the framework for implementation of a new project office, the Project Office Implementation Kit.

The 3M case illustrates the one-step-at-a-time approach to implementing the project office, beginning with the need to assess the value to the organization of instituting the PO concept, and to see if enough accumulated pain exists in the company for stakeholders to recognize a need for help. It was decided at 3M not to plunge immediately into creating a formal organization, but rather to use more subtle approaches involving temporary support and stealth missions aimed at resolving pending challenges and at the same time demonstrating the benefit of project management. Further steps, in an articulated political approach, were taken to strengthen the project management cause. These included launching the PMSIG, identifying PM champions, creating a PM curriculum, and developing maturity and project leadership models.

Once the basics were in place, the group of PM change agents perceived the need to spread the word, that is, to do marketing on the topics of project office and project management. Through the PMSIG, 3M project practitioners were brought together for the first time. PM education and networking opportunities were also made readily available and visible. PM best practices were gathered. More information began being disseminated. People given project leadership positions, such as technicians, could realize a whole new career path in project management. The PMSIG leadership created a new and significant realization among management ranks that project management is a viable career path. Potential pilot projects and programs using more explicit project management techniques were undertaken.

Periodically the movement was reinvented to keep it fresh, relevant, and visible. To do this, assessments were applied to determine the organization's requirements. After the assessments were completed, rollout plans were made for the distribution, training, and implementation of various PM techniques, tools, and methods. Project offices serve as a mechanism to keep activities on track.

Storeygard also evangelizes for a stronger link between project decisions and for translating them into business success, formulating a balanced scorecard set of metrics as suggested by Cohen and Graham (2001) and covered further in Chapter Ten.

As project offices mature, they need to get involved with benchmarking projects and networking relationships with other companies and associations. Project offices can also contribute to the company during major organizational change. As ambassador and caretaker of project management applications and techniques, the project office can make significant contributions in virtually all organizational settings. The recurring theme is to continually harness internal support.

PART TWO

MAKING CHANGE HAPPEN

In this part of the book, the emphasis changes from planning to doing. The first part was concerned mainly with creating conditions so that change could happen. Entering this part it is assumed that many of those conditions are in place. Now it is time for the project office team to make contact with those people in the organization who must actually carry out the planned changes. It is an accepted military dictum that "no plan ever survives contact with the enemy." The members of the organization are not enemies in the classic sense, of course, but they can be expected to respond in ways that are not expected, not planned, or not even imagined. From this we can construct a parallel organizational change dictum: "No change plan ever survives contact with the members of the organization for whom the change is planned."

The following observations will ease the transition:

- Be flexible—a plan is a metaphor, not a law. Treat the organizational change plan you have developed as a guide to behavior and not as an imperative. This is the essential idea behind another accepted military dictum: "A plan is nothing, but planning is everything."
- Beware—things may go too easily at first. Change agent teams often report that initial efforts meet with quick acceptance. This often instills a false sense of security, an idea that things will continue without much resistance. However, what it usually means is that the opposition has been caught off guard. It is

easy to prevail until the opposition gets organized. An example of this is the "hundred days" that new presidents have to actually make some changes, until the opposition in Congress gets organized.

- Be alert—unforeseen opposition could arise at any moment, and it may go well beyond verbal resistance. We now enter the middle section of Figure I.1, where the beasts come out of the jungle in response to invaders. For example, the second case study in this part discusses a runway repaving project that was delayed because a group with a political agenda backed up by sledge hammers destroyed some crucial equipment.

- Be ready—you will need to improvise and make changes in the plan to adapt it to reality. Remember that you have three choices for every step in the plan. First, you can exit that step, leave it if it does not seem to be working. The second choice is to modify that step, making change based on the reality encountered. The third choice is to push on if the step seems to be working, even if not quite as planned.

The basic plan that has been suggested so far is to find a small project that is in trouble, show how standard project management methods can help the project, generate a win from this project, and then use that win to develop legitimacy and move on to larger projects. However, this may not be possible. The project office team may suddenly find themselves involved in a huge, highly visible, bet-the-company type project. This case requires a radically different approach, an obvious change in plan.

Some suggest that to develop broad-based actions toward a project office should begin with project manager training and then develop expertise so it can eventually help in project portfolio management. However, it may be that assisting in portfolio management is the first task that the project office members are assigned. Again, a change in plan would be needed.

The basic theme here is that contact with the organization can often result in situations that seem chaotic. Given the uncertainty involved in organizational responses, it is not easy in a book to present an organized approach to responding to chaotic situations. As a result, the reader may experience this section as a bit chaotic itself as we present a series of organizational situations and the responses of the project office teams.

Chapter Six presents some structure to help understanding by giving creative and flexible ways to manage chaos, manage complexity, assist in project portfolio management, and generally operate in an organizational environment. This is followed by two wide-ranging case studies of project office implementation. The first example is in a high-tech office environment and illustrates the evolution of a project office within a business organization. This example shows the typical life cycle of a project office; it follows a process much like that outlined in Part One of this book. The second example is from a U.S. Air Force base in Italy. This example is a bit more chaotic as a project office was created to help make sense of a large, multiproject construction program. This example also shows how a project office can work with a coalition of organizations where the only thing constant was the construction site. The examples are then followed by Chapter Nine, which uses lessons from the case studies to suggest techniques for staffing and operating the project office.

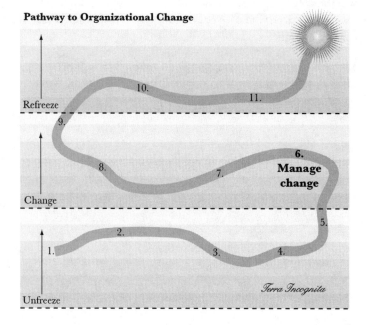

Pathway to Organizational Change

First contact with significant resistance typically occurs when you start doing something instead of talking about it. This chapter covers creative and flexible implementation of the change process, managing complexity in a turbulent environment, conducting effective start-ups, implementing project portfolio management, and working the plan. We describe the role of a project office to assist in a project prioritization process.

CHAPTER SIX

CONTACT: MANAGING THE CHANGE

At this point the reader has read about the change process and may be ready to go on a *quest:* an act or instance of seeking defined as pursuit or search, or as a chivalrous enterprise in medieval romance usually involving an adventurous journey.

Don Quixote immersed himself in reading tales of chivalry; he then exchanged a modest country life for that of a knight-errant full of zeal to perform heroic deeds. His exploration of life's biggest questions, in which he discovered things and people were not what they seem, develops through a series of ingenious and animated anecdotes, such as tilting at windmills believing them to be opponents in battle.

Like Don Quixote, modern managers may read all the literature about project management and want to embark on a quest to implement a project office—only to find themselves dreaming what appears to be a dream as impossible as Don Quixote's. The vision is there but implementation struggles. Too many projects are under way, cooperation is lacking, and chaos reigns.

People may not pay much attention to the project manager-errant during the planning phase, but their resistance will surely arise when they discover how the change affects them. Contact occurs. All animals emerge from the jungle to challenge intrusion by new players into their territory. It is now time to manage the change.

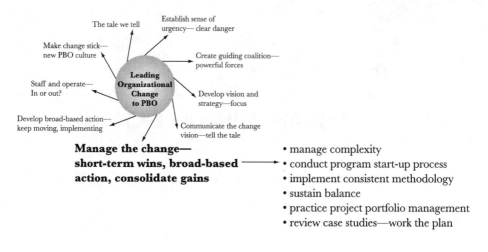

Manage the change—   • manage complexity
short-term wins, broad-based ——→ • conduct program start-up process
action, consolidate gains   • implement consistent methodology
                                       • sustain balance
                                       • practice project portfolio management
                                       • review case studies—work the plan

The dream of implementing a strategic project office requires a clear linkage between strategy and a portfolio of projects. This needs to happen at the front end of every product life cycle. Our earlier work (Graham and Englund, 1997) put together ten pieces of a puzzle (each piece a chapter in the book) that create an environment for successful projects. This chapter expands on one of those concepts, linking projects to strategy.

Managing Complexity

Remember Sisyphus, from Greek mythology. The gods condemned Sisyphus to keep rolling a rock to the top of a mountain, whence the rock would fall back of its own weight. They could think of no more dreadful punishment than futile and hopeless labor. Sisyphus is the absurd hero, as much through his passions as through his torture. His scorn of the gods, his hatred of death, and his passion for life won him that unspeakable penalty, in which his whole being is exerted toward accomplishing nothing. This is the price that must be paid for the passions of this earth, says Albert Camus ([1942] 1991). Sisyphus, proletarian of the gods, powerless and rebellious, knows the whole extent of his wretched condition; it is what he thinks of during his descent. The lucidity that was to constitute his torture at the same time crowns his victory—there is no fate that cannot be surmounted by scorn.

Sisyphus is without hope. He abandons any illusion that he might succeed at the assigned task. Once he does so, Camus considers him a hero because Sisyphus begins to view his ability to do the task again and again—enduring the punishment—as a form of victory. Unfortunately, too many modern organizations create heroes just like Sisyphus, trying to do too many projects with no hope of complete success.

Instead of pushing incessantly, it is far more productive to create a center of pull and channel energy. Compare how difficult it is to push a piece of string and how easy it is to pull it. The challenge is to access power and overcome inertia. Reframing mental attitude is a good start. Success also requires patience, because you cannot push a river, either. Things go at their own speed.

One way to reframe attitude to be more effective during implementation is to create new metaphors and name the chaos. This works because naming obstacles removes ambiguity and fear of the unknown. The unknowns now have names that we can talk about and address. The next step is to tame the chaos. Think of the fox in Antoine de Saint Exupery's *The Little Prince:*

> "If you tame me, it will be as if the sun came to shine on my life. I shall know the sound of a step that will be different from all the others. Other steps send me hurrying back underneath the ground. Yours will call me, like music, out of my burrow. . . . One only understands the things that one tames. . . ."
> "What must I do to tame you?" asked the little prince [(1943) 1971, p. 83].

He learned:

- Patience
- Dependability and predictability
- The need to spend time together
- The need to take care of what you tame; protect and nurture it
- The need to choose the very few to tame that you will commit to

Margaret Wheatley (1994) says that to survive in a world of change and chaos, it is necessary to accept chaos as an essential process by which natural systems, including organizations, renew and revitalize themselves. Information is the primary organizing force in any organization, and should therefore be shared widely. Successful change agents develop the rich diversity of relationships that are all around to energize teams; they also embrace vision as an invisible field that enables re-creation of workplaces and the world.

A change agent cannot rush into implementation alone or armed just with a plan. Resistance will erupt. The theme of chaos recognizes that project environments often appear unpredictable, disorderly, and sensitive to small changes. However, through all this, people respond in remarkably similar ways. The skilled program manager looks for patterns of similar behavior and for patterns in the chaos. Small changes in initial conditions have enormous consequences that can work to your benefit . . . or detriment. For example, if people did not participate in the planning process (initial condition), a program start-up meeting may be a disaster (consequence), with new objections arising that you never thought of before.

An adjunct of chaos theory—fractal geometry—says that similar patterns take place across layers. It is not only upper managers who care about purpose and vision but also the rank and file. In an organization—as you move up or down—you find many similar needs and corresponding responses.

The hope is that working together is a source of meaning and purpose in life, not just the requirements of a job. People aligned with their passion fully engage, and this leads to extraordinary achievements. Managers in organizations manage complexity by establishing a shared sense of purpose and an environment for people to interact.

Program Start-Up Process

Lewin and Regine advise people to "embrace chaos as a process of creative destruction, a time for fundamental change, to reorganize, to rearrange" (2000, p. 34). Effective teams emerge out of shared purpose, urgency, mutuality, and care.

The first step is to examine your own ideas, thoughts, and sources of influence. Reread Chapter Three on powerful forces. People who are good at getting results have a process they use—it comes from experience, best practices, proven processes, and research. They tame chaos by applying a systematic, repeatable process for building relationships.

The process of operating across organizations involves several discrete steps:

- *Prepare.* Do your homework, be clear about expected outcomes from the implementation project. Stay focused on a clear, convincing, and compelling outcome. A clearly articulated, compelling vision is an organizing factor in the chaos.
- *Establish.* During the start-up step, get explicit commitments from the people who will support or use the project office based on a vivid, shared vision statement. Use reciprocity—what you exchange with people is a powerful tool for influence. Determine how all people will work together and make decisions.
- *Maintain.* This is the steady state throughout the program life cycle. Focus on trust and integrity as enduring values, and point out the benefits of working in an open environment where people find more value in cooperating and communicating than not. Trust seems intangible but it is built with every contact; the more personal and respectful the contact, the more trust.

- *Adapt.* Adjust to changes, whether through enforcing commitments that are not being upheld or changing your attitude toward other organizations.

Attitude comes across like a half-peeled orange—people smell it across the room. Expect some level of chaos as a good thing. Using a model to manage chaos is a means to demonstrate confidence and provide a role model for others. The effect is more control over the environment and more order in it.

To engage others, recognize the problem of *entropy*—the degradation of matter and energy in the universe to an ultimate state of inert uniformity. When entropy takes over as a result of lack of attention either by management or by project leaders, what appears is reduced energy and increased chaos. When everything is a priority, nothing is a priority. It is hard to find focus in all the chaos, in a situation of "too much of too much." Implementing a change starts with overcoming inertia and then maintaining momentum. Be prepared to expend tremendous amounts of energy. People respond to that energy because it brings life and order. Just make sure it is energy with good purpose. When you lose people, a leader, a team member, or a sponsor from a project, you also lose their vision, focus, and energy.

As a change agent, you face an environment where you are asking people to act differently, on something they may not understand or agree with, and you have very little authority. That makes it appear unpredictable and chaotic. The organization almost certainly expects the implementation project to create something specific in a deterministic manner, and your support may grow shaky when people perceive that is not happening.

No matter how much others urge you to try for deterministic results, however, do not expect complete control and order—they are illusions. You can still get results without experiencing complete control and order. Control what you can and deal with what you cannot by designing contingency plans as part of a risk management process conducted with the implementation team during a start-up meeting.

Recognize that command and control, hierarchy, and unquestioned authority are on the wane in modern organizations. Electronic communication, cross-functional teams, globalization, and the free flow of ideas and people are on the increase. The bottom line is that the environment we work in has shifted a lot. This values shift requires moving from Know How and Know What to Know Why. "What should I do," shifts to "Why should I do it?" The changing role of program manager is in moving a team forward. You no longer drive a project; you have to create pull.

Focus on tactics to tame the organizational chaos. As part of the project office start-up process, begin relationship building with definitions and your role in supplying clarity to other people in the organization. From your preparation work, described in earlier chapters, put these statements on the table for review, discussion, refinement, and agreement:

- Define a *purpose statement*—the enduring reason for a group of people to work together.
- Define a *driving vision*—a vivid description of a future state associated with program success. One of the biggest gaps in organizations is between current reality and a future vision. Energy can be released by exercising the tension between the two, as in an outstretched rubber band. (And like a rubber band it could mean trouble if you release it too fast, such as in a reorganization.)
- Translate the vision into *mission statements*—specific deliverables the program will achieve.
- Then define *goals* for individuals, including action items and due dates.

Another factor for building energy around the change process is the emotional intelligence of the implementation team. Emotional intelligence has been cited as being as critical as cognitive intelligence (often referred to as IQ) to an individual's effectiveness.

New research shows that emotional intelligence at the group level is just as critical to group effectiveness. Teams that develop greater emotional intelligence boost their overall performance (Druskat and Wolff, 2001). Three conditions are essential to group effectiveness: mutual trust among members, a shared sense of identity as a unique and worthwhile group, and a sense of group efficacy, that is, the belief that the team can perform well and members are more effective working together than apart.

Building group emotional intelligence is about bringing emotions deliberately to the surface and understanding how they affect teamwork. It is also about behaving in ways that build relationships both inside and outside the team and that strengthen the team's ability to face challenges. "Emotional intelligence means exploring, embracing, and ultimately relying on emotion in work that is, at the end of the day, deeply human," say Druskat and Wolff (2001, p. 83). They depict group emotional intelligence as the platform that leads to trust, identity, and efficacy—which lead to participation, cooperation, and collaboration, all of which lead ultimately to better decisions, more creative solutions, and higher productivity.

Starting up the change process is an appropriate time to factor in group emotional intelligence. Some professionals find this uncomfortable, preferring to stick to the tasks or technical challenges of running a program. Nonetheless, creating a safe place for discussion and taking the time to talk, perhaps even vent frustrations, is a necessary investment. It honors people's willingness to change when they come to understand how the change affects them personally and positively. For example, finding a great group of interesting people to work with may be sufficient to overcome resistance to aspects of the change project perceived as onerous.

Creating conditions for creativity, productivity, and innovation to emerge requires complex interactions. You do not know where the next great ideas will come from, but they are out there, in people's minds. Encourage cross-communication and informal networks. Successful people make contacts with a wide variety of other people, sharing ideas and experiences.

Modern work already requires much time to communicate with people. Perhaps it is bad news, but the lesson is that it may take even more time to be effective in truly communicating with people. That extra effort is vital to success.

The extra effort invested in the time element is an increasing requirement because so much of our vaulted technology is impersonal. The author of *Megatrends*, John Naisbett, prescribes in *High Tech High Touch* (1999) that it is necessary to balance high tech with high touch to recover the personal element that is so important to effective relationships. Although technology is an integral part of the evolution of culture, it tends to pull us into a Technologically Intoxicated Zone. High tech high touch is a human lens that embraces technology but preserves our humanness. Take the effort to be a real person and acknowledge others as real people trying to work together.

Ask what kind of problem are you solving. Globally dispersed teams and project offices may struggle for weeks or months to resolve a critical issue remotely. An in-person meeting where you finally understand each other's issues often solves the issue in hours. One U.S. program manager, on vacation in Ireland, stopped by to visit a counterpart in person. Months of resistance and frustration subsequently resolved themselves within several weeks.

Match your approach to people based on the context of the situation. Building trust happens best when people are in the same place at the same time. This is why in-person program start-up meetings are so important. Later in the program you can use other tactics of anyplace or anytime interactions because you already built personal relationships. Consider the severity of the issue you are communicating—if high context, such as significant changes, personal or emotional issues, use in-person or person-to-person phone calls. Lower context items such as the current state of project work may easily be communicated in e-mail or memos. If it is important to get the words correct, write it down.

Program managers are partners with upper managers to create an environment for successful projects. Generate pull and excitement. Enforce discipline, follow through on commitments made, and tap support of management to create consequences for people to change behaviors. One of the competencies of effective program managers is their ability to operate in ambiguity, especially at the beginning of the program, and move into clear deliverables and results by the end of the program. The way to get things done is through influence; create an environment where you can be influential. Influence comes from relationships based on trust, mutual beliefs, and comfort in working with each other.

How you view your role will affect how you behave toward people. If you think you are the only driver of the change, the strongman leader, you unwittingly set yourself up as a bull's-eye or target. People will miss no opportunity to take shots at you. To proactively start up the change effort:

- Be clear about reasons for starting the effort. Give people time to become acquainted and begin working together.
- Prepare to overcome barriers:

    Time. Getting focused on common objectives and language minimizes misunderstandings and saves time in the long run, even though it may appear to take time at first.

    Travel. Rework and inefficiencies are reduced by the trust, relationship, and sharing of perspectives that develop during an in-person start-up workshop.

    Schedules. People make time for what is important.
- Allow more time when working with global teams. Design an agenda with sufficient time for discussion of major elements associated with the program. Cover important, high-priority items first.
- Encourage discussion and clarifying questions so that each person understands, shares, and takes ownership for creating a future state that is clear and compelling. A shared vision builds motivation. Be careful about proceeding without complete buy-in to the vision because progress is difficult when people work toward different ends.
- Develop a program objective statement—a one-sentence description of what you are going to do (scope), by when (schedule), and for how much (resources). Use ordinary language, not jargon or buzzwords.
- Validate all objectives, deliverables, schedules, roles, and responsibilities with the program sponsors. Reconcile any differences with the team.
- Identify assignments, owners, and due dates.

Methodology

The steps just outlined hint at a common methodology. Managing change is greatly facilitated by implementing a consistent approach to projects, using language that all project participants understand so they all know what to expect.

The HP Project Management Initiative taught a generic model in a three-day course titled "Project Management Fundamentals" that could be applied to any type of project in any business. It included simple templates but not thick binders of forms. Too much paperwork would be counterproductive to the goal of first understanding and then being willing to apply the process.

At this stage of the change process, the change agent should vigorously employ the organization's existing project management methodology—or seek one out if the organization does not have one. Having a repeatable methodology right now is better than waiting for a perfect one. Many experienced practitioners say it does not matter what process you use so long as you use a process. A very good place to start is with the five steps shown in Figure 6.1.

Take time to train people on use of the methodology. IBM's Project Management Center of Excellence developed a core course and then customized modules and case studies for different business units.

Once the basic course is in place, the next, or parallel, step is to include training on the behavioral, organizational, and business aspects of doing projects. Although not common, a preferred approach is to train upper managers on these topics first, then roll out the training across the organization. The project office may also want to offer, or broker, consulting to help people implement the steps learned in the training. Plan to include project portfolio management training and facilitation services, either as the organization is ready for it or as a way to capture attention about the organization's project culture.

Unintended Consequences of Change

Change agents, the people proposing and pushing for change, usually stress the positive consequences of change as they see them. That is, they stress how people will be better off—given their interpretation of *better*—and often ignore, or are

FIGURE 6.1. A PROJECT MANAGEMENT METHODOLOGY.

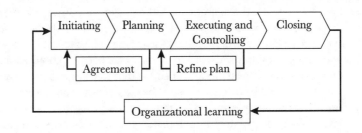

Source: Adapted from *Project Management Body of Knowledge* (Project Management Institute, 2000).

unaware of, potential negative consequences. It turns out that people often find themselves much worse off, usually because they have a different interpretation of what is better *for them*. Anthropological studies are replete with descriptions of situations where people from outside a culture attempted to make life better for its members but actually made things worse from the point of view of those they were trying to help. Figure 6.2 provides valuable modern lessons for change agents.

Despite the fact that the proposed change looks good and righteous to you, it may not look that way to others. It is possible that there will be unintended consequences to the proposed change, and these consequences may do more harm than good.

The change agent should be on the lookout for such unintended consequences and make adjustments to minimize them. In the Yir Yoront example, distributing axes directly to women and children contributed to the confusion of

FIGURE 6.2. UNINTENDED CONSEQUENCES IN REAL LIFE.

Spicer (1952) describes a typical example in *Steel Axes for Stone Age Australians* (pp. 69–90). Missionaries in Australia, as part of their plan for raising native living standards, made it possible for aboriginals to earn Western goods the missionaries considered "improving." Under certain circumstances these goods were handed out gratis. The handouts included steel axes that replaced old stone axes. Perhaps unknown to the missionaries, stone axes had gained a position of cultural significance in certain aboriginal tribes. For these tribes, the introduction of the steel ax degraded their life as they experienced it.

In the society of the Yir Yoront, the process of making a stone ax helped to define masculinity. Only men were allowed to make stone axes, and this required much skill to find a right wood for the handle and find a right tree for the gum. The stones were obtained from a distant quarry so this required trading during great ceremonies and fiestas. Production of the stone ax was a symbol of reliance on nature rather than technology. The ax was a pride of ownership—once it was created as it was associated with its creator. Other members of the family would borrow the ax from the father, solidifying various kinship relations. Once the steel ax was introduced, this change weakened the values inherit in their reliance on nature, weakened the prestige of masculinity, the age prestige, and various kinship relations. Family members became confused and insecure. Ownership became less well defined, so that stealing and trespassing were introduced into the society. Some of the excitement from trading surrounding great ceremonies evaporated, so that the only fiestas that people had became less festive and less interesting. Indeed, life itself became less interesting.

ownership, which was then partially responsible for the introduction of stealing and trespassing. Perhaps if the axes had been distributed only to the men, then ownership would have remained clear, and stealing might not have arisen. Of course, this is speculation and a change in distribution might have had no effect.

In addition, there was little incentive for missionaries to change their ways because the indigenous tribes were not in positions of power. But in organizational situations the people affected by the change program often are in positions of power and thus their points of view need to be taken into consideration.

The change agent should be particularly sensitive to other people's points of view when beginning to implement changes. Investigate or speculate about what unintended consequences may occur or simulate or prototype what might happen in the organization when a project office takes on increasing responsibilities in new territories.

Sustaining Balance

Managing change requires a balancing act. Project management deals with the triple constraints of scope, schedule, and resources, but it has another triangle to consider as well (see Figure 6.3). Management charters projects to achieve a level of *performance*, getting results. But what is the *experience* of team members on those projects—what do they encounter as they work to create those results? Is it stress, burnout, and fatigue that leave them thinking, "never again"? Or is it energizing, fun, rewarding, productive? Do people at the end of projects rapidly disappear or do they say, "Call on me next time you're doing a project—I really enjoy working with you"? If the experience is not good, over time project performance goes down. What type of *learning* takes place, both during and at the end of the project?

FIGURE 6.3. THE WORK TRIANGLE.

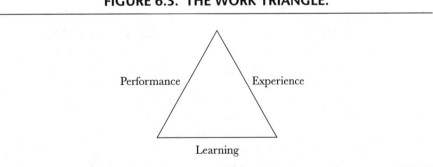

Performance   Experience

Learning

If people (and organizations) do not learn from mistakes or get reinforcement for what they did well, performance over time goes down.

Informal surveys among workshop participants typically reveal that most attention is focused on results. Very few program objectives include "have fun" and "get better at doing projects." When they do, however, you find an energizing atmosphere where amazing and wonderful things happen.

Timothy Gallwey says, "The three sides of the work triangle are part of an interdependent system. When either the learning or the enjoyment side is ignored, performance will suffer in the long run. When it does, management feels threatened and pushes even harder for performance. Learning and enjoyment diminish even further. A cycle ensues that prevents performance from ever reaching its potential" (2000, pp. 86–87). He adds, "When a few individuals make the commitment to their own learning and enjoyment, they serve as catalysts for others by the qualities they express while doing their work. Those who accept such a challenge may accomplish much more as a result of their work than the performance results they are compensated for" (p. 106).

To implement a project office for organizational change, strike a dynamic but balanced relationship among these three factors. The project office is in an ideal location to do this.

Sustaining balance requires great care when working among a variety of situations. Managing change to a project environment involves a similar quest to the story in Figure 6.4—and sometimes the same outcome. All too often, in working with good people and the best of intentions, we engage in too many projects with unclear objectives, fighting for resources, and the politics get ugly. To create a different scenario— *the good, the true and the beautiful*—the three factors we need to balance are professional project managers, upper management, and the enterprise project management process. All three viewpoints need to be balanced and integrated. Good people are essential to make the project office successful. Upper managers need to act with authenticity and integrity. Processes are the methods and tools to get the job done.

FIGURE 6.4. WORKING TOGETHER: THE PESSIMIST'S VIEW.

The movie *The Good, the Bad and the Ugly* is about another triad: Blondie (the Good) learns the name of the grave under which the gold is buried, Angel (the Bad) rounds up everyone in search of the gold, and Tuco (the Ugly) knows the name of the cemetery where the gold is buried. It's a quest for money: man against man against man, and may the fastest draw win. No one person knows the whole picture and they depend on each other. In the final gunfight, tension mounts higher and higher until it erupts in a blaze of gunfire.

Be guided by an inner knowing that the practices and processes employed, in the hands of master program managers and teams, are proven tools to craft outstanding results. All three categories or players are necessary before you have a decent story to tell. Help people sense the excitement that comes from creating something wonderful together.

Several cautions are in order, however. Watch out for these potential sources of sabotage:

- Staffing the office with the wrong people, both in abilities and attitude, can be disastrous.
- Upper managers who go through the motions of support for the sake of action provide only an illusion of productivity. People in the organization sense the lack of authenticity and integrity and do not put heartfelt effort into the process.
- Most managers say they want results, but careful observation of actions often indicates they are more interested in control. Control is usually an illusion, so focus effort on results, not on controls.
- Software tools are not project management. Implement common tools and procedures, but only after the process resides in the heads, hearts, and souls of participants.
- If organizations do not clarify and prioritize strategic goals, individuals decide on their own. Then you get whatever people want to do, not necessarily what is strategically important. The de facto strategy for the organization becomes the sum of uncoordinated individual actions.

Noted systems thinker Peter Senge (1999) offers another caution related to purpose and direction of the organization, "Conversations about power structures or control, without including consideration of where the organization needs to go, are counterproductive. They lead to organizations where control itself becomes part of the organization's purpose" (p. 367). He also goes on to suggest that people with internal networking capabilities are the ones who make change happen, "Ironically, those with the least formal organizational authority may hold many of the keys to better understanding the leadership communities that will determine organizational vitality in the future" (p. 568).

Project Portfolio Management

Managing or overseeing a portfolio of projects to achieve strategic goals is starting to come under the purview of a project office. It is one of the last areas to be developed or usually occurs at higher levels in a project management maturity model. Investing in a project office to implement this process offers perhaps the highest potential for significant return to the organization. Its political nature also makes it one of the most difficult areas to implement.

Robert Cooper (1998) describes the way many organizations flow projects through a tunnel: all projects or product ideas begin (go in), are in the dark most of the time, and all attempt to go to market (come out), most resulting in failure. A preferred model is to funnel good ideas into the critical few projects and focus on making them successful—*funnels not tunnels*. The linkage to strategy via a disciplined process can make this happen. A project office is the means to apply the discipline.

EXFO, an electro-optical engineering company in Canada, uses the concept of "funnel-to-tunnel" process to meet system objectives. Early product decision checkpoints focus on strategic fit and the business case. The middle checkpoint evaluates the technology fit and the ability to execute the project. From this point, projects are expected to go all the way through even though there are more checkpoints. The PMO coordinates the process and provides data.

The advantages are products that meet market requirements, better control of project time-to-market, and increased return on investment (ROI). Since its founding in 1985, EXFO has achieved 50 percent annual growth and employs over a thousand employees. About 20 percent of those people work in R&D. Product development process principles include concurrent engineering, product evolution through complete operational iterations, and built-in flexibility to adapt phases to each project.

Embarking on a strategic process for linking projects to strategy is a bit like the song "Three Coins in a Fountain"—everyone wants to make sure their projects survive the funneling process.

A *vicious loop* ensues (Figure 6.5) if there is no time to create a clear and widely understood business vision: with no consistent prioritization of work, the vast diversity of activity leaves even less time to prioritize; then choices are made in isolation, which creates duplication of effort or gaps in the product line; business results are unsatisfactory and that brings us full circle around the loop to the lack of a clear business vision.

Managers better serve their organizations when they focus attention on areas that can make the greatest impact. Focusing on individuals affects only 1 to 2 percent; doing training covers only 10 to 15 percent. Research shows that greater impact is achieved when 80 to 85 percent of managerial effort is focused on the environment—setting expectations and standards, providing more feedback, pointing out consequences, job engineering, and strategic alignment.

Steven Wheelwright also made the point for a PDMA International Conference audience that greater impact is possible when upper managers invest more

FIGURE 6.5. A VICIOUS LOOP.

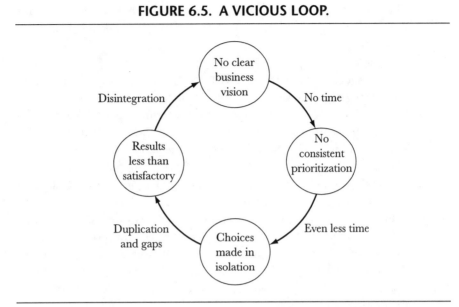

time in the front end of a product life cycle, when most important decisions are made. Instead they often wind up spending too much time on eleventh-hour crises. Such firefighting tends to look like an easy choice because the issues are clear and rewards are evident, whereas the fuzzy front end requires operating in greater ambiguity and with less tangible rewards, but more effective front-end work would lead to less need for firefighting.

The Linking Process

There is an inherent conflict between how a corporation gets measured by the outside world and how businesses are run. Portfolio management generally tries to work within these conflicting systems by focusing on businesses that are creating value, but there is no one right method for portfolio management. Most project management entities focus on new business, but some are starting with exit strategies—getting out of existing businesses—in order to free up cash.

In general, groups respond favorably to the idea of portfolio management, but few yet appear to do it particularly well or systematically. Divisions like the idea of tailored measures and clear strategic direction from above, but they also respond defensively as the resource evaluation process progresses. Many entities discover as they begin talking about the portfolio that they lack a commonly understood strategic direction, or that they are unable to define their strategic business units.

You can manage this change by operating in a *virtuous loop* (Figure 6.6) that addresses most of these issues. This loop represents an experiential mental model for linking projects to strategy (see Englund and Graham, 1999; Englund, 2000). The emphasis is on a process approach to selecting a portfolio of projects to meet strategic goals. It begins with a focus on what the organization should do; then moves into what it can do; a decision is made about the contents of the portfolio; and the portfolio plan is implemented. The steps continue in an iterative fashion.

Each step has a series of outputs, and outputs of succeeding steps build upon predecessor steps. The steps and outputs are interdependent, as in a true system dynamics model. Developing and implementing a process such as this means that a successful approach can be achieved, replicated, improved, and shared.

An imperative for management is to work together as a team to implement this process. The ancient Hermetic principle of correspondence says *as above, so below.* The idea is that the world is a mirror of heaven—a reflection. Dissension in the ranks of upper management will be reflected in the behavior of project teams. By working together, especially on project prioritization, instead of bickering across

FIGURE 6.6. A VIRTUOUS LOOP.

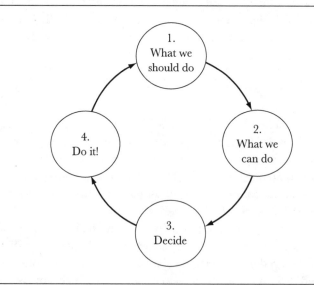

the organization, upper managers model the behavior they want from project teams. The commitment becomes to fully fund and staff projects selected for the *in-plan*. Getting people involved in the process is about the only antidote to avoid or ameliorate the political behavior that erupts anytime a change is introduced.

Stephen Bull, VP of engineering for EXFO in Canada, reports that their management team spends a full week each quarter on its portfolio review process. During the first three days they review strategy, business plans, project results and reviews, and new project presentations. The next two days they go through marketing prioritization and final prioritization with "loading." Managers from engineering, logistics, production, and marketing must all work together. Criteria to select and prioritize projects include company strategies, market potentials, financial estimations, and R&D forces. The process allows them to coordinate R&D resource availability with project priorities. They balance the portfolio with 65 percent new product projects, 25 percent incremental improvement type projects, and 10 percent for platform and research projects. Their complete new product development process system organizes project selection, prioritization, planning, following, and closure. This system is based on three axes: project portfolio management, product development process, and project environment. The PMO is at the heart of the system. This management and process commitment is key to the company's market success and maintaining its 50 percent annual growth rate.

At the end of a process like this you have

- A system of interrelated projects that all help implement strategy.
- A priority for each project that all department managers agree upon.
- A list of funded projects based on current resources.
- A list of future projects to be launched when more resources become available.

It is important to have a process person involved to guide this activity. Ideally that capability resides in a project office and is available across the organization. The role is to guide teams to implement this process and provide the linkage, invoking creative involvement from team members, discipline, dialogue, and work plans that support organizational goals. A project office that attempts to take over project prioritization from the business unit is asking for trouble. Ownership needs to reside with the people responsible for the outcome. A PO serves best when it shares its expertise and skill in guiding a business to prioritize its portfolio of projects.

This process is not meant to consistently score a portfolio no matter who does it. Depending on the strategy and criteria that a team selects, the outcome is a unique portfolio of projects that reflects the ingenuity, capabilities, and commitment of the people involved. This is a recipe for successful innovation:

- A process is repeatable and improvable.
- Selecting among choices happens at all levels in an organization.
- Defining criteria clears up misunderstandings.
- Criteria for success vary depending on business and development stage.
- Pairwise comparisons of projects under each criterion ease decision making.
- Explicit commitments create action.
- Prioritizing and selecting fewer projects creates greater capacity within the organization.
- A balanced mix of projects within a program portfolio supports strategy.

Organizational Approaches

Other stories document the rise and fall of a PMO. A project management office usually starts with good intentions, and often with initial good results:

> A steering committee comprised of representation from upper management as well as key functional units developed a prioritization process. The first step in this process was to define existing projects and create an inventory of current and requested work. Each function then brought to the table their prioritized requests. At a subsequent working session, the prioritized requests were then reprioritized based on benefit to the organization. The result became the priorities for IS project work and the beginning of the need for portfolio management. This was the first time the organization prioritized projects across functional areas based on business needs. While this process was painful the first time, it became a way of doing business and was repeated on a quarterly basis. The other directors became converts as they saw the entire picture and began to understand some of the unique challenges facing IS [McMahon and Busse, 2001, p. 2].

Sometimes the motivation to do these good deeds does not last. Y2K programs drew a lot of attention and a lot of resources. Surviving this effort—although a general relief—reduced the incentive for developing an enterprise-wide PMO in many organizations. There was even a backlash: "Functional groups resented the budget dollars spent for Y2K and felt IS had dominated the budget process and now it was their turn for their initiatives" (McMahon and Busse, 2001, p. 2). Many factors led to final dissolution of the PMO, including reorganization:

> One of the first acts of the new IS Director was a reorganization. Staff were shifted into various inappropriate roles in a newly created group, yet were still expected to function as project managers. This was an unrealistic expectation

for the staff to attain. There was no solid future direction provided to the project managers. The impact of these organizational changes was:

- Low morale
- Increased use of sick and vacation time
- Staff turnover
- Impact to productivity

The IS reorganization was the final blow to the PMO; in effect, the organization came full circle back to the chaos that existed prior to the establishment of the PMO [McMahon and Busse, 2001, p. 3].

Project Office Facilitation Role

Here's a tale to illustrate how this all works: Greg was the process manager for his business group, not his usual assignment but another accidental responsibility the group manager asked him to take on. Projects were not getting completed on schedule, and business commitments to customers were not being met. People were confused—should they focus on completing financial transactions or on an assignment to develop a new service? Frustrations mounted from arguments about what services to offer and how they would operate. Changes constantly interrupted work flows. Too many disparate activities were under way. Greg's assignment was to set up a process to prioritize projects in the organization.

The business team got together out of town and went through a prioritization process. People had their say, and they left with action items. However, Greg got no response to his requests for completed assignments.

Prior to the next meeting, Greg contacted his corporate project office that offered training, consulting, and best practices documentation. He asked if anyone had experience on project portfolio prioritization, because he was floundering on his own. A journal reprint (Englund and Graham, 1999) described the exact approach he was looking for. He found somebody in the project office who had gone through the process before, could steer the team along a proven path, and help them avoid the inevitable pitfalls.

The project office facilitator conducted a series of discussions and interviews with key players to assess the current situation. The group general manager was a forward-looking visionary, conjuring up multiple possibilities for new businesses and stretching his staff to determine feasibility. Division staff people were overwhelmed, however, by a series of current contracts they were struggling to execute. New business ideas were low priority for them. Recurrent communication conflicts were the norm.

Together they established a plan. Conduct a series of three meetings with the group management staff that would result in a prioritized plan of record, realistically staffing in-plan projects and listing future projects in an out-plan. Start with a vision statement, develop criteria for selecting projects, and apply to all projects.

The first meeting was set. The forward-looking vision was distributed in advance. The day before the meeting, the group manager reported a change in his travel plans abroad that prevented him from getting to the meeting. The meeting was held anyway and almost resulted in disaster. How can we discuss the vision without the general manager present? Feelings of powerlessness emerged but were quickly squelched by the facilitator, who pointed out that the business team now had an opportunity to express their own dreams and concerns, which could then be reconciled with the general manager's.

The group chartered a subteam to suggest categories and criteria for project selection. The project office consultant facilitated several subteam meetings. Individuals brainstormed criteria on Post-it notes and put them on the white board. The next exercise was sorting them. Categories emerged, not out of discussion but naturally from people concurrently moving sticky notes around the board. They ultimately labeled the categories as *sustaining business, new business,* and *must-do projects.*

How much should each category be weighted? Strong feelings emerged that sustaining projects were desperately needed to resolve current problems and keep the company in business. They gave that category a weight of 50 percent. New business came in at 30 percent and must-do at 20 percent. The must-do category recognizes that legal, environmental, or safety issues preempt resources from other projects.

Developing criteria within each category was a struggle until they came to realize, at the facilitator's unceasing prompting, that a core set of criteria, which they could influence, would support organizational goals. See Figure 6.7 for the criteria they developed. For example, ROI is a calculated number and is based on many factors beyond or indirectly related to project results. However, projects either support the ability to achieve revenue in the numerator or reduce costs in the denominator. Revenue directly relates to retaining sales from existing customers or to gaining new customers. So they selected criteria for the ability to retain and gain customers; projects enabling more of both scored higher. The subcriteria listed under Competitive Offering provide tangible means to compare projects.

Individuals on the subteam voted their relative weightings for criteria, and the average was computed to establish criterion weights:

Ability to execute	35 percent
Productivity and competency	25 percent

| Strategic fit | 20 percent |
| Competitive offering | 20 percent |

Despite initial doubts that their input would be valued, team members designed a plan for balancing the general manager's forward-looking vision with realities of executing current projects. Upon reconvening the management team with the subteam, the facilitator reopened discussion about vision and direction, since the general manager was now present. A welcome surprise (and an *Ah ha* entered into the facilitator's knowledge base) was that starting with a sense of direction and defining categories and criteria and weighting factors offered a convergence path. They would and could do it all (but not do all projects). The lesson learned was that the iterative process of forming goals and defining criteria to assess whether they are being met are inextricably intermixed—each supports the other and both are required.

The general manager and his staff embraced recommended criteria that came out of intense collaboration within the subteam. Instead of pushing his own agenda, the manager was pulled by the thoroughness and integrity that emerged from this work. Everyone agreed to move on to the next step—capture a project list and apply the criteria.

Using electronic media, the project managers used the criteria from the spreadsheet in Figure 6.7 to self-score their projects against the criteria. The project office consolidated all projects into a master list. Scores were presented and discussed at the next meeting to ensure agreement.

"How many people are available to do projects?" The consolidated worksheet indicated 224 people were required to do all fifty-one projects that needed to be completed over the following year (Figure 6.8). Silence. Finally the IT manager led the group to guesstimate that seventy-five people were available to work on projects that year.

At this point it is not important for the numbers to be totally accurate. The broad-brush picture shows too many projects under way or contemplated by too few people. It also shows underinvestment in sustaining projects and overinvestment in new business projects, compared to the desired mix. The first task is to get assignments in line with organizational goals and capacity. Fine-tuning happens later based on actual project planning after adjustments are made—projects funded, postponed, or cancelled. Careful review becomes especially important for projects around the cut line.

Note that headcount resources are the constraining factor in this example. Other cases may use total dollars or other units pertinent to the business.

The *cut line* in each category is a product of resources times desired mix. For example, 75 people × 50 percent = 37.5 head count (HC) that can be applied to

FIGURE 6.7. WORKSHEET OF SAMPLE CRITERIA.

Ability to Execute					Productivity	
Time to complete	Resources required	Right resources available	Geographic dispersion	Full time versus part time	Workload reduction, productivity improvement	Time and breadth

Sustaining business 50%

Strategic Fit				Ability to Execute	
Market attractiveness	Supports business strategy for business	Importance as a core competency (strategic leverage)	Worldwide or multinational benefit	Time to complete	Resources required

New business 30%

Ability to Execute			
Time to complete	Resources required	Right resources available	Geographic dispersion

Must-Do 20%

sustaining business projects. Apply the same arithmetic to the percentage desired for each category to determine cut lines. Figure 6.9 shows these calculations.

The true test came when the group assessed the prioritized project list. One business manager felt threatened when a large project within his department fell below the cut line. In the past, this particular manager would have found a way to implement it on his own. He argued the project was a good one and promised high return on investment. This pattern of behavior had created some of the unit's current problems—all projects under consideration were good ones, the resources just were not sufficient to do them all. The team usually operated virtually across international boundaries, allowing autonomous action, free of challenge. But this was a mandatory in-person meeting. The project office facilitator drove the process and kept the managers on track to achieve a plan they would all support. One manager openly questioned if the other would stick to the plan. This was not a com-

Strategic Fit				Competitive Offering	
Supports business strategy for organization	Critical to maintain business	Importance as core competency	Worldwide or multinational benefit	Builds competitive advantage (attracts new customers)	Customer loyalty (keeps existing customers)

Ability to Execute		Competitive Offering		
Right resources available	Geographic dispersion	Builds competitive advantage (attracts new customers)	Market acceptance	Customer loyalty (keeps existing customers)

fortable moment. She persisted in questioning, and he hesitated to commit. A safe environment allowed this confrontation to happen without doing any damage.

What happened next was creativity forged out of desperation. Instead of doing the whole large project, the manager agreed to start with a small subset whose return potential was high and whose profile more closely aligned with the criteria. Besides, the resources required were overseas and could not be deployed on projects above the cut line because of either skill set or geographic location. The group agreed to take an option on this project—start with a small investment and reevaluate later if further investment is warranted. Another approach would have been to invest *seed money*—usually a small amount—in an idea or venture, and fund the project fully later if a harvest developed.

Through open, face-to-face discussions, led by an outside facilitator from the project office, the entire group came to agreement on how best to achieve division-wide

FIGURE 6.8. SUMMARY OF PROJECTS.

Category	Head Count	Actual Versus Target
22 Sustaining projects	80 Person-months	36% versus 50%
23 New business projects	120 Person-months	54% versus 30%
6 Must-do projects	22 Person-months	10% versus 20%

goals. The leader's support for the integrity of the process created an environment that allowed this team to succeed.

The general manager demonstrated further integrity when he asked the team to help him identify the top three projects. Since he had a meeting with his manager the next day and needed to report how the organization would meet its goals, the general manager solicited input from the team. Now they knew he seriously wanted their involvement and would act on it. This was not a "going through the motions" exercise; the business would be run according to the results of the process that they were part of creating and implementing.

In this example, the project office facilitator came into a chaotic situation and invoked portfolio and behavioral processes to manage the complexity. Greg went back to his "real job," happy that experts from the PO were available when he needed them.

Portfolio Tools

A typical way to prioritize items is to brainstorm and then have people vote their top three favorites. Type the items into a computer, arrange them in categories, project them onto a white board, and mark votes on the board. Record results with a digital camera. The most popular items become quite evident.

FIGURE 6.9. WORKSHEET FOR PROJECT PRIORITIZATION.

	Category	Project	Head Count	Cumulative Head Count	
1	Sustaining	ATLAS	4	4	
2	Sustaining	Scancom	2	6	
3	Sustaining	Voltaire	3	9	
4	Sustaining	Data Mart	3	12	
5	Sustaining	Rational	17	29	
6	Sustaining	Migrations	3	32	
7	Sustaining	Rulings	2	34	
8	Sustaining	Back office	1.5	35.5	
9	Sustaining	Supplier payments	2	37.5	75 x 50% = 37.5
10	Sustaining	Hoshin2000	12	49.5	
	Category	Project	Head Count	Cumulative Head Count	
1	New Business	E-commerce	2	2	
2	New Business	Transfer channel	5	7	
3	New Business	Enhancements—New sales	1.5	8.5	
4	New Business	Hoshin2000, Stage 3	12	20.5	75 x 30% = 22.5
5	New Business	Global??	6	26.5	
6	New Business	Total E-finance	14	40.5	
7	New Business	Quote tools	5	45.5	
8	New Business	Online financing	6	51.5	
9	New Business	E-Finance	4	55.5	
10	New Business	Service line	13	68.5	
	Category	Project	Head Count	Cumulative Head Count	
1	Must Do	Star$ roll out	2	2	
2	Must Do	Hoshin2000, Stage 1	12	14	75 x 20% = 15
3	Must Do	Phase 1	3	17	
4	Must Do	Phase 2	5	22	

This does not, however, deal with varying degrees of interest or complexity.

A simple alternative is to list projects and criteria in a matrix like the one in Figure 6.10, assign weightings to the criteria, and vote each project a score from 1 to 5 for each criterion.

The spreadsheet computes the math. This way items that have medium importance across the board start surfacing because they do not lose out to the popular vote. They may represent an excellent compromise. For example, Project 4 would not have made the cut because of low profit potential, but it has excellent strategic fit and market growth and is valuable to keep in the portfolio. Here is how to use the matrix:

- List projects in the left-hand column.
- List criteria in the top row; weight each criterion as a percentage of 100.
- Working vertically, evaluate each project on how well it meets each criterion.
- Use a 1–5 scale.
- Multiply each cell by its weighting; add the product of the multiplication across the rows.
- The end of each row is a total priority score; indicate or sort the relative rankings.

The examples present a spreadsheet approach to the plan of record. You can also display the plan in project management software, using one of the enterprise project management software packages available in the marketplace. These are especially helpful to capture project data over an intranet, display either summary or detail project information, and access reports from anywhere in the company.

FIGURE 6.10. A SIMPLE PRIORITIZATION MATRIX.

Criteria / Projects	Market Size 40	Profit Potential 25	Strategic Fit 20	People Development 15	Totals 100
Project 1	5 x 40 = 200	3	1	1	310
Project 2	3	5	5	5	420
Project 3	2	3	4	2	265
Project 4	5	1	5	5	400

Be careful of software that requires the entry of extensive project data before doing anything useful. People weary of this process before getting to the good stuff. Start instead with a top-down approach. Structure the desired categories and prioritized projects that support what the organization should be doing. With a proposed in-plan, capture more detailed project information from core teams that are assembled to determine feasibility. Then reconcile efficacy of the portfolio. A plan of record might look like Figure 6.11.

Start-Up Example: Timbrasil

One organization that incorporated elements of group effectiveness in its program start-up efforts was Timbrasil, a wholly owned subsidiary of Telecom Italia Mobile. In 1999, the company won a bid to privatize part of the state-owned Brazilian telephone system. Timbrasil then set up headquarters in Rio de Janeiro to manage the installation and operations. The geographic area covered included the states of Rio de Janeiro, Pará, Federal District of Brasilia, Rio Grande do Sul, and part of São Paulo. These were the required activities:

- Set up offices in Brazil.
- Recruit project office personnel.
- Develop detailed implementation plans.
- Initiate operations.

The TIM Brazil project office, called Business Support and Integration (BSI), consists of ten people responsible for accompanying the start-up projects in Brazil. The group tracks critical activities and reports progress to the Boards and CEOs of TIM in Brazil and in Italy. BSI's principal scope is to provide support and troubleshooting to ensure that objectives are met within the established time frame. BSI's primary functions are to promote integration, provide coordination, facilitation, and support, and consolidate information.

Three categories of projects make up BSI's portfolio: marketing mix, client interface, and business operations infrastructure. Project activities include finance and logistics, interconnectivity and roaming, market demand, value-added services, network processes and HR, information technology, call centers and indirect sales, market analysis, launch program, communications plan, network construction, and direct sales.

In November 2001, BSI's director decided to carry out a two-day program aimed at creating a stronger team spirit with the group itself and with principal clients and interfaces. The program used outdoor experiential learning techniques on the first day. The twenty-five participants executed tasks that required strong

FIGURE 6.11. SAMPLE PLAN OF RECORD.

ID	Strategic Category	Priority	Project	Head Count
1	Platform (Mix = 40%)			
2	In-Plan	1	F	2
3		2	G	2
4		3	H	4
5		4	J	5
6		5	K	3
7	Out-Plan		Next Step	
8				
9	Enhance (Mix = 20%)			
10	In-Plan	1	B	2
11		2	C	1
12		3	D	1
13		4	E	2
14		5	I	1
15	Out-Plan		Fat City	
16				
17	R & D (Mix = 30%)			
18	In-Plan	1	A	7
19		2	L	5
20				
21				
22				
23	Out-Plan		Blue Sky	
24				
25	Infrastructure (Mix = 10%)			
26	In-Plan	1	Business Plan	1
27		2	Portfolio	1
28		3	Update Plan	1
29				
30				
31	Out-Plan		Corner Office	

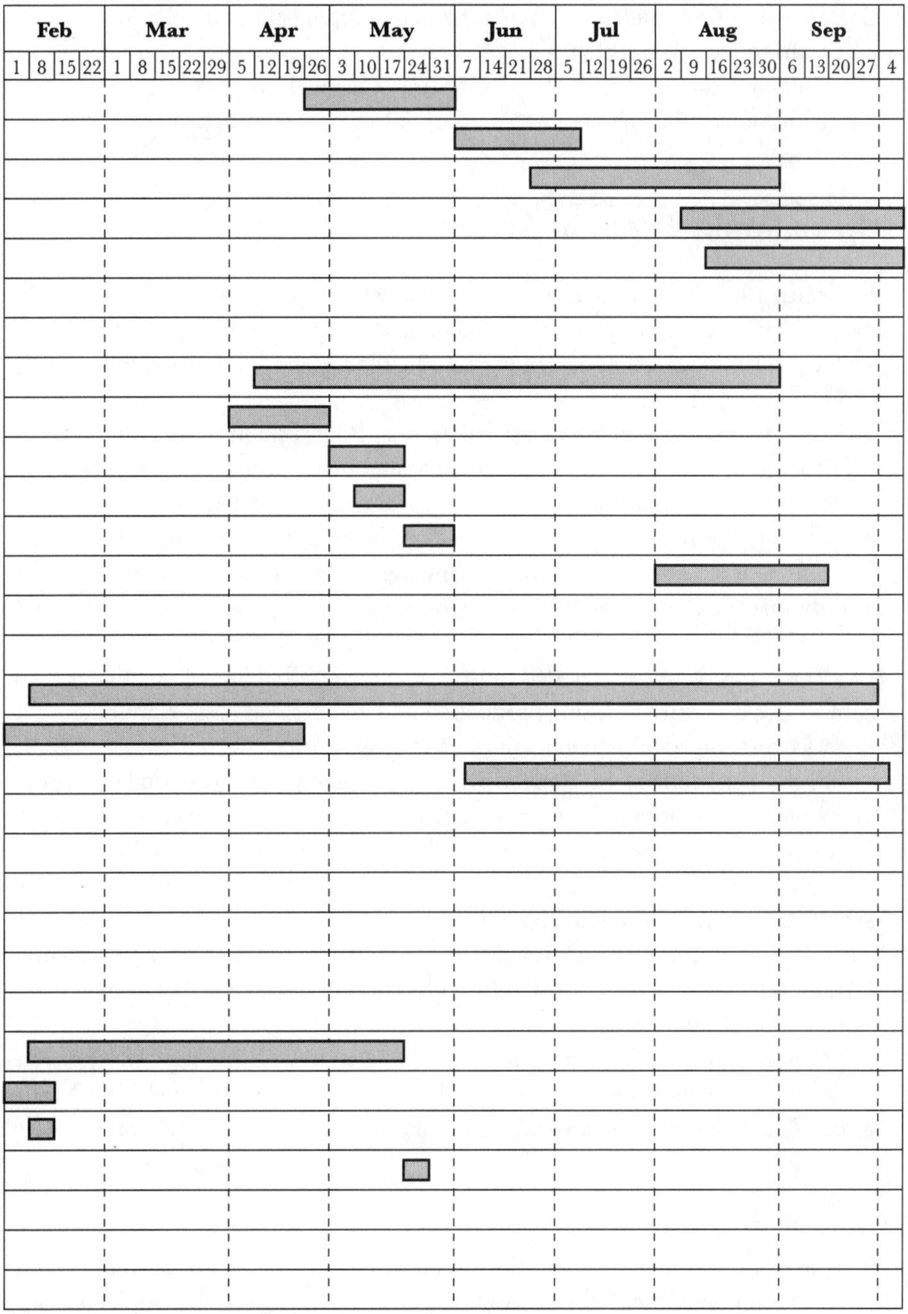
Feb
Mar
Apr
May
Jun
Jul
Aug
Sep
1 8 15 22 1 8 15 22 29 5 12 19 26 3 10 17 24 31 7 14 21 28 5 12 19 26 2 9 16 23 30 6 13 20 27 4

team interaction. The second day involved a forum of discussions regarding the role of BSI. It focused on the challenges to obtain timely and accurate information. The event was hailed as a milestone in developing effective relations between BSI team members and clients.

This case illustrates the role of a project office with the project portfolio plus a start-up process for managing expansion into a new territory.

Start-Up Example: Brazil in Action

In August 1996, the Brazilian government launched a program of forty-two strategic projects designed to promote sustainable development and new investments, and to reduce social inequities. In early 1999, that program increased to fifty-eight projects.

During the first four years, approximately R$70 billion (US$35 billion) was invested in the projects, with over 60 percent going toward improving the social welfare of the population and the remainder aimed at infrastructure projects. The key strategies for the program included careful selection of projects, use of project management approaches, and partnering agreements between the government and the private sector. Of the forty-two initial projects, twenty-five met or exceeded initial objectives at the end of the four-year period.

The projects chosen included those with a high probability of creating a more competitive economy, reducing production and commercial costs, eliminating bottlenecks, and improving qualifications of the labor force.

A good example is the Bolivia-Brazil gas pipeline. For every dollar invested in the pipeline, an additional seven dollars is expected to be generated in new capital projects such as power plants that will burn Bolivian natural gas.

Likewise, the modernization program for the Port of Suape plans to generate at least 3.5 times its initial investment, with the installation of port support services and plants for ceramics, textiles, metallurgy, and packaging. The widening of the highway from Belo Horizonte to São Paulo is also calculated to provide similar spin-off investments.

Other important infrastructure projects in the Brazil in Action program include the jungle highway from Manaus, Brazil, to Caracas, Venezuela, the North-South Transmission Line, and the Araguaia-Tocantins river navigation project.

Project Management

The program was managed by using an innovative approach not normally found in Brazilian government circles. A management by projects philosophy was applied, aimed at completing projects on time, within budget, and to specified requirements. The objective was to implement a results-oriented approach using modern management techniques. These principles guided the management model:

- A project logic is used in organizing actions and tasks.
- Each project is assigned a project manager.
- Adequate resources are assigned to each project.
- Managers and project staff have online project information.
- Barriers are dealt with through cooperation.

Each assigned project manager was held responsible for obtaining desired results. Criteria used for selecting managers included leadership, negotiation skills, proactiveness, and troubleshooting abilities. Managers carried out their missions with great success, proving that there is a high degree of competence available in the public sector. Maria Lúcia Sotério di Oliveira, manager of a financing project for low-income housing, stated that the project management approach "contributed substantially towards meeting the goals of the Letter of Credit program within the three-year timeline established."

The "every project has a project manager" approach represented a significant change from the previous mixed-responsibility model. Says Ludgério Monteiro Corrêa, program manager for the National Family Agriculture Program, "Having an available and willing person with name and telephone number responsible for achieving project results" made a vital difference in implementing government programs.

An online management information system was implemented, providing interconnections among project managers, partners, and government administrators. This allowed stakeholders to access up-to-date information on project status and apply timely corrective measures.

Tracking and Support

To support the project and provide reliable tracking information, a task force was organized within the Planning Ministry. The task force used the management information system to provide information to various governmental levels, including other ministries and the office of the president, so that decisions could be expedited and roadblocks could be removed. The task force's hands-on management approach yielded dividends both for infrastructure projects and social programs. For instance, the Bolivia-Brazil gas pipeline was completed 20 percent under budget; the North-South Transmission Line was finalized on schedule; and the Port of Sepetiba, near Rio de Janeiro, was terminated prior to the scheduled date of completion. Even for social programs, traditionally difficult to control, the management approach proved effective for many programs—Line of Credit,

Agrarian Reform, Basic Sanitation Reform, Direct Financing for Schools, and National Program for Requalification of Labor—all of which surpassed the original goals established in 1996.

The Brazil in Action program finished in December 1999 and set a new standard for project management in the Brazilian Government. The subsequent program for the 2000–2003 period, called Advance Brazil, came about from lessons learned on the pioneering Brazil in Action program. Municipal and state governments were also influenced to use similar approaches in their respective administrations.

As a result of the groundbreaking successes in the Brazil in Action program, the Brazilian government budget system was altered to better reflect the interdisciplinary reality of projects programmed for the 2000–2003 period. The old functional criteria for budgeting gave way to a project-based approach more consistent with the nature of the projects.

Projects must make a significant contribution to improvement of society in some manner. These are the criteria that govern project selection:

- Create a macroeconomic setting that helps stimulate sustained economic growth.
- Stabilize the government's finances.
- Raise the educational level of the population and increase the skill level of the labor force.
- Reach US$100 billion in exports by 2002.
- Become more competitive in the agribusiness sector.
- Develop the tourism industry.
- Develop the arts and culture as an industry.
- Modernize basic infrastructure and improve the quality of service in the telecommunications, power, and transportation sectors.
- Promote the modernization of production methods in order to stimulate competition in the internal Brazilian market.
- Increase access to work opportunities and the quality of jobs.

The Advance Brazil program includes investments of approximately R$317 billion (US$150 billion) in energy, transportation, telecommunications, social development, ecology, information, and knowledge, all necessary to obtain the growth and modernization desired for various regions of the country. The projects were designed and chosen to have a strong impact on society in terms of subsequent investments, additional jobs, increase in income and, social development. The projects were chosen in integrated clusters. For instance, a railroad is associated with highways, river transportation, ports, electric power, and telecommunications, which subsequently will have an impact on social development programs, technological capacity, and the ecology.

Initially, private sector investment in the Brazil in Action program amounted to 25 percent of the total investment. In the beginning of the Advance Brazil program, that investment percentage rose to 33 percent. The Brazilian government hopes to increase that private sector contribution to 50 percent.

Working the Plan

There are other roles a project office can play. Birkinshaw and Hood (2001) suggest ways to unleash innovation, especially across geographical boundaries:

- Give seed money to subsidiaries.
- Use formal requests for proposals.
- Encourage subsidiaries to be incubators.
- Build international networks.

These suggestions come in response to observations that no one has a monopoly on great ideas, least of all headquarters, and that bright ideas can get marooned on desert islands.

A project office needs to avoid positioning itself as a bureaucratic harpoon. One mind-set is to recognize how distance can become an advantage: distance allows remote units "to experiment with unconventional or unpopular projects that would be closed down if they were more visible to headquarters. It allows them to become incubators that can provide shelter and resources for businesses that are not yet strong enough to stand on their own," say Birkinshaw and Hood (2001, p. 135). They point out that Ericsson became successful in digital radio technology and handsets although both businesses struggled to gain acceptance during development. A unit president moved himself and his team to southern Sweden so as to gain the time and space to establish the business without interference from corporate executives.

This strategy, however, represents a risk that the new business may not achieve in-plan status within the corporate portfolio. "The critical success factor is typically how well the project champion is connected with other parts of the corporation." A key role for upper management teamwork is to serve as idea brokers, balancing the portfolio of businesses by staying connected via international networks. The project office can be the conduit for these communication paths.

Distance can also become a disadvantage. Levy (2001) documented five steps to failure that first arose out of observing the Nut Island sewage treatment plant:

- Management attention was riveted on high-visibility problems so it assigned a vital, behind-the-scenes task to an autonomous team that self-organized around a distinct identity.
- Management ignored the team's requests for help.
- An us-against-the-world attitude developed into an isolation mentality, but management viewed the team's silence as a sign that all was well.
- Management did not expose the team to external perspectives and practices so the team made up its own rules—which masked grave deficiencies in team performance.
- Management and the team held distorted pictures of reality until external events broke the stalemate. The Nut Island program was finally disbanded after thirty years of effort left Boston harbor no cleaner than when the core team first came together.

How to stop this effect?

- Install performance measures and reward structures tied to internal operations and company-wide goals. Reward mission-oriented rather than task-driven results.
- Establish a hands-on management presence to detect early warnings of problems and give the team a sense that they matter and are listened to.
- Integrate team personnel with people from other parts of the organization to expose them to new ideas and practices and encourage big picture thinking.
- Rotate managers and workers to discourage institutionalization of bad habits.

In essence, a project-based organization supports multiple reporting relationships, shared accountability, shared rewards, team effort, and shared decision making—all capable of generating increased chaos. The project office is a facilitator of this culture and its salvation for creating results.

Summary

There is no more magic to tame organizational chaos other than basically putting in extra effort focused on relationships. Win over allies by the ability to influence people. Especially in the beginning of any change effort, influence early and often because the more influence exerted at the beginning by getting explicit commitments from people, the easier it is later.

"Separate organizational from technical issues" is a lesson learned when working with a large cross-organizational effort on computer architectural issues. We kept engineers working alone far too long on issues that required more cross-organizational assessment and a business decision. If issues are truly technical, by all means keep engineers working on them. Be sensitive, however, to situations where trade-offs among competing solutions will be required. Escalate these decisions to the core or functional team.

Chaos builds tension and conflict but it also breeds creativity. Out of creativity comes closure so you move forward. With the focus that closure brings, you gain people's commitment, but you still need the power of a coalition. Effective communications are a face-to-face process to build trust.

Organizational chaos in fast-moving organizations behaves much like the turbulent flows often seen in air or water, and many of the same concepts apply to overcoming social entropy and channeling human turbulence to get results. Chaos theory, when applied to managing complexity in organizations, helps us to look for patterns in randomness and understand that behavior in each fractal layer is a reduced-size copy of the whole, exhibiting all its similar but chaotic traits—unpredictable and sensitive to small changes. A few rules of human behavior turn out to guide many patterns or responses. Look for these behavioral patterns and build up your internal alliances by mastering the universal principles they embody:

- People respond to energy; otherwise entropy sets in.
- People make the difference, not tasks, tools, or processes. Put extra effort into establishing and maintaining effective relationships with partners.
- You learn more by asking true inquiry questions than by telling people or advocating your own points of view. Effective leaders are known by the quality of the questions they ask.
- To influence others, use hard data and big numbers; then describe in vivid word pictures how the future will be different when the program is successful. Ask people for their commitment to this endeavor because people are more likely to follow through when they make explicit commitments. Tap the power of the word *because.*
- Commitments are not effective if there are no consequences for not following through. Processes that support consequences can change behavior. Be an enforcer through positive reinforcement.

People put in effort where they find value. Provide more feedback to others than they get anywhere else, employ currencies of exchange such as recognition and inspiration, and create learning opportunities to tap into the universal innate curiosity to learn. Put fun on the agenda. Create positive experiences where people keep coming back to work with you again and again.

A complete successful change agent

- Applies effective strategies for managing change and achieving successful contact across the organization
- Expects resistance and plans for surprises
- Tames organizational chaos through a clear sense of purpose and robust interactions
- Is creatively adaptable
- Watches out for unintended consequences
- Involves sponsors, change agents, and change targets in formulating and implementing effective process changes
- Conducts a start-up process that gets people connected
- Implements standard procedures, gets groups to use those procedures, and manages the resistance that arises
- Facilitates prioritization of projects in the portfolio based on their contributions to organizational goals
- Focuses on the critical few projects
- Recognizes and operates by the few simple rules that guide human behavior in organizations
- Continually applies the lessons of complexity science

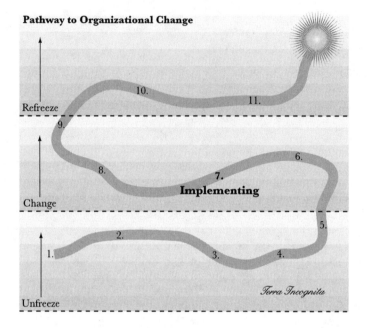

Pathway to Organizational Change

Refreeze

10.   11.

9.

Change

8.   7.
Implementing   6.

5.

Unfreeze   1.   2.

3.   4.

Terra Incognita

This chapter describes how program manager Alfonso Bucero and his team implemented a project office and managed the cultural change using project management skills in a professional delivery organization—Hewlett-Packard Consulting in Madrid, Spain. A project office implies innovation because it changes the way an organization proceeds, in this case creating the ability for project managers to keep focused on the client and perform high-quality project management. The office needs to analyze all internal and external stakeholders and their expectations, assign the team, divide all activities into functional groups, and, most important, create a very effective and empowered team. Also included is the evolution from a local to a global PMO.

CHAPTER SEVEN

IMPLEMENTING THE PROJECT OFFICE: CASE STUDY

Alfonso Bucero, PMP

Foundation work on the HP Spanish project office began in September 1999. As the organization grew in terms of projects and people, knowing more about project status became a real issue from management's perspective.

The Spanish project office arose from the need to relieve project managers of administrative tasks associated with managing projects in the "solutions business." The Hewlett-Packard Consulting Organization (HPC) provides solutions to "implement a customized software solution that migrates from a mainframe infrastructure to Open Systems." The management team often focused only on numbers and outcomes, wanting good project results but not worrying about creating and maintaining the right environment for project success. The project manager is supposed to manage customer expectations to get things done. It becomes difficult to maintain this focus while also dealing with many internal organizational concerns. Management came to believe there should be help for project managers to improve their efficiency, facilitate getting the right tools, and align services with the needs of the project environment.

Communication and documentation with the client and within the delivery organization are key to the project delivery process. Difficulties increase when the culture does not support project work. Project managers often find themselves on their own when dealing with internal and external stakeholders during the project life cycle. Sponsorship was an unknown term.

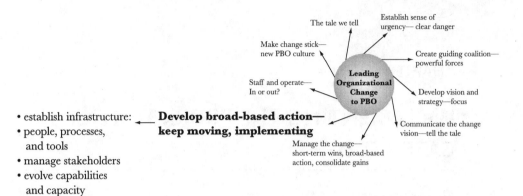

- establish infrastructure:
- people, processes,
  and tools
- manage stakeholders
- evolve capabilities
  and capacity
- review case studies

At the beginning of the project, Bucero—the assigned senior program manager—ran a survey to determine how well HPC supported project management. Sixty-five percent of the staff answered the survey. The results identified specific areas where the project culture was weak:

- No holistic view of the project portfolio
- Lack of knowledge or access to reuse previous work
- No consistent approach for complex projects
- Lack of project culture
- No consistent PM skills
- Poor scope definition, validation, and management
- Bad risk identification
- Lack of sponsorship
- Project closing delays

The results indicated HP needed an effective infrastructure for people, processes, and tools in the project office.

Mission and Objectives

People who have never worked on a project have difficulty understanding that, to achieve project success, the organization must support the project manager. It took almost six weeks to get an agreement with the management team about the reason for this project.

The big question Bucero had to deal with was, "Why do we need a project office at all?" He explained to the management team that the project office adds value to project team members by providing mentors, consultants, training, structured intellectual capital, and tools to be more effective. The project office also adds value to HPC by providing culture shift to project management, reusable tools and techniques, document and methodology support, global recognition, profitability improvement, and quality support. And the project office adds value to customers by providing visible signs of HP commitment, competent HP team support, and quicker and more effective answers. The key to setting upper management support at this point was showing how the PMO solved current problems and provided immense business impact. A complete business case was presented to the management team in the language and format of "management think."

The business case presented tangible benefits that could be achieved in a short time. The content of that presentation was to explain the PMO value to the organization, cost, flexibility and creativity obstacles, PMO functions, staffing, location, virtual teams, and establishing the project office.

Bucero defended the value of a PMO to project team members, providing mentoring and consulting services, training, tools to be more effective, a project library, global recognition, profitability improvement, and organizational improvement and quality support.

Explaining the value to the organization, he described the benefits of the cultural shift to project management, in terms of reusable tools and techniques, administrative support, visible signs of management commitment, competent project team support, and quicker and more effective answers to questions.

In terms of cost, he argued that although establishing and running a PMO would not be cheap, it would be worthwhile because it would be no more expensive than the cumulative cost of conducting project efforts without such an office, and might well cost less in the long run. A major feature of a PMO would be a comprehensive approach to PM, and it would pay for itself very soon. The PMO would help project managers feel they were not alone on the customer site. Somebody was supporting them from the HP organization in a way that would make them feel more comfortable not only to implement and execute projects but also to sell more.

The business case also included a role for the PMO to support creativity, reflecting a bias toward centralized decision making, and supporting team members to be more effective. The PMO team would be there to help project managers and project teams, not thwart their efforts to do the right thing. The first key success factor is to support project managers.

In terms of services, he proposed to start with a Document Management System group (DMS) as a first priority, helping PMs and consultants to generate bids faster and with higher quality.

Regarding PMO staff he proposed two alternatives:

- To serve in a simple support and facilitation role, the PMO would only need three or four people.
- To play a central role in guiding an organization's project efforts, the PMO would need up to a dozen people.

He argued the approach selected would make a big difference to the kinds of efforts the office would carry out.

One key factor considered was the visibility and accessibility of this group of people. The PMO should be located where it made most sense, in this case inside the existing department where it is accessible by all project managers and consultants. The HPC Project Office belongs to the Business Operation group at HP Consulting. They assigned a physical location for the office at the beginning of the project and hung up a poster with the words "Project Office" above the physical space designated for the office. The advantages were that everybody could see where the project office was located and identify where to go to request services. Eventually the team members all added a PMO logo on their badges. Project office members identified as a team and worked in that way.

He also included comments about their virtual world, arguing most projects are in remote sites. The PMO, as the link between project managers and the rest of the organization, greatly facilitates the reuse of libraries, methods, and standards. He told them establishing a PMO requires a lot of effort, and it demands thorough and careful planning.

Finally he got management agreement about the mission and objectives for this project. Some discussions were kept between the management team and himself to achieve this agreement because some people perceived the PMO was a bureaucratic organism. He demonstrated there were more and more projects under way; lack of knowledge about project management existed; and new people in the organization had little experience in project management. Following the approach in Figure 7.1, the proposal was presented, studied, discussed and finally accepted by the management team in February 2000. The PMO project started on March 1 at the Madrid office.

Progress was aided by collecting data on current projects that encountered extreme deviations and showing this information at management meetings. He audited projects that suffered from lack of scope and risk planning, noting the cost impact on the organization. He demonstrated that most projects had no formal sponsor and explained that impact on the organization. Making a presentation to the management team and setting clear expectations and deliverables at the beginning were key to achieving the go-ahead decision.

FIGURE 7.1. APPROACH TO PROPOSING AND IMPLEMENTING A PMO.

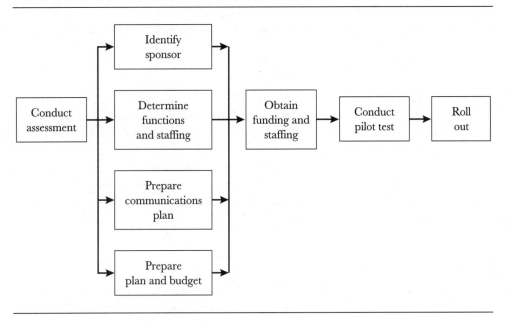

Because project managers were used to doing all the work themselves, including documentation and project file archiving, and did not know that help was available, a marketing campaign was necessary to communicate the existence of the PO and sell its benefits to the whole organization.

Bucero announced the PO's mission statement: *To support HP Project Managers during the project selling and delivery processes so they can focus on high-quality project management and added value.* He followed up by describing its objectives as follows:

- Relieve HP consultants of standard activities (low added value)
- Provide quality assurance within the project delivery process
- Serve as a breeding ground for knowledge sharing, conducting project snapshots
- Be the home front for all PM initiatives

Scope

The project office was born to relieve consultants and project managers of some administrative activities in the delivery of customer projects, helping them to focus on project management activities. Project office duties include managing the project file—the documents to be authorized during the project life cycle—as well as supporting proposal development, taking project meeting minutes, distributing documentation, managing labor time registration, assuring invoicing schedule is followed, and backing up the project manager.

After breaking down the first objective into smaller activities, one question came to mind:

How did the end users feel about it?

The program manager had several meetings with consultants and project managers to verify the initial scope. Figure 7.2 shows the different types of meetings he conducted.

These meetings were extremely valuable. Getting these people involved from the beginning was the only way to convince them to use the project office. Bucero notes that being aligned with real user needs was his personal objective during the whole project.

PMO Meetings

These meetings were conducted on a monthly basis and tremendously aided the scope verification and management processes. "All the time invested preparing

FIGURE 7.2. SCHEDULE OF MEETINGS.

Meeting Type	Attendees	Presenter	Duration	Preparation Effort	Material Delivered	Objective
Management Meetings	Management team	PMO lead	1 hour	2 hours preparing strategy and material	Slides copy and PMO white paper	Inform and get upper management commitment
PM Meetings	Project managers	PMO lead	2 hours	4 hours preparing material and examples	Slides copy and PMO proposed services	Share plans and ideas and ask for feedback
Presales Consultants Meetings	Senior consultants in presales activities	PMO lead and PMO coordinator	1 hour	3 hours preparing material and slides	Slides copy and presales PMO services	Share information and ask for feedback and validation

and running these meetings was extremely helpful for me to implement the PMO," says Bucero.

Participants in these meetings defined the following responsibilities for the project office throughout the project delivery process:

- Make sure that mandatory documents are used.
- Improve quality system.
- Guide project manager through PM methodology.
- Report to project manager about project status and progress (alerts!).
- Monitor outstanding actions.
- Track labor time.
- Provide third-party and subcontractor management.

Knowledge sharing is another key element in project office success; it is even more relevant when the project culture level is very low. The PO also needed to support project snapshots and establish a PM coaching program.

The project office advises Resource Management personnel regarding project manager allocation. This includes sharing knowledge about PM soft skills and best practices in conjunction with the Human Resource manager. It acts as a centralized organ that collects documentation for reuse and provides collected documentation when needed in other projects.

The project office is the home front for all PM initiatives, facilitating PM Forums and establishing a PM coaching and mentoring program.

Outside the Scope

The project office must not be a black hole that absorbs everyone's project problems, logistical glitches, and other difficult issues. This group is not covering nonoperational activities, not doing all activities presently executed by administrative people, not substituting PM work, and not curing all the organization's ills. It is providing support and information for project managers, and needs to keep the difference straight.

Critical Success Factors

Bucero sums up his experience as follows:

In all the projects I managed in my professional career, I found that project success depends on how well you work with and lead people. The project office approach must be aligned with the culture of the organization. Technical problems can be solved with new releases or different hardware or software, but it is different when we talk about people interactions and relationships among team members. Although we identified some factors as critical in the PMO implementation project, one of the most important things is to focus on being prepared to answer questions and demands. Each consultant and PM expects the PMO to be there to help them on a daily basis and that means to be prepared for a world of uncertainty. Many times the type of demand is driven by pressure in terms of time or expectations, and we as PMO members need to transmit feasibility and security. I always ask for proactive behavior from each PMO team member.

Bucero's critical factors:

- Scope agreement and setting clear expectations between all users and stakeholders. (This took some weeks of meetings and validations.)
- Forming, storming, and norming the PMO team. (In this case, 80 percent of the team were contractors rather than employees. This required additional time for initial training on methods, tools, and procedures.)
- Clearly defined functions, roles, and responsibilities for the PMO. (Bucero verified each person's expectations in one-to-one talks.)
- Sponsorship from upper-level management. (Bucero asked the general manager to request that people use the project office services.)
- Clear communication plan deployment. (A stakeholder map guided this activity.)
- Periodic communications to the management team and to the end users about project status. (Bucero participated in meetings at all levels of the organization.)

The Plan

Starting with a deliverables-oriented work breakdown structure (WBS), Bucero elaborated a plan among team members. Elapsed time for completing the implementation plan was eighteen months, but he had to demonstrate that the PMO added value to the business month by month. That made the two first months difficult as it was hard to come up with concrete results so quickly, especially given that all team members were new hires. He received much pressure from the whole organization. Reducing the time to prepare proposals and clarifying scope helped to ease the pressure.

He organized the PMO project in the four stages outlined in the center of Figure 7.3 and described in subsequent sections.

Stage 1: Set-Up and Rollout. Project managers know that starting up a project is always hard. First, you have to "create the basement for the building." The first

FIGURE 7.3. A PMO IMPLEMENTATION PLAN.

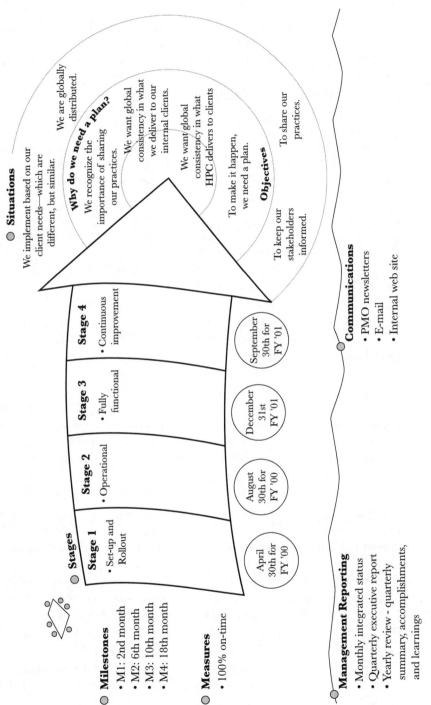

activity was to establish the necessary infrastructure, staff the PMO, and define roles and responsibilities with clear objectives for all team members.

Due to internal resource restrictions, Bucero had to use outsourced people. As soon as the PMO project was approved, he asked the project sponsor for six resources to staff the PMO. Management suggested they start with three people and look at the results. He then asked for three people but started with two, following this process:

After explaining the main functions and responsibilities to each candidate, questions that helped understand their people skills were "Will you be able to contribute added value?" and "What does customer service mean to you?"

Team member selection followed these steps:

1. People solicitation from third parties according to document management skills (office skills were previously defined)
2. People interviews (face-to-face interviews with the PMO lead)
3. Dry run test (documents and presentation elaboration)

Initially Bucero focused on finding people with office and administrative skills because the document management system was their first priority for PMO implementation. He also observed desire for the job, looking for assertive and proactive people. "I appreciate the attitude of people during the interviews more than having the best skills. I selected open-minded people who are ready for action. I try to transmit the need for proactive behavior and transparent communication. Sentences like 'passion, persistence, and patience' were ways to involve new people in the PMO. We are customer focus-oriented. Since the PMO must help project managers to focus on project management practices, PMO team members cannot wait around; they need to move forward."

This process worked during the first six months; acquisition of the three initial members enabled Bucero to demonstrate performance improvements to the management team in the process of generating project documentation. "That fact proved PMO people were adding value to the organization and enabled me to ask for more resources."

Sharing the PMO project vision among team members was another key to project success. Every team member knew project goals before starting their tasks. Bucero delivered presentations to the whole team that shared the project mission, the objectives, the stakeholders, and the environment. In that way people took project ownership and felt more identified with the main objectives.

Since most people staffing the PMO were outsourced, he provided them with internal training to get them more involved and prepared in terms of tools and internal organizational procedures. These circumstances required him to put a lot of care into the team-building process. People came from different organizations with different skills and patterns of behavior. "I had to establish clear and simple rules from the beginning to work quickly among team members to define 'how to understand and serve our customers.'"

He employed these tips during the PMO implementation project:

- I always assumed that people working in the project know more about how to do their job than I do. I listened to their ideas and suggestions.
- While team members planned for execution, I as program manager planned for contingencies.
- When my team did good work, I told them.
- I never delayed dealing with bad news; tomorrow might be too late to address critical issues.
- I never delegated tough decisions.
- I communicated, communicated, and communicated, having lunch with my team, meeting them weekly.
- When people came with a problem, I asked them for a solution. I empowered people because they usually know better what needs to be done than I do.
- When I observed bad performance I spoke directly with the person who was not performing well.

At the end of this stage the group published a *PMO Services Bulletin* that was distributed to the whole organization. The elapsed time for this stage was two months.

Stage 2. Operational. This stage started as soon the team started to work together and all the initial PMO services were defined, published, and distributed. The elapsed time for Stage 2 was four months.

As a team the group delineated the structure of the PMO and used the PM software defined at corporate level for assigning communication, methodology, training, and tracking processes. One key activity during this period was defining PMO success metrics. Bucero attended most management meetings and dealt with the critical stakeholders. In those meetings he requested feedback from all attendees in order to address problems and fine-tune the affected processes.

The establishment of priorities was another important activity. Bucero used a stakeholder analysis tool to find out where and for whom priorities existed, applying his best efforts. The final objective for this phase was to have a database with historical data, which helped show results to upper management.

Stage 3: Fully Functional. The main objective for this stage was automation of all activities. Elapsed time for this stage was four months.

All initial activities needed to be more effective, adding value to project managers and also to an achievement-driven organization. Measurements included achievements defined and assigned for accountability, automated and implemented assignments, templates created and being used. Major processes must have automated trend analysis conducted and mentoring in place, and 70 percent to 80 percent of all projects must have a project plan and activity duration derived from historical data.

Stage 4: Continuous Improvement. This stage is in process as we write. They estimate an elapsed time of eight months.

They employed their standard quality assurance system. They updated software tools according to PMO user needs and tuned the success measures. They planned key areas to improve such as project numbering, tracking of project success, decreasing the number of failed projects, and increasing the number of professional project managers on staff. They expect 90 percent of all projects to have a project plan.

Quality Assurance

Project office employees need many skills to perform quality assurance within each project. A wide range of methodologies, software applications, procedures, tools, and templates are employed. Because project office employees all work on multiple projects, knowledge and experience with methodologies, software applications, procedures, tools, and templates builds up faster than it does with project managers on single projects. The reason to make the project office responsible for quality assurance is that improvements can be implemented and communicated faster than when the task is left to the individual projects.

The project manager is responsible for the overall project delivery process. Project office employees are not expected to know the project technical content. Standardized project planning and frequent project delivery process experiences are two aspects that give the project management team a standardized quality improvement process. Knowledge sharing is a major factor for both those aspects.

Figure 7.4 shows the quality cycle. This is a proposed model combining strengths that the project office has proven. Quarterly they ran a PMO customer survey to check the satisfaction level of PMO users (project managers and consultants). During the first quarter participation was low (25 percent), but more people participated and provided feedback about the usability of PMO services, which allowed them to improve their service level.

FIGURE 7.4. STANDARDIZED QUALITY IMPROVEMENT PROCESS.

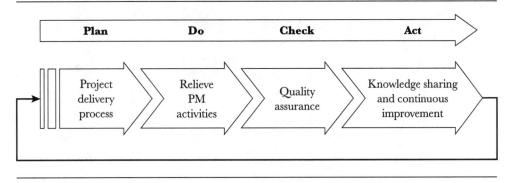

The PMO surveys cover these areas of customer satisfaction:

- General PMO perception
- PMO Services provided (deliverables)
- Response time
- PMO—project manager relationship
- Web services availability

Also the management team used the results of the PMO surveys to encourage people to use the PMO. Figure 7.5 shows a graphic example of a survey response.

Stakeholder Analysis

The HPC project office stakeholders were the managers of the businesses and solutions that influence end users and upper managers alike. A stakeholder analysis helped Bucero understand the way different individuals influence decisions throughout the project.

He used a process based on asking four basic questions and brainstorming for answers:

- *Who are the stakeholders?*
  Identify all possible stakeholders.
  Identify where each stakeholder is located.
  Identify the project team's relationship with each stakeholder in terms of power and influence during the project life cycle.

FIGURE 7.5. SURVEY OF PMO USAGE.

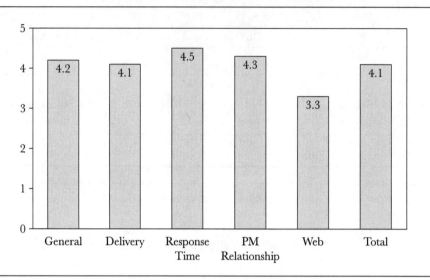

- *What are stakeholder expectations?*
    Identify primary high-level project expectations for each stakeholder.
- *How does the project or product affect stakeholders?*
    Analyze how the products and deliverables affect each stakeholder.
    Determine what actions the stakeholder could take that would affect the success or failure of the project.
    Prioritize the stakeholders, based on who could have the most impact on project success or failure.
    Incorporate information from earlier steps into a risk analysis plan to develop mitigation procedures for stakeholders who might be disposed to harm the project.
- *What information do stakeholders need?*
    Identify what information needs to be furnished to each stakeholder, when should it be provided, and how. The answers to the first three questions should provide a basis for this analysis.

The stakeholder analysis is fundamental to PMO project success. Bucero uses the type of map illustrated in Figure 7.6 to keep track of all political issues during the project office project life cycle. For example, "One political issue that I observed using the map was a middle manager who had a lower level of concern

FIGURE 7.6. A STAKEHOLDER MAP, EACH BUBBLE A KEY PERSON.

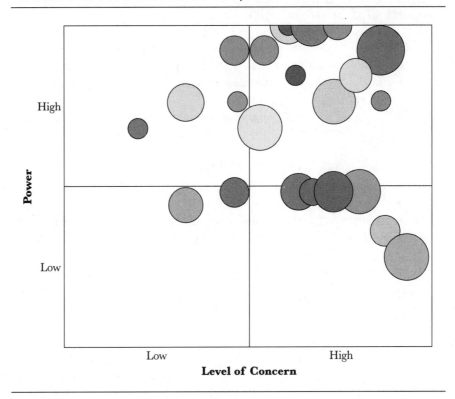

regarding the project office implementation. I then prepared a communication plan to address that issue."

That plan reflected actions such as these:

- Face-to-face meetings with each middle manager, explaining the PMO mission and objectives, and most important, getting them to share their expectations from the PMO. These meetings helped Bucero understand their real needs and expectations.
- Brainstorming sessions with all middle managers, using mind-mapping techniques. These sessions helped brainstorm ideas, suggestions, and real needs from various perspectives, which helped develop a more aligned vision for the PMO.
- Identifying barriers such as organizational climate, perceptions, customer pressure, too many communication links, and too many projects, and working to avoid or minimize them by talking with the middle managers.

Support and Sponsorship

The stakeholder analysis tool helped get more support from the management team through business needs identification. The PMO program manager acts as facilitator, promoting, managing, encouraging, and optimizing relations among all stakeholders.

Here are a few of the things the program manager did to achieve sponsor support:

- Explaining and validating the PMO mission and objectives periodically
- Keeping management in the loop (sharing real PMO status, problems, and issues)
- Using a PMO selling presentation
- Showing small deliverables very quickly to convince them with tangible facts
- Showing passion, persistence, and patience (different people, different behaviors, different culture)
- Offering all services without charge to any solution area, PM, or consultant

Sponsors' Role

How did sponsors demonstrate support?

They pushed the rest of the organization to use the PMO services and also use the PMO as an example. They asked the PMO manager to attend management meetings to inform them about PMO implementation status and to escalate any issue or problem. When managers saw how the PMO was helping the organization, they began talking outside the organization about the benefits of using a PMO. For instance, one said, "The PMO is alive because everyone who asks for a service is given an answer and the PMO team never refuses any demand; they proactively search for solutions." They recognized the effort of PMO implementation at the end of the fiscal year, giving a prize to the PMO team during the kickoff meeting.

Other Assistance

Who else helped Bucero implement the PMO?

Team members work in an open climate of communication and transparency. After doing the stakeholder analysis, he identified key players and project managers who could help him sell the advantages and PMO benefits. Those colleagues were great ambassadors for PMO services and also supported him during the continuous improvement cycle.

Many people provided constructive criticism and positive feedback. People became convinced they should use the PMO services also because the program manager inspired truth and passion in getting tasks and activities done. When consultants and project managers see enthusiastic people in the PMO who exude desire to do the job, they ask for more services.

Key Ideas in Sponsorship Training

Sponsorship is a commitment by senior management and leaders to support and be involved in major projects and initiatives from launch to finish. In the training Bucero focused on these points:

- Every project needs a sponsor, but sponsorship is most critical and essential in complex and large projects, projects with large risks and investments, projects spanning different company departments or divisions, and projects with the potential to lead to large business opportunities.
- Project sponsors should be members of the local management team, empowered by all businesses, and assigned for the full project life cycle.
- Sponsors should plan to invest a considerable amount of time: 10–20 percent in working with project team and client, equivalent to the workload of a senior partner at system integration or consulting companies.
- Key responsibilities for sponsors:
  Drive the pursuit process.
  Negotiate the project with customer within agreed-upon framework.
  Engage in the delivery process.
  Serve as focal point for escalation for both HP and client.
  Look for new business opportunities: up- and cross-selling.
  Set project strategies. The sponsor has full ownership and accountability, but is not the "super project manager."
- Understand and position client culture.

Measures for the project sponsor include customer satisfaction, overall margin in project, achievement of business mix, growth in project, and feedback from client, project team, and involved organizations.

Sponsorship is a question of mind-set, commitment, and competence. *Mind-set* means the desire to get involved, understand the role, and ask questions, and the confidence to deal with customers and clients. *Commitment* means structuring sponsorship with project reviews, investment of time, and work with the project team. *Competency* means understanding the basics of project management and having the ability to coach the external client and internal stakeholders with understanding of the business and the change process, and also of the people involved.

Bucero offers, "My personal opinion is that excellence in sponsorship has an impact on project financial performance. Strong sponsorship assures that projects are properly structured and delivered on budget, schedule, and quality. Strong sponsorship drives prospecting and selling of follow-up and new business."

Value Added

Sponsors provide support when they clearly understand how a PMO adds value. The following structure, services, and activities were carefully crafted and communicated up and down and across the organization. Bucero's objective was to manage perceptions about the value added to the organization by the PMO.

The Organization

As soon as the PMO proposal was accepted, the management team approved the PMO budget, and Bucero started to hire people for his team. Although he had a structure in mind, some constraints arose.

Most of the people on the team were subcontractors. That restriction reduced the effectiveness of his plan, but the only way to be successful in the PMO implementation was to continue with the goal and achieve some results very quickly. He followed the rule "if you need to eat an elephant, eat a bit each time." It was really effective.

Week by week, team members joined the PMO team. Initially he delivered one day of training just to set up rules of the game. Also he dedicated days to train people in basic knowledge about HP projects and the PMO scope.

After that they reviewed responsibilities of all team members. Bucero assigned people to the groups shown in Figure 7.7.

At the HPC organization, there appeared to be a general lack of appreciation for the importance of project planning. Upper managers often did not appreciate the necessity and thus did not allow enough time for proper planning. But after team members were assigned and began planning, upper managers reviewed the project WBS, focusing on deliverables to be built and their acceptance criteria.

The management team asked for results at once, but the process took time. Some weeks later Bucero presented a document explaining the initial PMO deliverables. This document was distributed to the whole organization.

FIGURE 7.7. CHART OF ASSIGNMENTS.

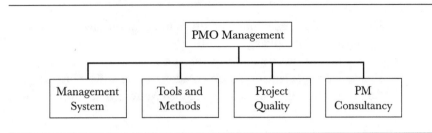

The Services

Relieving project managers of standard activities was the initial driving force for the project office. Decreased labor costs directly contribute to the organization's profit. Nevertheless, the project office proved that combining all its people's strengths was what made it successful. These functions fully align with organizational strategy. Indirectly, they deliver enormous contribution to profit and revenue for the organization.

Consultants and project managers need to focus on using data and information to work through critical issues, defining and validating the project scope, analyzing risks and starting project plans in order to be able to develop and present the "solution proposal" to the customer. The project office team relieves the consultant and the project manager of many tasks so they can use their time more effectively by working with customers and defining the scope of their projects.

In terms of project delivery, the project office can relieve project managers of tasks such as filling forms and templates and getting these forms signed off internally. Regarding project management skills, the project office can help the project manager in scope definition, project kickoff preparation, and planning tasks through mentoring and coaching on project office services. These are the combining strengths that help project managers move forward and achieve project success.

These services create capacity for organization to take on more business and complete it successfully, winning bids because of the PMO.

Document Management System

This functional area was priority one for the implementation. The functions covered produced these deliverables:

- Proposal generation and support (using standard templates and customized as needed)
- Documentation generation and distribution (according to the PM methodology forms and templates)
- Taking minutes (internal project meetings)
- Project file management (documentation sorting and archiving)
- Authorization management (relieving the PM from getting sign-off by managers)

Tools and Methods

This functional area is dedicated to support local tools and methods that help project managers use the HPC methodology and manage projects. They provide application maintenance (local application maintenance and improvements), Web updates and maintenance, PM methodology localization and support, tools support (automated forms and templates), and project management information system (PMIS) tools—Microsoft Project, weekly reports, configuration management, risk management, change and issue management.

Project Quality

This is one of the most important areas in the project office because customer satisfaction is a must in every project. That means completing the full quality process (quality planning, quality assurance, and quality control). The functions covered in this area are

- Quality plan support (helping the project manager to create a quality plan)
- Preliminary audits (project reviews according to the PM methodology)
- Quality reviews (solution review process followed during the whole project life cycle)
- ISO audit support (review aimed at ISO 9001 certification)
- Customer satisfaction survey (hearing the voice of the customer and taking action in case of problems)
- Process documentation

PM Consulting

In this area the PMO provides these services:

- *PM mentoring:* Junior project managers need senior colleagues to support them as they manage projects. The PM colleague establishes deadlines for project reviews, results analysis, and action plans for improvement.

- *PM coaching:* The organization needs on-the-job coaching and advice about career paths, for both PMs and their supervisors. The PMO also provides advice to the management team about sponsor role implementation.
- *PM skills training:* PMO personnel plan and deliver training sessions locally according to PMO user needs. Bucero notes, "In my experience training is necessary, but we also need to test the PM maturity level of the organization from time to time. This helps us discover areas where people lack experience."
- *PM forums:* Project managers profit by getting together to share PM knowledge inside the organization. A different PM assumes the leadership role for each forum. These meetings foster an environment for improvement by allowing people to share thoughts, ideas, best practices, and failures. The effort to prepare presentations for other colleagues is a worthy part of the PM development plan of the PMO.
- *PM newsletters:* The PMO produces a monthly publication for sharing PM knowledge, skills, experiences, theory, and practice. Each newsletter focuses on a specific learning area. These newsletters cover all PMBOK areas.
- *Sponsorship training:* The PMO is also responsible for preparing, planning, and delivering training for project sponsors in a workshop format. Allowing mistakes and working in teams is included in these sessions.

What Made It Work

The management team was very committed to PMO implementation from the beginning. Without upper-level management support this project would have failed.

Communication with and among team members went smoothly. The team had weekly meetings and also the extended team had lunch together from time to time. At the department level, PO staff participated in all area meetings to explain the progress and services of the project office. In addition, the PMO program manager participated actively in upper management meetings to report status and issues of the PMO project on a monthly basis. And publishing project status on the intranet allowed the PMO to spread the word company-wide.

The participants in the PMO accepted ownership in the operation. Bucero empowered team members but also coached them to help them work around their lack of experience. As noted earlier, they all wore badges to increase their affiliation with the group.

Measuring the Use of PMO Services. The main objective for this particular project was to get HP people using and asking for project office services. The PMO provided general help for project managers, document management support, project management skills development, PM methodology support, quality management support, PM library, project management forums, and PM fundamentals training.

Then they measured participation on a monthly basis, and worked to improve the level of service through analysis of this data. They also ran an end-user survey on a quarterly basis. One thing this report revealed was the high volume of demand for documentation and proposal generation, support, and PM methodology support. No demands for PM mentoring and coaching were realized.

Status of the Local PMO. Bucero proceeded in a step-by-step process to staff the PMO. He started with two people, then added two more at one-month intervals until he reached six people. He could increase the number of people because their actions demonstrated added value to the organization. They all focused on the DMS (managing and elaborating proposals, presentations, methodology forms, and templates). As soon as project managers felt supported and relieved of those tasks, they indirectly began selling PMO services to the whole organization. Face-to-face feedback also provided a valuable mechanism to sell high-performing PMO services.

Currently there are ten people on the team (five DMS specialists, two tool specialists, one Quality specialist, and two trainees). The focus going forward is to get more project managers involved in PMO activities and able to mentor and coach junior PMs. One key success factor has been to create a knowledge-sharing culture inside and outside the PMO. Project retrospective analysis is an ongoing and helpful activity for sharing case studies among project managers and team members.

The forecast is to have two full-time project managers working with the program manager in the PMO delivering project management consulting services inside and outside the organization.

The PMO Evolution

Project management offices were started in different sites and countries but without common objectives. However, the HP Consulting organization as a whole understood the tendency in the project business was to be more and more global. Reinventing the wheel every time in each country was not effective. They were creating project offices in each country but not able to share things because of different approaches. They needed to define a common approach to move forward.

They had a lot of professional project managers with a lot of experience, a Project Management Initiative, a Quality Initiative, a Knowledge Management

Initiative, and the need to share real cases and experiences was a reality. How to manage that puzzle? How to fix all the parts?

From their Project Management Initiative (PMI) meetings, people were escalating local problems with PMO implementation. Then a task force was created and managed by one of the upper managers. This professional organized the first meeting in California, asking PMI leaders to participate. Ideas were collected before the meeting from PMOs around the world so basic ideas could be shared. PMO leaders from different countries participated, sharing their opinions and validating both the idea and potential structure for the Program Management Office.

During the meeting they discussed the content, services, roles, responsibilities, and priorities for a proposed Global Program Management Office. At the end of the meeting they had an action plan for moving forward. After this meeting, the manager heading the initiative delivered the proposal in a presentation to the upper-level management team at the corporate office. The team also organized monthly teleconferences to keep in touch.

Status was shared among the team by e-mail. Some weeks after the first meeting the idea of a Global Program Management Office was accepted by upper management and other organizations joined in. Two months later, the organization changed. The leader retired. Then the initiative was stopped for some time. Since the HP and Compaq merger, the new Consulting and Integration Services is being redesigned around the PM Compaq methodology. As of late 2002, the PMO leaders are expecting movement about the Global Program Management Office implementation.

So far the focus has been on practical experience to implement a local PMO, but additional efforts are in place to manage different project office implementations for each location depending on the needs and project requirements, the project culture maturity level, the resources and type of projects, and the business. When an organization wants to become project-oriented, a common model is needed.

The team of PMO leaders identified the factors listed in Figure 7.8 as essential to support the project office evolution. Bucero adds,

> The team documented the following unifying assumptions: To implement this model a Program Management Office structure needs to be created and implemented at multiple levels. To successfully implement this mode we need top management sponsorship and all stakeholders must be involved. That requires a cultural change and measures and metrics that need to be changed in our organization.

FIGURE 7.8. KEY SUCCESS FACTORS.

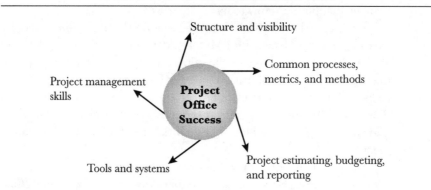

We will focus on our customers, covering all phases during the project life cycle according to the PMBOK. We will demonstrate to our customers that all parts of the organization support the project manager along the complete project life cycle to achieve customer requirements.

We will implement a quality assurance process along our whole organization, convince people of the added value of this process, and be aligned with customer needs, values, and culture.

We will have a common approach from all organizations inside our company. Each department, organization, or division should work together with common objectives and think about customer satisfaction. There should not be different projects for the same customer inside our organization. This common approach must be agreed upon as the strategic plan for the company as a whole.

The quality assurance process they developed is outlined in Figure 7.9. Bucero goes on to note,

The Program Management Office consolidates all project support activities that have resided in the different company organizations or departments. It supports the local implementation of a common model based on processes, skills, and project management development, coaching, and mentoring, providing a structured monthly project status report.

The proposed model should have a Global Program Management Office established that defines all processes, practices, and tools associated with the common model. This organism must manage and support complex and global

FIGURE 7.9. A COMMON QUALITY ASSURANCE PROCESS.

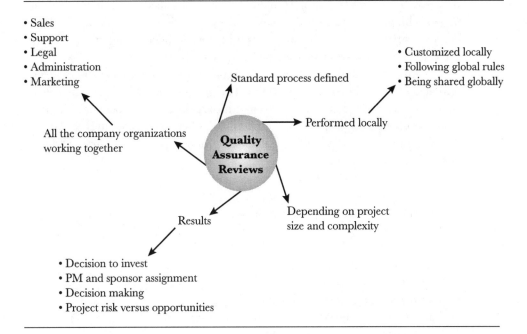

- Sales
- Support
- Legal
- Administration
- Marketing

- Customized locally
- Following global rules
- Being shared globally

Standard process defined

All the company organizations working together

Quality Assurance Reviews

Performed locally

Results

Depending on project size and complexity

- Decision to invest
- PM and sponsor assignment
- Decision making
- Project risk versus opportunities

projects, lead the project management learning communities, and produce periodic project status reports. On the other hand, the local Program Management Offices must support local implementation of the common model established, manage the local project portfolio, lead project managers, be responsible for local project management, and sponsor development programs.

The charter of the Program Management Office is to ensure that the processes, practices, capabilities, tools, and systems are in place to effectively support the project business and thus establish the foundation for improving the maturity level of the organization.

Geographic PMO Responsibilities

The main responsibility for the geographic PMOs is managing the project portfolio. This entity is responsible for reviewing portfolio reports and providing business management with recommendations. It also ensures follow-up and implementation of decisions made by upper management. The geographic PMO is measured and accountable for planned versus actual gross margin for the project portfolio.

It is responsible for driving knowledge creation and reuse according to defined processes. It ensures that project managers are well skilled by leading PM training, coaching, mentoring, and professional certification. The geographic PMO conducts sponsorship training and mentoring for business managers and deploys the necessary processes, practices, capabilities, tools, and systems.

Resource planning is another key responsibility tied to business planning, potential deals, and the existing portfolio. The geographic PMO plays the role of project sponsor for projects as necessary and provides bid management support to geographical area projects—collecting client references, generating proposals, managing the bid, and providing quick quote service, project planning, and proposal review facilitation.

The geographic PMO provides these services:

- Snapshot and retrospective analysis facilitation
- Customer surveys
- Quality audits
- Methodology support
- Schedule management
- Cost management (overall tracking and control)
- Time management (WBS development and support)
- Risk management (overall tracking and control)
- Communication management
- Procurement management
- Document management support
- Technical writing support

Global PMO Responsibilities

The Global Project Management Office leads the PMO Council formed by global and geographic PMO leaders to determine the processes, practices, capabilities, tools, and systems that will be implemented by the geographic PMOs. The Global PMO reviews company project portfolio reports at the global level, provides business management with recommendations and drives follow-up on those recommendations, and conducts global analysis on trends to determine good practices and training and process improvements. One key responsibility is to support international opportunities and projects during selling and delivery phases, conducting project reviews and recommendations, supporting resources and staffing, assessing the risk, escalating problems when needed, conducting local team start-up and on-the-job training, and conducting sponsorship training and mentoring for business managers.

Project Reporting Information

Several key elements are involved in the report generation activities: the financial system, the status provider, the client status, the history and trends, and the project manager. Each of the items mentioned is consolidated for project report generation. The PMO facilitates the necessary infrastructure (methods, processes, and tools) to help the project manager have all information as up to date as possible.

Critical Success Factors

Because of different behaviors, local needs, and culture, some key factors are critical to the PMO evolution:

- Upper-level management sponsorship (from all departments, divisions or organizations)
- Local management team involved and measured through defined business parameters
- Changes in the measurement system to be consistent across a business
- Adoption of reward and incentive system
- Sponsorship capability development

Addressing these factors means changing the culture of the organization.

What Has Changed

The PMO evolution is not complete. Some of the steps are covered—HP has a global PMO and have some global standards defined in terms of processes, methods, and tools. The local deployment is coming slowly and it is planned to happen in the next year. The main objectives for the current year are focused on project management skills development and sponsorship culture within the complete organization.

Upper-level managers better understand the sponsorship concepts and needs, and all departments are beginning to work together, discussing global decisions before acting. Bucero says, "After the last two years of experience implementing a local PMO, I really believe the organization has learned that the PMO is worthy—because our customers appreciate that we work as a unique organization with common methods and tools and common objectives, not as separate departments with different visions and objectives."

Lessons Learned

The PMO cannot be successful without upper-level management support. Stakeholder analysis is fundamental for success. In addition, despite the time required for PMO planning and organizing, it makes a big difference to create an identity and communicate through multiple channels.

Every PMO team needs time for the traditional stages of forming, storming, norming, and performing. Priorities definition is a must-do step.

Most of the work of the project office is like educating children—trying to convince people they will have better results if they change their way of doing things. A key difference, however, is not to create a parent-child relationship but to develop trust and collaboration among colleagues. People will support a project office (and communications in general) when they see its value and how it links directly to positive business impact. It is essential to constantly demonstrate that the organization is better off with the project office than without it.

Summary

The latest results of the "PMO services survey" were very good. The country manager showed the results to all employees to demonstrate improved PM efficiency using the PMO. Basically they found the following:

- More bids are generated more quickly.
- Quality reviews help the PMs and their supervisors detect project deviations (cost, time, scope) early in the project.
- Project snapshots are very helpful to share project success and failures across projects, helping the organization to learn from the practice.
- Project methodology use has grown to 85 percent.
- Project managers felt supported and coached by the PMO.

Generally, at a corporate level, project offices are regarded as project management centers of expertise. HP decided that the professionals who staff these project offices should be experienced and trained in project management skills. At the local level, the project office can change the culture from reactive to project-oriented. This culture shift largely occurs by demonstrating or modeling the new behavior. The approach selected is to get results on a subset of projects initially, and use these successes as models for others to adopt the process.

Bucero says, "My final conclusion is that implementing project and program management offices takes time, commitment, sponsorship, and upper management support, along with leaders at all levels who want to get things done."

Author Comments

Bucero encountered common forms of resistance to implementing a project office. Initially the project culture was weak, even for an organization used to doing projects. Staffing was not plentiful, and he had to depend on outsourcing. This is not a preferred way to operate but can work if the people brought on board have the right skills.

This case demonstrates another example of the implementation approach generally recommended in this book: start small and plan to expand. Bucero identified current inefficiencies, developed a plan, and used ramped-up staffing, a marketing campaign, metric reports, and ceaseless communications to support expansion of the project office services.

The political climate became manageable via stakeholder analysis. A stakeholder map was a valuable tool for identifying and positioning all key players according to power and level of concern, then using that diagnosis in working with them.

Training plays a major role in creating a successful project office. Everybody learns what the plan is and what their roles are. Sponsorship turned from an unknown concept to full training on roles and responsibilities. The PMO manager further supported the training with real-time coaching.

The effort toward establishing a global office benefited from a strong sponsor. Then the sponsor left the organization, and efforts went on hold. Only the perseverance of dedicated program managers kept it moving. By having strong local PMOs, the organization was set to expand the effort worldwide and link the local offices under the umbrella of a global PMO. This facilitates extensive knowledge sharing—especially about work estimates, pricing, documentation, and experience levels—that directly leads to increased shareholder and customer value.

This case study demonstrates that it takes many small things done right to accomplish the goal. Going to many meetings and publicizing the activities to get the word out finally paid off. Bucero still attends and participates in many PMI activities to constantly refresh his knowledge about project management and document his findings (Bucero, 2002). He is an exemplary model.

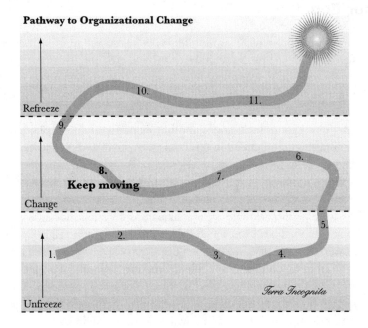

Pathway to Organizational Change

Refreeze

10.   11.

9.

**8.
Keep moving**

Change

7.   6.

5.

2.

1.   3.   4.

Terra Incognita

Unfreeze

This chapter tells Colonel Gary LaGassey's story of a project office implementation within the U.S. Air Force. It describes a chaotic environment that had been operating for years without a project office and how it transformed to a new standard of excellence. LaGassey describes his approach to the people, processes, and structures within an international, intercultural organizational setting. Troubled projects become less the norm, replaced by the means to manage multiple projects and quickly respond to fast-moving programs. Here all the elements from earlier chapters get put into play to create outstanding results.

CHAPTER EIGHT

KEEP MOVING: GETTING YOUR ARMS AROUND CHAOS

Colonel Gary LaGassey, USAF

An air base construction program provides an ideal case study. Like the Veneto plain surrounding the base, the program is a fertile ground where literally hundreds of lessons have been harvested. Many involve simply adapting well-known principles, while others involve developing entirely new ways of doing business.

In early 1999, the U.S. Air Force (USAF) established the Aviano 2000 Program Management Office (PMO) at an Italian fighter base near the town of Aviano in northeastern Italy. The PMO's primary task was to deliver a $530 million, 264-project base upgrade to support the USAF's 31st Fighter Wing with its forty-two F-16 fighters, a military and civilian workforce of more than forty-five hundred people, and approximately four thousand family members.

Aviano 2000 is the largest base infrastructure upgrade cosponsored by the North Atlantic Treaty Organization (NATO) and the USAF. The operating environment includes multinational funding and project approval systems, international acquisition methods and pitfalls, bureaucratic systems of NATO, Italy, the USAF, and the U.S. Navy, and the interaction of construction designers and contractors from various NATO nations in different time zones.

Each fiscal year the USAF submits projects to the Italian Defense General Staff for approval. Following initial review the defense staff farms the projects out to regional authorities for their review and approval based on environmental, cultural, and economic impact on the communities surrounding the base.

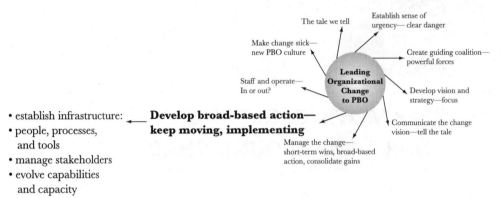

A few years ago the mayors nearest the base decided they would not sign off until the Italian government recognized and compensated local municipalities for the U.S. impact on their respective infrastructures. A boycott of the annual projects had the potential to bring the entire program to a halt because the projects involved were on the critical path.

This scenario represents one example of the challenges that affect program managers working in international, intercultural environments. Responding to these challenges requires team-building and partnering with local political and regulatory agencies, introducing modern project management to international and national organizations, promoting the value of program management, and effectively integrating a myriad diverse projects into a cohesive program.

Vision

In December 1998, the commander of U.S. and NATO air forces in NATO's Southern Region stepped in with a vision of creating a single, full-time program office to build the base for its customer—the 31st Fighter Wing—freeing the wing commander and his team to concentrate on the flying mission. Signs from program reviews indicated something was wrong. A program that had been under way since 1994 was in serious trouble—delays, snafus, and lack of focus were just the symptoms. The Aviano 2000 PMO was to be the "single belly button" for execution of the program. A program manager (PM) was selected from within the base organizational structure and instructed to "make it happen."

Sense of Urgency

Sorting out the players was a critical first task for the program manager. Evaluation of available resources revealed no slack available to start up and run a program office. He would have to establish requirements and compete for each and every resource.

The NATO screening process, by which the alliance reviews proposed projects at the 35 percent design stage, approves individual project scope, and authorizes final funding, had bogged down due to a lack of project screeners and a heavy workload. This action delayed final designs and construction awards, putting the program at great risk against the schedule.

The PM's assessment of his tasks, program scope, operating environment, resources, and program status indicated that, despite the extraordinary work put in by everyone involved in the initial years of the program, it was now at a point where drastic change was needed to avoid failure.

What had been a hair-on-fire approach to project management between 1995 and 1997 had gradually turned into business as usual. Top-level leadership, which had been the key to early success in the planning stages, no longer participated frequently in program reviews. Functional managers were executing this multiple-project program as routine work—emphasizing individual projects, not the overall program. Despite the fact that there were sixty major NATO projects to be completed in the program, formal project teams were not established to manage any of them.

Project managers had been assigned from three different organizations: Headquarters, U.S. Air Forces in Europe (USAFE), the base civil engineer squadron, and the two design and construction agents—Italy and the U.S. Navy. Project managers from each organization thought they were in charge of the project. In reality, their responsibilities, which had not been formally defined, were shared, and no one really had authority or accountability for the projects. As a result, decisions were frequently kicked up to senior management and, in many cases, to program sponsors. Problems began to arise together with finger pointing. It was impossible to pinpoint root causes for actions not completed, delays, or other problems.

This situation manifested in poor communications, busted deadlines, disproportionate workloads, crisis management, lack of budget controls, functional managers who were not supporting the program, minimal customer focus, a limited quality program, and a lack of basic processes for change, issue resolution, decision making, and financial choices. The process was loose and inefficient. Project controls were lacking, and there was no schedule to track status. Most critical, there were not enough people available to handle the enormous workload.

The fundamental disconnect? No one was truly in charge of either the overall program or individual projects. Despite being the USAF's largest ground-up construction program, it was managed by functional managers at headquarters in Germany and spread throughout the engineering, contracting, and communications functions of the fighter wing. To complicate the effort, the fighter wing in 1995 was occupied full time with the planning and execution of air combat operations in the Balkans.

Course of Action

The program had two critical needs: a program management methodology and a formalized, project-based approach.

Conscious of the need to attack the dual challenges of keeping the program moving and establishing the PMO, the program manager plotted his course of action. He struck a deal to take immediate operational control of a number of engineers assigned to the wing's civil engineering function. He assigned projects and gave engineers authority as single project managers to keep their projects moving forward—a cradle-to-grave approach—that included leading project delivery teams and acquiring furniture and equipment. The next complication was his discovery that, although the assigned engineers were called project managers, they were not really project managers at all. Only one had actual project management experience or formal training. They were technical project engineers. It became a matter of turning those who showed the desire into PMs—easier said than done. Instead three elected not to remain with the program for personal reasons, and their departure left the program shorthanded.

The program had to move ahead. Because the personnel system did not work fast enough to hire permanent staff, the program manager brought in replacements on Temporary Duty, known as TDY basis, to fill the gaps. Four engineers for ninety days cost about $75,000 for transportation, billeting, and per diem expenses. Had the people who were already present filled the bill in the transformation to a project-based organization, those costs could have been avoided.

A call went to all Air Force engineering units seeking TDY personnel who could "work in the largest AF construction program and enjoy Italy at the same time." The urgency of the situation required the program manager, for the first time, to outline what he was looking for in project managers for both the short and long term. The outline set one of the baselines for their Program Management Methodology. He sought experienced construction managers (engineers or architects) who were technically qualified in large construction projects (ideally in multiproject programs), and who had actual project management training and experience plus appraisals that showed they had supervisory, team leadership, and communicative skills—that is, a mixture of technical competence and skills, a grounding in project management, and proven leadership ability. He also sought people of higher rank, at the GS-13 level, with long experience in Air Force engineering. That was not easy because GS-13s are already in good jobs, usually as deputies of civil engineering squadrons. The enticement was the chance to come to Italy, a new overseas experience for many of them.

Colonel Gary LaGassey, the program manager, says,

> I determined that as long as I was going to shell out so much money, I would go for the best. We canvassed all major Air Force commands asking for help. We had many takers because there were lots of people who wanted to come to Italy for a ninety-day stint. We had the luxury of being pretty selective, therefore, I set the marker as high as I could in terms of technical qualifications, experience and, enthusiasm.
>
> I have long been a believer in enthusiasm as a prerequisite in hiring. Project management is all about team building, and team building is all about passion for a task and enthusiasm in carrying it out. Also, I'm a believer that enthusiasm can make the average person great. In my career I've seen many "big brains" or "hotshots" that don't work well in the team situation. I'll go with the above-average person with enthusiasm every time!
>
> An interesting side note, we took the same approach twice in 1999 and again in 2000 when we experienced additional shortages. Of those people who came here TDY, we later hired two of them permanently. What we established as our prerequisites (technical and PM experience, team leading skills, and so on) still stand as part of our evaluation process in the hiring game. The best part of our success had been the fact that we earned Air Force-wide reputation as a quality organization so we can screen applicants and select only those who meet our standard. That's a good position to be in.

With the goal of obtaining a systematic approach to the workload and creating balance among the PMs, he reassigned work and laid out a priority of action. Realizing that it all could not be done with the resources available, he developed a plan to seek additional people.

The next step was building a preliminary (and very rough) program methodology, called the "Approach for Aviano 2000 Project Managers." The basis of this methodology was a back-of-the-envelope work breakdown structure that focused on overall goals for the Aviano 2000 program. Looking back on the methodology (see Figure 8.1), it is easy to see just how primitive it was—but it worked.

FIGURE 8.1. APPROACH FOR AVIANO 2000 PROJECT MANAGERS.

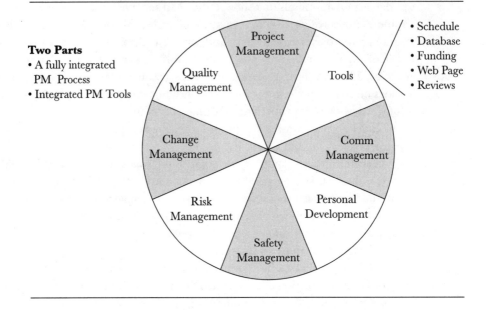

Using principles of project management contained in *A Guide to the Project Management Body of Knowledge,* established by the Project Management Institute (PMI), the centerpiece of the methodology was that for the eighty-five NATO projects, the PMO would become a truly project-based organization. Steps included

1. Sort the elements of a successful program and individual projects.
2. Assess tools needed by the program team to achieve success.
3. Draft simple mission, program scope, charter, and vision statements. Again, these were rudimentary in nature. The principal objective of having these in the *Approach* was to get preliminary buy-in from players who felt they were being forced into a program management system.
4. Develop a nominal organizational structure, a rough framework to be used to convince the project sponsor of program needs and to gain his support in the fight for resources.
5. Rough out an operating budget. (Including salaries for temporary hires and contract personnel, the Aviano 2000 budget was initially estimated at $1.8 million a year. Sticker shock ensued!)
6. Lay out a preliminary scheduling program that would be used to manage the projects from a programmatic view.

7. Accelerate a dormant facility upgrade to house the program team. Set a fast-track construction schedule and order furniture and equipment. This single step of housing all sixty players involved in the program under one roof improved communications by 50–100 percent.
8. Obtain sponsor buy-in for the approach and take it to HQ USAFE in mid-March 1999 with the objective of obtaining headquarters' functional buy-in for the concept along with the resources necessary to execute the program.

The "Approach" document was as much for the program manager, who was "getting his arms around chaos," as a tool for defining the change that would have to take place for the organization to execute the PMO. LaGassey was "breaking lots of glass," and not everyone who had been working in the program for some time was happy with the change being introduced. The difficulties to effect change apply both to people and to processes.

Sponsorship

Since developing a guiding coalition is a common theme and success or failure factor throughout the change process, what are a few things LaGassey did to achieve that support? How did sponsors demonstrate support?

> We have had two sponsors since the PMO started up: Lt. Gen. Mike Short, who actually stood us up and created the organization, and Lt. Gen. Ron Keys, who replaced Short in May 2000. Both embraced the Aviano 2000 Program as theirs and supported the team in every way they could. Their enthusiasm and support as senior Air Force leaders is not unique to the Aviano 2000 program. Both are exceptional military leaders, both combat warriors, who clearly understand the value of mission, teamwork, and taking care of our most valuable resource—our people. Getting their buy-in on our approach was not difficult.
>
> Nonetheless, we worked very hard to make sure the program team understood the support it has from those gentlemen. As we began the program in early '99, we had Gen. Short do a team kickoff meeting where he laid out the sponsor's view. This gave people a chance to hear his objectives and philosophy firsthand. Then, periodically, as we did program reviews, we would build upon his views. That made it easier for us (and me) to carry out our tasks on a daily basis. When Gen. Short left and Gen. Keys took over, we gave him a full orientation and a chance to do his own kickoff meeting.
>
> Fortunately, Gen. Keys had been involved in a major construction program earlier in his career as a base commander and understood the difficulties. He

expressed his philosophy to the team and set the tone for his watch. He's been great, letting us do the job and weighing in when we need his help. Again, each program review gives him the chance to reinforce his views.

We've been blessed. The sponsor supports us all the time and when we need specific help, he's there. More importantly, he has given me the authority to decide and always supports my decisions.

I work sponsor support constantly, because it does two things for us: 1) It keeps him apprised on our progress and an advocate for our needs, and 2) it reinforces his support for the team, who need to know it more than I do. Whenever we can we have him present awards and recognition to the team members for their hard work.

Gen. Keys will depart this summer and we'll be grooming another sponsor. I intend to approach it exactly the same way—orientation, kickoff, updates. . . .

Leading Change to Processes

An initial assessment showed the major cause of the runaway program was uncontrolled change across more than thirty major projects that were under way. They had to improve change management quickly.

Making change to change is difficult—it takes senior management attention. First, they implemented a change control board, applying basic change control procedures. They tailored the process and improved it by putting decision-making authority at the proper work levels. They installed a three-tier decision threshold process, gave authority to project managers for day-to-day decisions, and established an executive steering group to approve critical configuration changes that have high-impact cost and schedule challenges.

The executive steering group consists of the program manager (when he is there, which is only about half the time), his deputy program manager, the HQ USAFE program manager, the commanders of the 31st Civil Engineer Squadron and 31st Communication Squadron (the prime customers), the Italian program manager, and the U.S. Navy's resident officer in charge of construction. The voting members are the program manager (or his deputy in his absence), the USAFE PM, and the two squadron commanders. Italy and the U.S. Navy do not vote, because they are the design and construction agents, but they have considerable input to the process. The program manager's vote is the tiebreaker (and he usually leans in the direction of the customer). They meet weekly, and their deliberations focus on programmatic issues rather than specific technical challenges with individual projects (although occasionally they get bogged down in that sort of thing, too).

The focus of the executive steering group is multiple project integration. They also conduct three specialized reviews: the configuration control board, BOS control board, and cost share review board.

The configuration control board deliberates and decides on technical project changes that are required at the programmatic level. The configuration control board process is three-tiered, putting most of the responsibility on the PMs and project delivery teams. Cost and schedule thresholds determine what must be brought to the executive steering group for decision.

The BOS control board focuses on decisions related to the $40 million budget for items such as new furniture, equipment, and communications. The program manager manages that pot for the wing commander and, usually, his decision is final. Only twice since they started have they escalated approval to the wing commander.

The cost share review board addresses the application of USAF dollars that must be spent to buy scope not authorized by NATO. For example, they wanted a new security forces facility at a scope of $4.5 million. NATO said it would only pay for $4 million. They had to source the difference somewhere.

Across the $350 million NATO program, U.S. cost shares are about $50 million. There are many rules (congressional and USAF) about this, so it takes a lot of attention to avoid going to jail. One of the most important features of the executive steering group is its ability to get all leaders to the table once a week and sort out programmatic issues. Other meetings discuss pure project issues.

According to LaGassey, "Our requirement for project managers and project delivery teams to present and defend requested changes to the Executive Steering Group forces them to resolve 'bright ideas' during planning. Overall, this has been very beneficial, because customers now understand fully there's a price to pay for any change. They don't request them lightly. Change is under control. Our capability and maturity levels here are quite high."

People Development

A strong focus on human resource activities existed from the beginning. Training, career development and progression, awards and recognition programs, and social and recreational events are all part of the plan. A first initiative was to push authority to the right levels of responsibility. That is not easy, especially in heavily matrixed government organizations.

They spent considerable time developing clear roles and responsibilities for everyone assigned. These were captured in the Program Management Plan (PMP). In the early stages it took facilitated partnering meetings to reconcile a long-term program vision and the realities inherent in creating an organization five years into the program. There were lots of hidden agendas—"lots of rice bowls that needed breaking," as LaGassey says. The overriding challenge was to keep the program moving without criticizing those who were leading or working in the pre-PMO organizations. LaGassey's approach was to develop a "living" Program Management Plan, one that is readily changed by agreement at the executive steering group. As with most things in this program, tidying up the formal paperwork is the most difficult. The PMP is a guide, and success is in the way they partnered. LaGassey says, "My idea was to set the structures and processes in place, give the responsibilities to the right levels, and try and hold people accountable. For the most part it works. The leaders at all levels have their responsibilities, and they have gotten used to them."

LaGassey's role in defining roles and responsibilities:

> In the beginning, as we were standing up the PMO, I was working a fine line. Gen. Short decided and ordered that we "would have a PMO." That upset a lot of people who had been working in Aviano 2000 for a long time. Some saw this as a power play on my part, others saw their spheres of influence fading. I decided to go with a consensus-building approach at first. The program was in trouble, everyone knew it, but I couldn't survive an authoritarian approach at the time. Many people were tired, some demoralized by the workload and lack of progress, and there were lots of rice bowls. My forte, what got me to where I am in my Air Force career, has been good situational awareness and situational management.
>
> There were some tough days and some people were in need of discipline, so there were occasions when I had to go with the "Lion's Roar" approach. But, for the most part, that wasn't necessary—the "bring-'em-along approach" worked. We've got great people and they responded.
>
> The bottom line is that we brought drastic change to the program and the system and to people's lives. That's not easy for most people, so it's got to be done with compassion and understanding. I hope I contributed to that.

They invested heavily in training and skill development, because well-trained, skilled people drive maturity and success. Professional development of all team members is paramount. The goal is for each person who works three or four years in this program to be enhanced by it, to have a professionally rewarding experience, and to leave with an improved, highly marketable résumé.

They installed a healthy awards and recognition program. The Air Force has a well-developed quarterly and annual awards system at all levels. "We try to submit our people, operations and support staff, in every available category each quarter," says LaGassey, adding,

> We had some good success with this, to include our resource manager winning the wing's best resource manager of the year. This year we are submitting the program team for a number of military and civilian awards. As we are in our third year, we established a number of successes to support those applications. I've enlisted the support of our key sponsor, a lieutenant general, in that process and he's carrying the message to Washington. I want to win one big award for the team in 2002, something we can reproduce and frame for everybody to hang on their "I love me" walls. We have also pushed our people hard to expand their experience and training, so we can elevate them within the organization. We have promoted three (of ten) project managers in the past year and continue to offer that incentive as a reward for strong performance.

Communications

In the PMO context, *communications* refers to the ways people communicate with each other to achieve program and project management objectives. One measure for communications capability and maturity is based on getting the right word to the right place at the right time. There are literally thousands of players in this program, all trying to communicate. There are American and British English speakers, Italians, NATO international staff members from four or five countries, U.S. Air Force, Army, and Navy personnel (different service-specific languages), military and civilian engineers and architects, techies and nontechies, politicos and nonpoliticos, even lawyers. All must communicate.

Their approach to this complex area has been both technological and human. They give people the best possible tools to communicate and teach them how to use those tools. On the human side, by communicating principles, methodology, vision, process, and procedures they get everyone moving in the same direction. With a common understanding of the objectives and language used, it all becomes easier.

They recently surveyed team members using the Construction Industry Institute's "Communications Project Assessment Tool (COMPASS)." COMPASS provides an assessment of overall communications effectiveness and six category scores (accuracy, timeliness, completeness, understanding, barriers, and procedures) to assist in identifying communications problems.

The approach was to baseline the program and then methodically work on weak areas. The tool allows for reassessment at any time. Despite all efforts in this area during start-up, the results showed lots of work to do. Some fixes were implemented through focused training and dialogue on weak areas and then reassessed later in the year. One could make this a lifetime of work, but they do not have the time, so they plan to use awareness of these issues as a selective measurement for continuous improvement.

Results

The tremendous progress achieved since February 1999 includes the following achievements:

- Kept the construction program going through the seventy-nine-day Kosovo air campaign (March-June 99)
- Received final approval of the program and organizational plan (24 May)
- Met planned initial operating date (1 July)
- Completed a $6 million runway restoration project in just thirty-two days (August-September 1999), which was necessitated by operational considerations and the possibility of a Balkans follow-on air campaign
- Opened a $13 million, 150,000-square-foot commissary and base exchange that is now the standard for worldwide consolidated stores for the military services (November 2000)
- Won numerous design awards
- Successfully recovered when three construction contractors were terminated for nonperformance, reprocuring the work in record time

LaGassey describes the PMO as "self-actualizing." He adds,

Team members feel great about what they are doing, the responsibilities they have, and their contributions to the program. Our reputation in the Air Force goes all the way to the Chief of Staff in Washington, D.C. We've got applicant lists a mile long of people who want to come to work here. We've had a number of our people "stolen" off with promotion offers. One Italian engineer who had been with us only ten months was hired away at four times his current salary to run the infrastructure effort at Bologna airport. He was one of seventy applicants. He was told his Aviano 2000 experience pushed him to the top of the list. Two sponsors in a row, Lt. Gen. Mike Short, who successfully ran the Kosovo war from Aviano, and Lt. Gen. Ron Keys, the current commander, 16th Air Force, said many times that the Aviano 2000 program "would be dead if it hadn't been for the PMO." The biggest flattery, of course, is that HQ

USAFE has stood up two additional PMOs in Germany based on the success model (and structure) of the Aviano PMO. Tangible value? We have proven that to recover a program in trouble, a PMO is the only approach to take. The kinds of challenges inherent in troubled programs can only be addressed with a comprehensive, systematic, programmatic approach. Of course, it would have been better to start with a PMO.

Program Assessment

LaGassey says, "We are in good shape." And he can cite a lot of evidence for that conclusion:

Our capabilities improve every day and our projects and program are maturing. We are seeing more and more on-time, on-track projects. Customers are pleased with what they are seeing in designs and construction. They feel more involved in the process and in the eventual outcome. Things are looking up. We're achieving success.

Our program management approach was developed in house. Except for hiring consultants for the project management information system and project management training, we pretty much built our methodology by applying the *PMBOK Guide* and other commercially available guidance. We burned a lot of midnight oil trying to grasp all of it.

Ours was a task of piecing together the elements of project management, extrapolating the right elements, applying them to our circumstances, and tailoring tools and resources for our situation. There has been a great deal of trial and error and frequent worries that perhaps it's not exactly the way the PMI Grand Masters would have done it. So be it, it's our program and our way of doing it.

When asked, what would you now do differently if starting anew, LaGassey responds,

If given the same state of play, that is, a troubled program that is five years under way, I would approach it just a little differently. For one, I would be more insistent in my battles to get the resources I need to get this thing off the ground and make the program go. Because I was breaking new ground each day and was not sure if it was going to work, I sometimes used kid gloves in my dealings with those who had the resources I needed. As a result, they sometimes slow-rolled me and I accepted it. With the experience I've gained, I now know that it works and I don't have to take no for an answer.

Two, I would have pushed harder to clarify the roles and responsibilities earlier and get them down on paper. We were making it happen, but I've seen that getting buy-in is one of the hardest parts of making this work. When you win a battle, you have to codify it. As time goes on and people transfer out, we lose some of the history. A lot of how we do it (organization, processes, our PM methodology, and so on) is in my head and we need to formalize them. If I croak tomorrow, we don't have it all nailed down. A PMP update (with signatures) is on our strategic plan for 2002.

Third, I would institute a more effective personnel assessment program. For the most part, I've been fortunate to have great people, but there are always a couple who I would like to change out if given the opportunity. The trouble with our system is that it takes lots of paper in the form of counselings and so on to effect a change. Because of the "bullet train" nature of Aviano 2000, such refinements weren't possible at the outset, and now we don't have the necessary documentation to effect additional personnel changes I might want.

Lessons Learned

Catching up with a program that had been under way for five years was much more difficult than anyone could have imagined. Achieving full operational capability meant assigned people, an organizational structure, processes and procedures in place, money flowing, and projects being delivered. LaGassey achieved some early successes, like the complete restoration of the runway in thirty-two days. There were also a number of failures, for example, unacceptable delays caused by nonperforming contractors. Many of those might have been resolved earlier had a PMO been established from the start.

LaGassey says,

Simplicity is imperative in all we do and our program success continuum is no exception. We have a tiger by the tail and, although we find all the current theoretical project management maturity models very interesting, the Aviano 2000 program team doesn't have time right now to study and analyze them.

We recognized from the start that application of standardized PM principles is critical for project management. Because of the imperative to start up a program office so late in the game, we needed a simple, commonsense approach. At the project level, we quickly settled on selective use of principles found in the *PMBOK Guide* because it was ready-made to help us. We figured we could develop our initial approach and fill in gaps later. At the program level, a considerable part of our approach was derived from the writings and teachings of Graham and Englund. Their 1997 book, *Creating an Environment for Successful Projects: The Quest to Manage Project Management,* became our bible for program leadership during PMO start-up and continues to be a fundamental part of our thinking as we work to attain recognition as a truly project-based organization.

We have learned hundreds of lessons from this experience of setting up a PMO five years after the program began. It's been a steep learning curve. While we will undoubtedly continue to learn through program completion in 2005, this next year of our activity, as we begin construction of fifteen new projects, will steeply accelerate our learning curve.

All stakeholders in the program are trained or oriented in the methodology, principles, and techniques of project management. PM basic training tailored to Aviano 2000 is given to each member, including customer representatives. This training has been a real eye-opener for many, especially those who had never been involved in large projects before. Core team members get specialized training on software, partnering, leading teams, and the tools to be used. LaGassey says, "Our capabilities and maturity have been increased a thousandfold because of training."

What effect is this work having on the larger organization?

We are beginning to create a mind-set of project management as the only way to do business. The successes of Aviano 2000 made believers out of those who knew we needed change but didn't know quite how to go about it. Now they see the benefits to an organized, structured, focused approach. We purposely included representatives of the user (customer) organizations during our PM 101 basic training as one step in the process, along with asking each of the four groups in the fighter wing to have a standing representative of the colonel group commander within the PMO. This has paid great dividends in spreading the word. Our goal is to have everyone thinking the same way.

How is it being extended?

We've also made a point to include the leadership of our major customer groups in quarterly program reviews. The 31st Fighter Wing structure is a straight military hierarchy—chain of command. The senior commander is a brigadier general. He's the wing commander. Beneath him are four groups: operations, logistics, medical, and support, each commanded by a full colonel. Beneath the groups are the squadrons, mostly technical in nature, each with a commander, usually a major or lieutenant colonel. There are about twenty squadrons at Aviano. We included both group and squadron commanders as our target market because every squadron on the base has at least one major construction project in the program. By creating "group representative" positions in the PMO, we formalized a channel for the group commanders to have a direct voice in the process. That way, the group commanders' concerns enter the system without anyone having to talk to me except on the most pressing issues. Each squadron in turn has "facility project managers" who are responsible for defining requirements and working with our project delivery teams. Everyone has a responsibility and a communications avenue.

The structure, training, reviews, and so on keep the project teams and customers interlocked through the entire process. In essence, everyone has ownership of a part of the process and in the final outcome.

Are other organizations adopting the same or a similar approach?

We are beginning to break through to other organizations on the base. Those mostly closely related to the Aviano 2000 program team, for example, the navy and the base civil engineer, embrace our PM methodology and use it routinely. The Italian program team is eager to learn. Our customers understand the principles and adapted to our way of managing the program. Whether all are true believers remains to be seen. Our biggest challenge is turnover of personnel. The average assignment tour at Aviano is three years—commanders two; therefore it's a constant orientation and learning process.

Have you established a standard?

Yes—a standard approach to execution of the program, the organization, and periodic reviews. We now speak the same language. When we talk about program or project issues, everyone understands a common terminology, schedule milestones and what they signify, requirements, and the project review grading system. This applies from the top sponsors to where the rubber meets the road at the project team member level. Our standard for success in terms of scope, cost, time, quality, and safety are also deeply embedded in the system.

What is on the horizon?

Integrating the newly established Italian program team is our challenge for 2002. They are starting construction on ten projects and will be working through all multiproject management procedures at once. One PMO objective over the past two years was to put all organizational, structural, procedural, and process systems in place so Italy could insert its team into the PMO and simply adhere and adapt. Their leaders, who have been with the program for many years, know how it works. It is now a matter of orienting new members to the program team methodology. We will include the team in the next round of PM 101 training.

How are the practices being disseminated?

Through the structure, training, and tools we have put in place. Also, a large part of our effort was to get everyone under the same roof. That paid off 100 percent in better communications. We get a lot of work done at the cappuccino machine!

What would you say to convince another organization to start with a PMO?

The most compelling argument derives from the basic premise of a PMO—to manage multiple projects to success. One can approach it smartly from the start or by recovering a troubled program. Unfortunately, most programs appear to fall in the latter category. That's how ours was, and just about everyone I've talked to at the past three PMI Symposiums and classes is in the same boat.

When sponsors realize their programs are in trouble, they begin looking for a programmatic fix, which usually seems to be a project or program office of some sort to bail the sinking ship out. But, at what cost?

The "react" method of creating PMOs may save a troubled project or program, but success has to be measured differently. Instead of excellence in project management, success becomes survival or project recovery versus failure. For example, our measure of success for projects that were under way (and in trouble) before our PMO stood up in early '99 is measured on getting them completed with good quality. Everyone has forgotten about the time, because it was already lost, or the cost, because we were already overrun. Our success on those projects is to avoid project failure. On the other hand, projects that we start have different criteria against the traditional scope, time, cost, quality, and safety. Psychologically, I think we approach them differently in terms of responsibility to the project and the customer.

The costs in terms of human resources differ also. The react mode always creates stress on program team members. They never catch up and never get ahead. It's a daily battle against failure or unrealistic time lines.

Instituting a PMO before you begin the program is the only way to go. You control your own destiny and success is measured by a plan developed from the start against the elements of success. When talking about flying with other pilots, many Air Force pilots say, "If I'm going to be part of the crash, I want to be part of the takeoff." The same applies to project management. If I'm going to be part of the project, I'd like to be part of the project start.

Could the runway have been completed without the PMO?

The runway restoration project was programmed in 1998, long before the PMO stood up. Team members did a credible job of planning the necessary steps to execute the project within the constraints of time. The Kosovo Air Campaign in March 1999 forced a postponement in the original project start, necessitating reprogramming.

The first project task of the newly formed PMO was to sort out this re-programming action. The task had to be done within thirty days because of two operational imperatives: the potential for follow-on air combat in the Balkans and projected costs of $1 million a week for the squadrons to be deployed longer than thirty days.

During the Kosovo Air Campaign, Aviano hosted up to two hundred fighter aircraft. There were additional aircraft stationed at six or seven Italian air bases in support of that effort. When Kosovo ended, all but Aviano's 31st Fighter Wing were sent home. The cost of replicating any or all of that force structure in the event of further Balkans hostilities without Aviano was prohibitive and would not meet a warfighter's expectations. We had to get Aviano done in thirty days or less.

As the program team reviewed the original plan and assessed it against our PM methodology, we found hundreds of ways to accelerate the process to meet the timing deadline imposed upon us and ensure the quality desired by the customer. This focused approach, which we fondly call "battle rhythm," is still in use by the PMO today as we approach time-critical projects. We focus all disparate players on hard-hitting action items and put a senior-level manager on the project to provide oversight at every juncture.

This is not the way we do every project, just the ones in deep trouble or that need special attention. The more our PMO matures, the less we have to take this approach.

The end result of the focused approach on the runway was delivery of the job in thirty-two days. By our actions we accelerated project completion by two days and finished exactly on target. The first jet touched down right on the money.

With project and program management, one can get a sense that everything is all lined up. Try as you might, unexpected problems will occur. How do you respond to chaotic events?

The runway terrorist incident best demonstrates the value of a PMO approach in getting your arms around chaos. As we kicked off the project after two months of "battle rhythm" preparation, we began production two days earlier than planned. It seemed like all our moons were lined up. We had a good plan, a great contractor, perfect weather, and all potential risks accounted for. The materials were on hand and people lined up; we were "rocking and rolling."

During the initial five days, the contractor did superbly and made phenomenal progress. Over the weekend, a revived Italian Red Brigades terrorist group broke into the asphalt contractor's compound and applied sledge hammers to two asphalt mixing systems, destroying state-of-the-art computerized production capability.

The terrorists, who were later identified and arrested, were working from an original schedule they had obtained; they wanted to do damage on the night the work was originally supposed to start. But they were mistaken about the date—the contractor was already well into his routine.

The contractor, on track for a world record, was not deterred. He called in computer specialists and had one batch plant up and running by Monday morning. He never missed a beat getting the job done.

Chaos? As soon as the incident was reported, key leaders from all teams came together, assessed the situation, and developed a fresh course of action. We reweighed the alternatives in the event the batch plants couldn't come up on time and plotted a backup plan. We could do that because we established solid rapport among all team players during the planning phase and were on the same wavelength about the desired outcome.

Every project has its rough moments, where the leadership must come together and face tough situations. Good planning, teamwork, and positive attitudes make "getting your arms around chaos" much easier.

Summary

Going back to the scenario presented at the beginning of this chapter, LaGassey sums up the situation as follows:

We now know exactly how to attack the challenge. In this case, because of PMO partnering with all the mayors and the Italian Defense General Staff, we would have gotten this issue on the table and resolved in short order. We resolve tougher challenges each day because of the relationships and working processes we've put into the program.

A PMO is the only way to go for international, multiproject, and fast-moving programs. There are simply too many complexities and challenges to overcome. If the team isn't structured and organized for a project approach to its desired end game, it won't get there. Project management excellence is what we are trying to achieve. You don't get it without focused management, continuity of effort, and a goal of excellence in everything you do. Those elements don't come from fragmented, business as usual work. It's all integration.

A further thought:

The PMI pros could come in and assess the "maturity" of the Aviano 2000 PMO and probably find lots of things to improve. We are working on that, too. But this year, for the first time, we are also shooting to become a project management center of excellence. Throughout the fighter wing, we are known as "the guys to go to" to get things organized and on track. We have been asked to pick up non–construction-related actions and put them on a track for success. Our approach to that is PM excellence. We do a kickoff meeting, bring all players together, get them started, and monitor their progress. We were just given the challenge of developing a base volunteer effort to support the Italian regional International University Winter Games in January 2003. These games, often referred to as the University Olympics, will host forty to fifty national teams with two thousand competitors. This has nothing to do with constructing our base, but we have the expertise on how to organize projects and the base leadership wants us to lead the charge. That's success!

Author Comments

It is no accident that people are drawn to this assignment, because LaGassey is an authentic leader who acts with integrity. His story clearly demonstrates progression along our path. The entry point came not initially as one would hope but with a hefty load of projects under way for several years. He personally has a sense of urgency to learn and apply all he can about program management. He has been fortunate with enlightened sponsors, but he does not stop there, continuously communicating and drawing upon them for support.

The elements of urgency, alignment of powerful forces, focused vision and strategy, and harnessing support are present in force. LaGassey manages complexity with incredible enthusiasm and adaptability, constantly seeking new or improved ways to work. He rewards these traits in others as well. His initial "Quaker" approach started with small wins and allowed him to expand the approach across the organization.

Managing multiple projects is the purview of the PMO. Projects have clear priorities. By focusing people on structure, practices, and processes, they get the job done. A positive effect is creating bandwidth to take on other interesting opportunities like the Winter Games. Other organizations notice the results and adopt his approach. This impact, plus the newfound ease of attracting quality people, is a very powerful, qualitative metric.

LaGassey successfully addressed the problem of troubled projects. No longer is that the norm—they created new criteria for success. When trouble strikes, upper management teams respond quickly and effectively.

The project office adds definitive value. It contributes focused effort on program success using a disciplined body of knowledge, coupled with effective leadership. This effort frees and actually empowers other professionals to focus on their responsibilities, at the same time drawing them together in cooperative teams.

Managing a half-billion dollars and hundreds of projects in an international environment can be chaotic, especially since a pattern of chaos had developed over several years of operating without a project office. The case demonstrates that chaos can be tamed, even though not eliminated or necessarily controlled, by a strong sense of vision, purpose, tools, methods, motivated individuals, and teamwork.

Pathway to Organizational Change

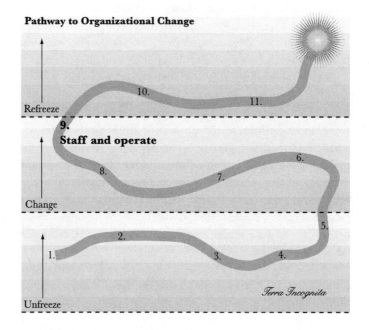

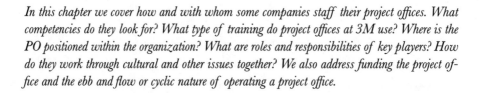

In this chapter we cover how and with whom some companies staff their project offices. What competencies do they look for? What type of training do project offices at 3M use? Where is the PO positioned within the organization? What are roles and responsibilities of key players? How do they work through cultural and other issues together? We also address funding the project office and the ebb and flow or cyclic nature of operating a project office.

CHAPTER NINE

IN OR OUT? STAFFING AND OPERATING THE PROJECT OFFICE

"Are you in or out?" is the tag line of the main character in the movie *Ocean's Eleven.* Dapper Danny Ocean (actor George Clooney) is a man of action, rolling out his next plan, one that's never been done before, to do it would be impossible, there are a dozen reasons why it won't work, a smash-and-grab job. Following three rules—don't hurt anybody, don't steal from anyone who doesn't deserve it, and play the game like you've got nothing to lose—Danny orchestrates the most sophisticated, elaborate casino heist in history. Knowing the difficulties of pulling off the heist, Ocean and his partner assemble a team, each person brought on board for a specific expertise and the lure of a big payoff.

The movie director made a conscious effort to have all the actors hang out together. The movie producer noted that as the actors started spending time together away from the set, real friendships developed. The actors wanted to go to work and work and be with one another. The movie's Web site describes how much fun everyone had on this movie.

Staffing a project office involves similar challenges, approaches, and desire to work together. Getting the right people and creating the environment for them to be successful will make or break a project office.

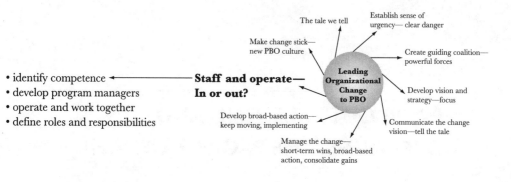

Competence

Sandberg (2001) writes, "Corporations need to shift the focus of their recruitment and training programs from flawed attribute checklists toward identifying and, if necessary, changing people's understanding of what jobs entail" (p. 28). He identifies three views of competence at work. *Sequential optimizers* see their work as a series of steps and value technical skills the most. *Interactive optimizers* see activities as interactive systems and value learning, teamwork, and knowing how performance categories influence each other. *Customer optimizers* are similar to interactive optimizers and see goals not through a technical engineering lens but from a customer's viewpoint.

Sandberg's research at Volvo revealed that customer optimizers were the most effective at their work while sequential optimizers were the least capable. Even the reasons given by employees for these assessments differed depending on how they defined the job. The conclusion to remember when staffing a project office is that a person's competence is not easily reduced to a standardized checklist of skills.

Competent workers see a particular vision of what their work is and why it is that way. Thus a project office is more effective when the people in it possess not a litany of project management skills but a clear view of the end result that is possible and a commitment to doing everything they can to make it happen. Recruiting these people means probing for their understanding of the big picture.

David Frame spent much of his career immersed in issues of project management competence. He notes, "Achieving project management competence entails the concurrent development of individual competence, team competence, and organizational competence" (1999, p. xii). In his work he explores the issues of competency and presents checklists of tools that competent project professionals should master. He also offers an interesting perspective about the demoralizing effect of *clueless managers:* "These are men and women who are oblivious to the impacts of their words and actions. Their attempts at humor are offensive. They provide little feedback about the job performance of their workers, and when feedback is forthcoming it may entail ad hominem attacks on the employees. . . . They wear the mantle of captains of industry and issue orders like generals running a military campaign. Regrettably these orders often have not been thought through and lead to predictably unfortunate consequences" (p. 39). Frame concludes that it is difficult to see how people who do not understand themselves can be expected to understand and deal effectively with others.

Beginning project managers may struggle with these issues as part of their development. They are not the best candidates for a project office. Since the change agent role is so relationship-dependent, look first for people who have the people skills and ability to see the larger picture. They may be a little weak in project management. That is probably OK because it is easier to backfill and train someone on project management skills than it is to adjust attitudes toward other people. One requirement, however, is passion and enthusiasm for the project management process. That could be long term or newly developed, but it is generally wise to seek out more experienced people to staff the project office.

Another area of competence for program managers is business acumen. While this competency is desirable in all project managers, a project office manager will be called upon even more often to speak in business terms and present the economic and shareholder value of a portfolio. To implement the project office for organizational change and build the value proposition talked about in Chapter Two, proponents need the latitude to think like CEOs and the information to act like entrepreneurs, taking responsibility for a program as a total enterprise. Such people see the world beyond the department, have a generalist, big picture, top-down view, and are system thinkers. They possess luck driven by intentionality. They are intrigued by how business runs and have the aptitude to stick to a program and make it successful.

Program managers need the ability to engage in meaningful dialogue with upper managers, and that means speaking truth to power (see Chapter Three) in a language that upper managers understand. This imperative, according to Cohen and Graham (2001), comes about because of an outmoded model for a standard way of interconnecting the business perspective of upper management with the technical and tactical perspective of the project team and project manager. "In quieter, more placid environments, management could set a strategy and then program it into a static set of project constraints. Today things move so fast, this method prevents rather than produces the desired results" (p. xii). Program managers need competency and commitment to make decisions in real time and extend their horizon over a complete program outcome life cycle.

The responsibility of most program managers is monumental—they have to get jobs done on time and within cost and quality constraints. Although the responsibility is gigantic, the authority to get things done is often on the short side. So program managers have more responsibility than they have authority.

Paradoxically, in more complex programs, this responsibility-authority gap is greater than in lesser projects—there are more players with technical, professional, or commercial stakes in the outcome. These stakeholders require political nurturing, so an authoritarian approach is inappropriate. That is why effective program managers are excellent influencers. They recognize that full formal authority is usually lacking in program situations, so they compensate by using other skills such as influence management, negotiation, and conflict management.

While at HP Consulting in Madrid, Alfonso Bucero (see Chapter Seven) developed the model shown in Figure 9.1 to staff his project office. It was especially important to get the right people on board because he had to use outsourcing rather than employees.

FIGURE 9.1. PROCESS STEPS AND CRITERIA.

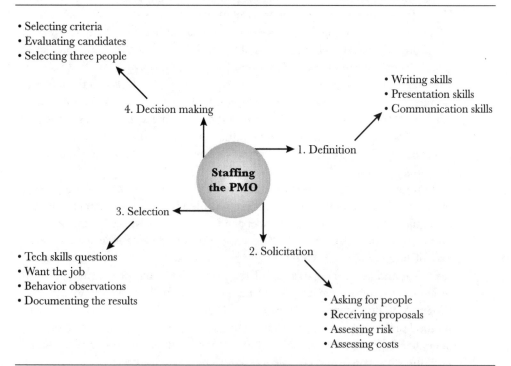

Buckingham and Clifton (2001) make a strong argument for building a strengths-based organization. Seek people and find positions where you do the job practically effortlessly because you are then putting your strengths to work. You "reach excellence only by understanding and cultivating your strengths" (p. 124). They advise being bold and perceptive, listening for performance feedback from the outside world, and continuing to investigate your strengths. *Manage your strengths, not your weaknesses* is a wise but often unpracticed approach. Many performance systems rub people's noses in their weaknesses instead of discovering, positioning in, and building on their strengths.

The Gallup organizations' research finds a connection between strengths-based organizations and the health of their employees. As senior managers at this organization, Buckingham and Clifton report that "employees who strongly agreed that they had a chance to do what they do best every day claimed fewer sick days, filed fewer workers' compensation claims, and had fewer accidents while on the job" (p. 244).

Evangelists

People staffing the Project Management and Teamwork Group within the 3M Learning Center, a quasi-project office, demonstrate evangelist personalities. They are enthusiastic about project management and actively make contacts both across and outside the organization. They speak regularly at conferences. This exposure offers dramatic learning opportunities where other people react to their message and share additional ways of approaching the issues presented. They also achieve renewed energy to spread good practices across the organization. Project offices need people like these who can stimulate vitality.

Siegfried Woldhek, former head of the Netherlands organization of the World Wide Fund for Nature, formed a new conservation environment. He writes, "we are learning that it is more effective to appoint a program manager and give him or her a budget and a relatively free hand. This person is responsible for the 'heart, head, and belly' of a project: the vision, the strategy, the day-to-day management, and the development of people. He or she goes to bed with the project each night, and gets up with it in the morning." Woldhek's group developed Target-Driven Activities with impressive results, doubling old-growth forest lands. He adds, "We develop these 'zealot-like' skills into the whole organization," and "Developing such a large-scale conservation operation is completely different from an ordinary project; it means collaborating with many constituencies, including local and regional politicians, businesspeople, and community leaders. . . . This was a passionate, collaborative endeavor" (Woldhek, 2001, p. 61).

On the other side of this issue, evangelists tend to see things from their side only, which could tend to make people angry. They might also not be the good customer optimizers suggested earlier. Demonstrative passion may be viewed negatively by some partners. A good compromise is to seek persons who combine the enthusiasm of evangelists with the credibility of effective leaders.

Developing Program Managers

One company's commitment to project management becomes evident in a published brochure of competencies and career path. It lists nine project management competencies the company has identified as important and five project management levels in a career path from project manager up to VP of projects. These are the project management competencies:

- Building customer relationships and stakeholder expectations
- Leadership
- Project management tools and information technology
- Monitoring project performance
- Business acumen
- Management skills
- Project execution
- Project management knowledge
- Project planning

Staffing a project office requires people especially strong in these competencies. The task becomes easier when potential candidates see strong evidence that an advancement path is available to them. It encourages and renews commitment to study, learn, and continuously update program management skills and project office best practices. Organizations that use the career ladder report high competency marks in the areas of program and project management on employee satisfaction surveys.

One program office effort started with a focus on reducing product development cycle time and schedule slippage. The vice president setting up the program achieved Project Management Professional certification from the Project Management Institute as a demonstrable commitment to the profession. By conducting assessments and driving changes through metrics, they exceeded a goal of 10X improvement. The people and organizations that embraced project management showed better business results.

The vice president retired, and program office staffing was reduced. Most of the corporation continued to move forward rapidly. A common enterprise-wide PM tool was adopted, as well as phase gating methodology. In some parts of the corporation, PMP certification is required.

In one organization, a setback occurred when some leaders received advice to focus on project management tools and forms (rather than on the PM process and benefits to the organization). In some cases people were selected as PMs simply because they could do the administrative job of filling out the forms, and they were classified as general administrative rather than professional staff. The people generally lacked knowledge about project management and received little training. When cutbacks became necessary, these positions, because of their overhead classification, were eliminated. This left organizations with even fewer resources to support a hefty load of programs.

Operating divisions that paid little attention to creating an environment for successful projects brought in program managers who had neither technical nor administrative skills. One person might have ten programs going on at the same time. They barely had time even to do status reports.

A program controller who is committed to improving the project management competency reports how one business brought in a skilled program manager who knew how to do assessments, drive the process, and resolve issues. The business achieved remarkable improvement. The program controller's strategy is to meet with general managers to help them understand the value proposition that project management offers, take advantage of the successes that occur when the right people are on board, and work directly with the HR function to help its staff understand the importance of people, process, and training. He believes that focusing on early adopters who have the best chance to achieve better business results will attract attention from others to want the same. His stake in the ground is to focus on product pipeline and portfolio management along with development cycle time slippage as a means to address the issues.

Integrated Project Management at 3M

This section describes how one form of a project office—a Learning Center—approaches the function to train and upgrade an organization-wide cadre of professional project managers. We include this example as a sample of the type of work that PO people may do and should be interested in doing. Use this material as a gauge to measure interest level among candidates and in forming interview questions.

For many years, 3M has provided extensive coursework and experiences for project leaders and teams in the areas of project management and teamwork. To help teams and project leaders get the learning that they need to be successful in their projects, the 3M Learning Center needed to organize the many courses and tools into clearer and more usable curricula that 3Mers could access.

The effort to provide better coordinated and rationalized team and project management offerings and skills resulted in the creation of two complementary programs designed to help teams and project leaders do their best for 3M: the "Corporate Project Leadership" and the "Project Team Management and Tools" curricula. These are comprehensive curricula whose goal is to provide the best training and tools in the industry to make project teams and leaders the most effective.

3M also realized, however, that leaders and teams needed a simple way to get started, so the company created a third "integrated view" (not a separate curriculum) that highlights the absolute essentials in both curricula to get projects going.

What Is the Integrated View?

The 3M Integrated Project Management, Leadership, and Teams View is the essential collection of courses and tools for a project team to get a quick start on a project. A project has a finite life, and if it is to be effective, that life is shorter rather than longer. The intent of these offerings is to supply the leader and team with the basic skills and tools to start quickly and to move at a fast pace through their project. The composite curriculum view (see Figure 9.2) shows the project team how to get the minimum training necessary to make fundamental agreements and work together on a specific project. 3M has found that people who work through process issues together as a project team can save time and increase team effectiveness, thereby accelerating and enhancing project completion.

Corporate Project Leadership Core Curriculum

The Project Leadership Curriculum was originally developed jointly by IT education and consulting professionals, technical developers, learning operations, and organizational effectiveness professionals to provide employees with a set of proven principles, methods, and techniques that help them manage both simple and complex projects. The 3M Learning Center eventually consolidated these efforts and coordinated the work of these professionals and is the current custodian for the curriculum.

Over the years, the curriculum kept pace with an evolving Project Leader Competency Model. This model reflects that many skill sets are necessary (see Figure 9.3) for effective project leadership, and is now an accepted industry stan-

FIGURE 9.2. AN INTEGRATED CURRICULUM VIEWPOINT.

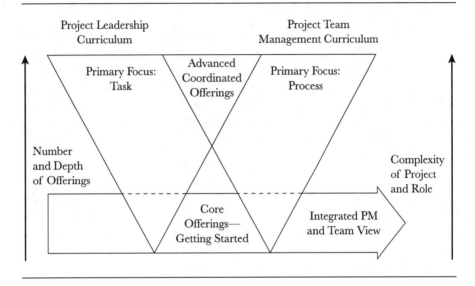

dard. The latest version reflects a corporate view across the various 3M groups providing project management training.

Bob Storeygard says, "The competency clusters at the lower right level of the structure break out into separate, testable, measurable skill statements. Several of the clusters, such as Group dynamics, Decision making, and Communications, repeat in each area and therefore have skills attached to them that are related yet somewhat different in focus, depending on the higher cluster in which they appear." The end result of the development efforts and the model was a curriculum designed for both flexibility and comprehensiveness, providing training for both novice and experienced project managers and leaders. This curriculum is reviewed regularly to ensure state-of-the-art PM training.

What Does the Project Leadership Curriculum Offer?

The Corporate Project Leadership Curriculum offers training both in core project management skills and in associated professional skill attributes of a successful project manager or leader.

Core skills pertain to the direct application of project management principles and activities. They include skill development in initiating, planning, estimating, scheduling, tracking, and closing projects. Associated skills pertain to the professional

FIGURE 9.3. PROJECT LEADER COMPETENCY MODEL.

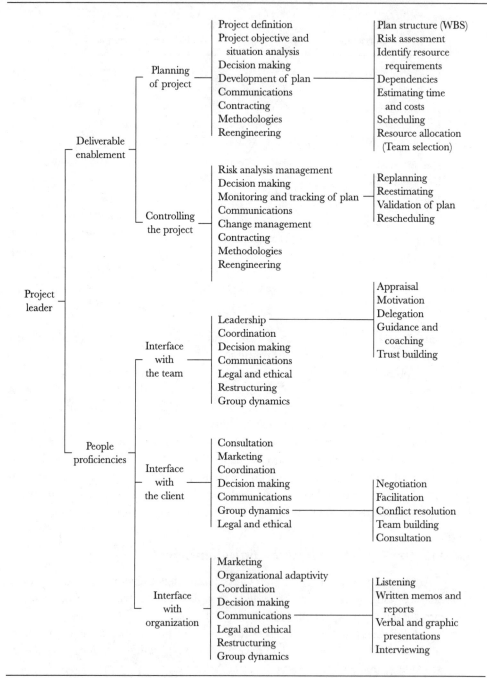

Source: Robert Storeygard (1999), 3M.

attributes a successful project manager or leader needs. Associated skills include things such as consulting expertise, risk management, decision making, and building professional and team relationships.

The initial guide to what it is to be a full-fledged, completely skilled project manager or leader is best described by the Project Leader Competency Model (see Figure 9.3). Novices get started in the discipline by attending project leadership core classes. However, that is not enough. The associated classes, in many cases, are just as important as the direct PM classes are to success as a project manager or leader. When it comes to project failures, problems with soft (people-related) skills are more often the problem than any lack of core PM skills.

Very little is prescribed in this curriculum in terms of sequence. Beyond the first few classes, which provide the basics and are called "quintessential" classes, modules are taken at point of need or when people identify a weakness or lack that they need to strengthen. Here is a sample listing of the Project Leadership Curriculum:

Building Core PM Understanding

- Project Management Basics
- Strategic Project Leadership
- Effective Technical PM (self-study)

PM Tools and Core Techniques

- PM Using MS Project
- MS Project: Basic, Intermediate, and Advanced
- Project Planning Workshop
- Gathering Complete Client Requirements

PM Methodologies

- Methodology for Small Projects
- PM Tools and Techniques
- Creating High-Performance Teams

Sharpening PM Skills

- PM Workplace Simulation
- PMI PMP Certification Test Preparation

Associated Support Skills

- Building Business Partnerships
- Systems Thinking
- Transition Management

Note that this corporate curriculum tries to leverage the "best of the best" course offerings to meet the competency model, whether they are offered in-house and taught by 3M instructors from various departments and divisions, or provided by expert consultants and vendors from outside 3M. They have all been brought together to forge a unified whole in helping people achieve maximum competency as value-added employees and project managers or leaders for 3M.

Reflection

The 3M approach is a model for what the right people in this position can do to make significant impact on the organization. The evangelists in the 3M Learning Center are a small group that mobilize others in the organization. They extend their impact by engendering enthusiasm in others through their example and the curricula they create and the programs they serve. Staffing and operating a learning center with people of this caliber enables a very worthy change effort across the organization—leading to improved competence in project and program management.

Operating a Project Office: EXFO's Approach to New Product Development

Canada is the home for electro-optical engineering company EXFO (the name derives from EXpertise in Fiber Optics). An interview with the VP of engineering, Stephen Bull, reveals an enlightened project culture.

Within the new product development process system, what makes up the project environment axis?

At EXFO, new product development is a corporate affair not just a concern of the R&D department. This means that all departments within the corporation are involved at some stage in new product development projects. To ensure success on projects, it is necessary to create an environment that will stimulate the teams. This is done through clear assignment to projects from each department and individual responsibilities for team members. Production pilot cells are colocated with R&D to facilitate product transfer to production. Finally a project manager is assigned to lead the project. Although coming from a technical background (but not generally the best technician), the project manager is a specialist in project management. The PM has all the authority necessary to coordinate the activities of resources assigned to his project from every department.

How did the project office get started?

The PMO started through the VP of engineering's initiative with the purpose of providing tools and project scheduling support to the project managers. He did not and still does not want project managers to become specialists in scheduling tools or other reporting tools. He wants them to concentrate on managing the project, which is, 90 percent of the time, managing people.

What was the vision, who supported it, and why was it formed? Is the project office supported by the whole organization? Why?

At the start the PMO was envisioned as I just described it. The PMO is attached to the R&D department under the VP's direct supervision (necessary to ensure its acceptance corporately). Since its inception, the PMO role evolved along three axes:

Process keeper. The PMO through its manager is the keeper for the portfolio and NPD processes. Responsibilities include rigorous application of the processes, coordination of portfolio and gate reviews, and continuous improvement of the processes.

Control center. The PMO team supports and provides project information such as schedules, dashboards, metrics, and loading. It also provides portfolio information such as resource usage and allocations, and overall metrics.

Competence center. Within the PMO, they have expertise to provide support in project management. The PMO is responsible for defining and implementing methodologies, standards, and tools. It also ensures the diffusion of best practices and provides training on project management. Finally, it makes an effort to promote project environment principles in other departments.

The PMO role today is strictly assigned to new product development. They are now seeing interest from other departments in the usage of tools and expertise within the PMO for their own functional projects.

Describe a typical role of the project office in the portfolio selection process.

Upper management does project selection and prioritization. The decisions are mainly driven by market requirements, and priorities are adjusted with corporate capacity. The PMO plays a coordination role and provides the data on actual loading and last quarter project performances. It also builds compilation graphs such as bubble diagrams and pie charts of all the projects being reviewed for analysis by the portfolio team.

Since the "PMO is the heart of the system," what does it pump out across the organization? What contribution does it make to implement projects? Does it have a significant role to make any changes in the organization?

The PMO is a service center. It has a coordinating and counseling role. It has no authority per se. The PMO manager is the owner of the processes, thus has authority in the application of the processes. It is strictly focusing on new product development.

How is EXFO weathering the current market situation? How has the PMO helped maintain success?

The current market situation is specifically difficult in the telecommunications sector. EXFO's strategy has been to concentrate efforts on new product development. The company launched more than twenty new products in 2001, and 2002 will again be a record year for new products. The company anticipates continued improvement due to market acceptance of important new products, contributions from acquisitions, and expected gains in market share due to the enhanced positioning of EXFO's entire product line in the marketplace. Germain Lamonde, our chairman, president, and CEO, says, "There's no question, these are unprecedented times in the telecommunications industry. We've taken appropriate actions to deal with this current situation, while protecting our long-term capabilities and intensifying our focus on gaining market share."

The PMO performs an activity of visibility to projects. For example, the PMO took the initiative to create a poster that shows all ongoing projects and put it up throughout the company. That helped to inform the staff and align everyone with their objectives.

What is management's view of the project office? What is the vision for the future?

Eventually, the PMO will move to a corporate level, instead of a function level (attached to R&D). Project managers will be attached to the PMO, who will have the responsibility to assign them to specific projects. Eventually, one can imagine that major corporate initiatives could be managed through project management and be part of the PMO portfolio of projects.

Working Together

Other aspects of staffing and operating a project office are the effects people have on each other when working together. Value conflicts often arise within a project office or especially with its clients.

Cultural Effects

Kleiner (2001, p. 77) describes the dilemma theory put forth by Trompenaars and Hampden-Turner: "We can never grow to become great business leaders until we actively strive to embrace the behaviors and attitudes that feel most uncomfortable to us." He reports that Trompenaars and Hampden-Turner suggest first naming the extreme positions or double binds between conflicting goals that groups of people find themselves in. Understand the reasons why each position makes sense. Then develop a strategy for cycling back and forth between the two approaches. When people gain experience over time with both sides, they develop their own new kind of system. For example, should program team meetings be formal (European) or informal (American)? Start out first with informal brainstorming and follow up with formal reporting on action items. Learning techniques such as these are indispensable tools for program managers to develop.

Here is one example of a manager's guide to cultural conflict. Americans believe that success stems from individual achievement (individualism). People from Asia assign primary responsibility to the group (collectivism). These diverging views often make it difficult to establish viable performance assessments. An IBM sales team dealt with the problem by awarding bonuses to excellent groups (those that had nurtured individuals) and excellent individual performers (especially those who had been the best team players). The advice is "to assimilate the ideas of the enemy until there is no enemy at all" (Kleiner, 2001, p. 85).

Creative ideas like these are vital to making change happen. A really excellent project office manager can hold two opposing ideas in mind at the same time. This is a skill that often develops with experience in applying effective processes. For example, the project portfolio management process invokes tremendous resistance because it says an organization cannot do everything. However, success in a marketplace often demands full-service capability, and people want to do everything. By having process-capable people in a project office, organizations discover that they can have it all. But they do not do all projects. Through the guidance of the project office facilitator to implement the process described in Chapter Six, they pick only the best projects in each category, and the categories represent a complete solution.

Staff Infection

One central lesson from the study of culture and society is summarized by the phrase "you become like the people you hang around with." It is easy to observe that through the process of socialization, people in any society learn to behave like other people in that society, particularly if they want to be accepted by the members of that society. This lesson is no less true in organizations as it is outside them. Years of observation of this process, watching people in organizations change their behavior because they find themselves in a new group, caused us to postulate a process of "staff infection."

For example, most organizations experience animosity between the people on the line—production people, salespeople, the ones who make and sell product—and the people classified as staff—home office people who produce regulations and paper. Staff people are often accused of nonproductive behavior: "they never answer their phone, they just quote regulations, and all they do is write white papers."

Occasionally, someone from the line is brought into headquarters to join the staff. The person coming in often sees this assignment as a mission to change the way things are done, to right the wrongs perpetrated all these years. They promise their friends on the line that they will answer their phone calls, not be a slave to regulations, and write no white papers. What often happens is that for the first month or so this is true. The phone gets answered, and the new staffer tries to help line people get around the regulations. No white papers get written. But shortly after that, the behavior begins to change. It starts to get more difficult to get the new staff person on the phone. When you do get hold of them they just quote regulations. It is not long until they produce a white paper arguing that the regulations are good for you. Sadly, they become like the people that surround them—they succumb to *staff infection*. Conversations littered with TLAs—three-letter acronyms—indicate when the infection is complete!

Keep this concern in mind when staffing and operating a project office. Bring in new people from varied experiences and raise the caution flag when too much agreement creeps in.

Structure: Roles and Responsibilities

Conflict often arises if people both in and outside the project office are unclear about roles and responsibilities. That makes it useful to examine how some organizations structure their approach.

Goodman Fielder is Australasia's largest food manufacturer, producing many of Australia and New Zealand's most popular and well-known brands as well as products and ingredients for the food service, commercial, and industrial sectors. The role of the Goodman Fielder Group Project Office (GPO) is to facilitate the successful delivery of projects (see Figure 9.4). GPO staff do this by partnering with project teams and business unit managers to establish a work plan, match up resources, provide centralized project coordination, and develop common disciplines, tools, and training across projects.

The Group Program Office commenced in August 1999, when the business had just completed a drive on projects. The delivery rate across the business was

FIGURE 9.4. GROUP PROJECT OFFICE STRUCTURE.

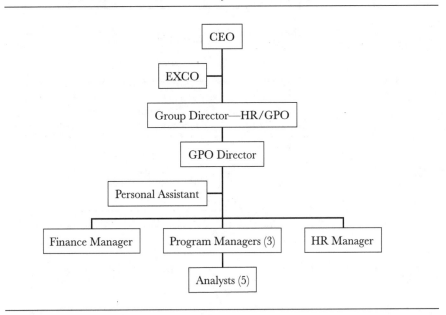

at around 40 percent (benefits achievement being the measure for success). During the same period one division achieved a result around the 80 percent delivery rate, assisted by the focus provided by Simon Rowe, director of the Program Office. The human resource director for Goodman Fielder at the time took the initiative to set up the Group Program Office based on Rowe's proven success. Rowe moved into the corporate group in August 1999 to facilitate the start-up of the Group Program Office.

Barriers were encountered across the whole business as the GPO was perceived as the corporate watchdog or policeman. The level of acceptance across the business was variable and progress was difficult. The process was assisted by having the CEO aligned with the concept and a strong senior director of the business providing great support.

Divisional Program Office Role

The Divisional Program Office (DPO) interacts with cross-functional project teams in the design, evaluation, planning, implementation, and monitoring and reporting of business improvement projects affecting all processes, products, and services (see Figure 9.5). The idea to create the DPO was to get the processes

FIGURE 9.5. DIVISIONAL PROGRAM OFFICE STRUCTURE.

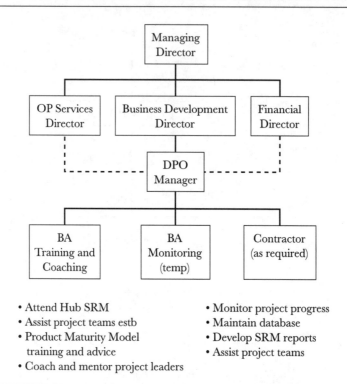

- Attend Hub SRM
- Assist project teams estb
- Product Maturity Model training and advice
- Coach and mentor project leaders

- Monitor project progress
- Maintain database
- Develop SRM reports
- Assist project teams

closer to the businesses in the same way that Rowe had been operating in 1998 and 1999. Before introduction of the DPO structure all program office support was held within the corporate team.

For a PMO to be a success as seen by PMs and their own managers (and hence survive for the long term), it must not come between them or add extra layers of bureaucracy to their work. It should function as a high-quality support department. It must be responsive to its PM and senior management customers in the best service-role traditions.

PMO staff can enable collection, consolidation, or reporting of multiproject information for senior management, but they must not do the reporting themselves. That is, they must restrict themselves to helping the projects with the reporting, because bad things happen to the PMO's reputation if it seems to be going behind the PMs' backs and spying for senior management.

This approach can easily lead to conflict for a status-seeking PMO director who wants to be active at the highest level of discussions on projects such as in senior management committees. However, if such a person can stick to providing help and stay out of the direct status reporting loop, Goodman Fielder's experiences indicate it might work well—as long as the PMO staff gets high marks from the PMs and their managers for their support work.

Simon Rowe, now director of the Group Program Office, adds, "We are definitely a more productive company due to the program office concept. However, we are in the phase where everyone wants to take credit for the success. I am a firm believer that the program office is not there to take the glory—the people doing the work at the coal face should be praised. The PO needs to be in the engine room ensuring success of the business, which has been the case to date. The wide recognition of our work has not been openly accepted by the business."

Key responsibilities for DPOs are as follows:

- *Project Register:*
  Maintain a project register for all divisional and relevant cross-divisional project activity.
- *Small Divisional Projects (up to $1 million in costs or benefits):*
  Ensure sufficient quality resources.
  Manage, coordinate, and report on execution and benefit capture.
- *Medium to Large Divisional Projects (up to $5 million in costs or benefits):*
  Support development of appropriate plan.
  Ensure adherence to the Project Maturity Model (PMM).
  Ensure sufficient quality resources.
  Manage, coordinate, and report on execution and benefit capture.
- *Group and Cross-Divisional Projects:*
  Ensure sufficient divisional focus and quality resources.
  Manage, coordinate, and report on local module execution and benefit capture.
- *Resourcing:*
  Allocate resources across range of divisional project activity.
  Liaise with GPO to resolve conflicts and shortages.
  Determine what projects are worth resourcing.
- *Mentoring:*
  Provide mentoring and training for divisional project teams.
- *Reporting:*
  Participate in monthly review with GPO.

The GPO during the major change initiative that took place got up to fourteen staff people (Goodman Fielder Limited at that time had around 15,000 employees total). As of this writing, the Group Program Office has been resized to four to meet current business demands. The three divisions that implemented Divisional Program Offices have two to three people in each office.

Lessons Learned

Setting up of a program office is all about improving business performance. Rowe believes the processes used need to become second nature to the people running the business. To achieve this they must be very easily integrated into the day to day business. Complicated systems with lots of bells and whistles are generally not acceptable as they distract people and prevent them from being high performers. Rowe also believes that there is not any one system or process that will fit every organization, therefore, a program office has to be tailor-made for the business. This means that the best people to set up program offices should have a good understanding of the culture of the business.

The program office must be closely linked to the top of the business and to decision makers. Progress on projects and programs is often slowed because managers do not understand or have not been communicated with. Therefore, one key role of program managers is to be able to influence key senior people. When this ability exists and is exercised, roadblocks get removed.

A program office should have clear and well understood processes, but should not live only by these processes. The role is to drive value for the business (and therefore for the shareholders). If PO processes are gold plated and business performance is down, then the PO is not doing what it needs to be doing. Rowe says, "Businesses that are doing this stuff well are getting results by integrating robust changes into the culture of the business; they are not shouting from the rooftops that they are running programs with great systems to drive improvement."

Project Management in Action

The following outline documents a response to the Australian Stock Exchange request concerning the Y2K problem as it related to Goodman Fielder Limited.

Background. Goodman Fielder's principal activities are the manufacture and sale of consumer foods and ingredients. Major product areas include grain-based products such as bread and breakfast cereals, edible oils such as margarine and cooking oil, food ingredients, and poultry.

Goodman Fielder recognized the potential seriousness of the Y2K problem in early 1997 and implemented measures in all its Australian and overseas operations designed to minimize exposure. The Y2K problem was addressed as a matter of priority, and Goodman Fielder aimed to be Y2K-ready by October 29, 1999.

Goodman Fielder's Y2K program commenced in mid-1997 with the engagement of a firm of independent consultants to conduct a comprehensive assessment of the extent of the problem within the organization.

The assessment, and the recommendations it contained, were the precursor to Goodman Fielder's formal Y2K program. The goal of the program was to ensure that the susceptible systems, suppliers, customers, and logistics chains critical to their organization continue to operate normally during the transition to the year 2000 and thereafter. In this way they minimized any adverse material affect on the organization as a whole.

Y2K Readiness. On its Web site, Goodman Fielder referred to Y2K readiness as: "Ensuring Goodman Fielder and its operations have addressed those components of the business that are exposed to the Year 2000 problem. In doing so, Goodman Fielder looks to ensure that the risk of any adverse impact to the conduct of business resulting from the issue has been removed or reduced to a level whereby it is not significant."

Project Structure. A program office was established to manage and coordinate Y2K activities across the organization. The project office was headed by the Goodman Fielder Y2K project manager, who reported to the Y2K Executive Steering Committee, which consisted of the chief financial officer, the chief information officer, and a representative from the internal auditors, Deloitte Touche Tohmatsu. A regular reporting mechanism was implemented, which included monthly reports to the Board of Directors, the Audit Committee, and the Executive Committee.

To facilitate the project, nine project teams were assembled, each representing a division of the organization. Each team was headed by a designated project manager who in turn reported to the Y2K Program Office.

A significant observation about successful project office implementations is that they occupy a prominent, visible, and important position on the organization chart. The Y2K example reflects a sense of urgency, a vision about the desired outcome, and how an important project needs a project office reporting high up in the organization (alignment with powerful forces), which offers them a prominent and authoritative role to complete a mandatory program that by itself is not a project people want to do.

Maturity

Maturity models offer a means to assess where an organization currently resides with regard to where it can be along a continuum of progression within a discipline of knowledge. Refer to Crawford (2001) and Kerzner (2001) for detailed descriptions of project management maturity models. A project office is usually established by the time an organization reaches higher levels of maturity. Keep in mind how many people accept, are uncomfortable with, or integrate the change when gauging the project maturity of your organization. Chapter Five describes the dialogue that a maturity model offers within the 3M Company. Here we offer a few more words about how maturity affects the operation of a project office.

A strategic project office monitors the progress and effectiveness of the change to the organization and makes adjustments as necessary. Kent Crawford of PM Solutions, a former PMI president, says it is possible to prepare people for cultural change by helping them accept ambiguity, prepare for possible scenarios, have fun in order to survive, forget consensus (conquer through collaboration), adopt to life in the chasm (that space between the known and the unknowns), and recognize a task is for today while the system is for always.

Implementing a project office is an organizational change project, and executive sponsorship is important. Crawford also believes that without an executive sponsor, the chances of successfully deploying a project office are very slim. The more influential the sponsor, the greater the likelihood of success. Identify a project sponsor and increase management participation by establishing a project office steering committee. This steering committee may be the guiding coalition you establish to begin the process, or it may consist during later stages of maturity as a dedicated group of upper managers committed to overseeing the continuous improvement of project management across the organization. As the organization matures further and the project management process becomes the normal operating condition, the role of this group and the urgency of its work may diminish.

Ideally, the head of the strategic project office is a director of project management who sits at a director or vice presidential level with other senior executives in the organization. Other members of the project office are project managers, project mentors, project planners, project controllers, and methodology experts, along with a library and documentation specialist, an administrative support coordinator, a communications coordinator, an issue resolution and change control coordinator, and a risk management coordinator. Higher levels of maturity display these titles prominently on the organization chart.

Other advice to increase program management maturity: Ensure that expectations and goals are shared and that the charter for the project office deployment project is endorsed by all stakeholders. Do not try to do too much too soon—start with the basic needs and start up the office to help project teams. One way to fail is to work in a vacuum. In a project office implementation, a team approach wins. Organizations advance as they formally recognize teamwork and as they flexibly modify the role of the project office to support changing organizational requirements.

Operating HP's Project Management Initiative

Since the rise and fall of a project office is another prominent theme, let us look at steps along this path. Previous work (Graham and Englund, 1997, Chapter 9) described the Project Management Initiative at Hewlett-Packard Company. This investment focused on corporate resources to help people anywhere and everywhere in the organization improve the environment and skills for effective project management. Figure 9.6 reflects a timeline and update.

Events in the company's response to competitive time-to-market needs invoked an assessment of its project management needs. The initiative has been a stabilizing factor. The PM Council, a guiding coalition, helped get it started but lost relevance when the initiative was established and self-funded. Figure 9.6 shows it disbanding after the first few years.

Training was an ongoing activity, supplemented by concise documented process sheets. Conferences were held every two years until large attendance made them too visible (and perceived as expensive).

FIGURE 9.6. A TIMELINE OF ACTIVITIES AND PEOPLE IMPACT AT HP.

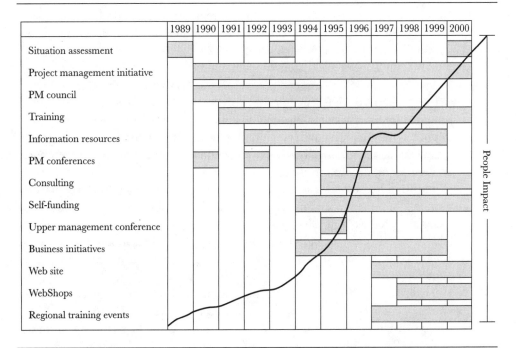

Consulting was added when everyone realized that training was not enough. Self-funding (an internal market model) came about as part of a corporate functions initiative to ensure corporate activities added value, not just expense. It changed the whole focus for the group.

An upper management conference helped address the leadership's role in creating an environment for successful projects. Business initiatives also addressed upper managers, working to ensure they were both supportive of the project management effort and trained on what project management involves.

The Web site and "WebShops"—Web-based workshops—facilitated widespread communications of the initiative offerings and online distance learning. Regional training events, where all courses are offered on site over an intense two-week period, helped fill the void left by discontinuation of the PM conferences.

The people impact line (cumulative) show a big increase when the initiative became self-funded, due to extensive marketing and introduction of new workshops. Progress was slow in 1997 because of company-wide cost constraints. Impact picked up again due to alternative delivery of WebShops and regional training events coming to division sites.

Funding a Project Office: A Cyclic Adventure

No simple answer exists for how to fund the project office. HP did it both ways and keeps swinging. It started with corporate funding, switched dramatically to a self-funding model, and then back to corporate.

Self-funding requires extensive marketing efforts to communicate offerings and motivate people to buy the services. It requires a focus on value—courses, written materials, conferences, consulting, and online workshops need to offer practical steps to take for immediate action. The HP initiative dramatically stepped up development of new workshops and other offerings when its survival depended on self-funding. This led to a positive quantum jump in its effectiveness and impact on the organization.

Self-funding requires shameless selling. That marketing effort may mark its downfall. Marketing takes time and effort, and that effort takes away from developing new products and value-added services (unless the initiative balances its portfolio to include these activities). Internal customers become annoyed with endless e-mail marketing campaigns about course offerings. The problem compounds when numerous corporate programs advertise through the same channels. Divisions typically ask corporate groups to get their acts together into one package. However, developing that package is a massive program itself—and is quickly abandoned.

Leadership needs to be clear about the purpose and focus it wants from the project office. Self-funding may be appropriate if the PO is viewed as a stand-alone activity that offers whatever its customers will buy. Corporate or overhead funding may be more appropriate if the PO is a strategic imperative that exists to discover new practices and lead the organization into new territories. Business units within the organization are usually too busy with new products to worry about developing world-class competency in project management as a competitive advantage. A hybrid approach with corporate and business funding could strike a good balance.

The HP initiative hit hard times in 1999 when company-wide cost cutting dramatically reduced its ability to recover costs. The director of its parent organization and the initiative manager became obsessed with finances and lost the drive toward value-added or development of new programs. Any strategic imperative was diluted.

Impact on team members? It certainly looked as though a high-performing team became stagnant. A couple of senior people took an early retirement package and another left to become a consultant. Staffing was down to a shell and by the middle of 2001, the initiative ceased to exist.

But life goes on. One author recently received this e-mail message:

> Years ago, much earlier in my career at HP, I attended a number of your group's project management courses, seminars, and WebShops (remember "Project Management—If it were easy, anyone could do it"?). I subscribed to the "Action Sheets" and became a devotee. They saved me more than once!
>
> You probably know that the Action Sheets are still alive. The Project Management curriculum is led by one of my colleagues in what is now the Technical Workforce Development (TWD) group within Enterprise Workforce Development (EWD).

Such cycles for a project office are not uncommon. In fact, the HP Initiative was blessed with more than a ten-year run from start to finish. Both staff and clients achieved significant personal benefit from the learning and sharing process. Many lasting values remain in the documented practices and workshop materials it disseminated. Once an organization is enlightened or high on the project management maturity curve, it is not long before new actions take place. Already a call has gone out from a reconstituted corporate education department for training on program management. The pendulum keeps swinging.

Summary

Staff the project office with people who want to be there, can see the big picture, possess requisite skills, and are enthusiastic about making a difference. Continue a training program to strengthen existing skills and learn new ones.

Operate a project office with clear roles and responsibilities. Position it strategically within the organization. Clarify whether it drives an organizational change or offers enabling factors such as training, expertise, or resources. Strive to keep people energized through recognition, rewards, and stimulating work. Making a contribution on a large scale across the organization is a key motivator.

Recognize the cycle of creation, recreation, and death of a project office. Times change. And so must the people.

The complete successful change agent

- Gathers people who are skilled and motivated to change the organization
- Seeks leaders who inspire—people will respond and achieve
- Operates from a power base within the organization
- Adapts the project office to meet changing times and conditions
- Drives increasing progression up a project management maturity model

PART THREE

MAKING CHANGE STICK

We are now ready to enter the final phase of the journey. If the change agent team has made it this far, anywhere between two and ten years have elapsed. The project office has no doubt changed many times, perhaps moving from a project control office, then to a project management center of excellence, and perhaps on to a strategic project office.

The organization itself has probably also changed many times, perhaps becoming more centralized, then moving to decentralized, then maybe back to centralized again. A chief project officer may have been appointed with power equal to the chief operating officer, thereby defining a matrix diamond form of organization structure. The CEO may have changed, perhaps several times. Several management fads have come and gone as people have moved from zero-based budgeting, been through a "Neutron Jack" type downsizing, tried reengineering and maybe even a balanced approach.

If the project office team has existed through all that change and has implemented the structures and processes suggested in this book so far, its staff may begin to feel that these changes have become permanent, that they have made a lasting change in the organization. Would that that were true.

Experience indicates a far different scenario. Think of the organization as being like a large rubber band. Adapting to all the project management changes has caused people in the organization to twist, turn, and stretch. As long as the tension is maintained, the organization remains in the stretched position. The moment the tension is released, the organization snaps back into its original shape.

Most large organizational change processes become identified with one person or one group of people. As long as those people remain in power, massive efforts are expended to help power the change. Meetings are held, conferences are attended, committees are formed, announcements are made in the annual report, all as organization members strive to show that they support the change. However, on the day that the lead person leaves or the change agent team falls from power, everything stops. Meetings on the change process are no longer held. The committees are disbanded—everyone suddenly has higher priorities. The announcement in the annual report is forgotten. The visitor coming to the organization the day after the lead person has left would have difficulty finding any trace of activity indicating that the change had ever been considered. The organization snaps back that fast.

The next two chapters address the problem of maintaining the change after the change initiators leave. Chapter Ten looks forward to a changed state to help you start building the framework to achieve it. Chapter Eleven offers summary reflections on the journey and discusses the templates on which to record it, which are included in the Appendix.

The key to success, of course, is to maintain the pressure for such a long time that there is no one left in the organization who remembers doing things in any other way. When that is the case there is no former situation for the organization to snap back into, and so the new processes become organizational reality. Good luck.

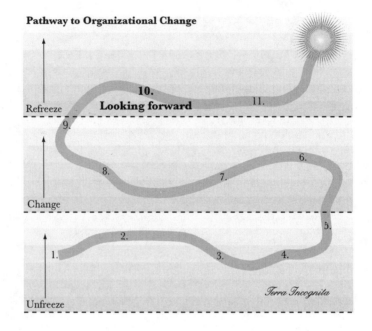

Pathway to Organizational Change

Refreeze

10.
Looking forward

11.

9.

8.

7.

6.

Change

2.

1.

3.

4.

5.

Terra Incognita

Unfreeze

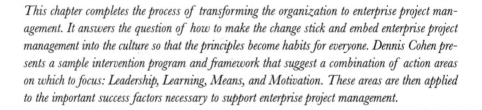

This chapter completes the process of transforming the organization to enterprise project management. It answers the question of how to make the change stick and embed enterprise project management into the culture so that the principles become habits for everyone. Dennis Cohen presents a sample intervention program and framework that suggest a combination of action areas on which to focus: Leadership, Learning, Means, and Motivation. These areas are then applied to the important success factors necessary to support enterprise project management.

CHAPTER TEN

LOOKING FORWARD:
EMBEDDING PROJECT PRACTICES
IN THE CULTURE OF THE ORGANIZATION

Dennis Cohen, Strategic Management Group

Once the project office begins to fully implement fundamental changes in the organization to support successful projects, a new problem emerges that is often ignored. The problem is how to consolidate the changes and prevent the company from sliding back to business as usual—the former steady state. Anyone who has been involved in large-scale organization change is always amazed at the resiliency of the old ways of doing things. Given the slightest misstep or the momentary drop in vigilance, what once seemed to be a successful change quickly slips back to the way things were.

In this chapter we focus on a number of methods to prevent this from happening. They are based on transforming the fundamental nature of the PMO—from center of excellence into cultural change agent. As a center of excellence the PMO is primarily the facilitator of a set of tools and techniques to run projects, programs, and project portfolios and the sponsor of a set of competencies for project managers to effectively use the tools and techniques. As a cultural change agent, the PMO becomes the sponsor of project management as a core business process. This requires increasing the breadth and depth of project management so that project practices reach all members of the organization. This process helps embed project practices into the culture of the organization.

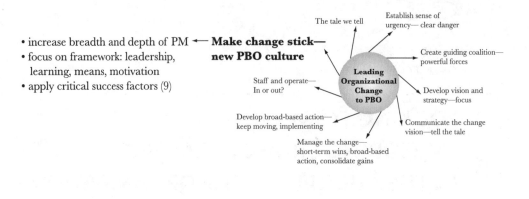

- increase breadth and depth of PM
- focus on framework: leadership, learning, means, motivation
- apply critical success factors (9)

Depth and Breadth

As seen in earlier chapters, when project management is first introduced into an organization, it often starts off as training for project managers. When projects are not going well, the first assumption is that project managers simply do not know how to do their job. If we just train them in a body of knowledge, the problem will be solved. This, of course, usually turns out to be a false promise. Education alone is never enough. Changing the organization so that projects become more successful is complex and time-consuming. And even implementing the tools and techniques, process, competencies, and best practices is not enough. Until the basic assumptions of project management become embedded in the underlying assumptions of the organization's culture, there will always be a tendency for the equilibrium of the system to swing back toward the original status quo.

Most PMOs focus on the typical PM community in areas that traditionally do projects—R&D projects for new product development, client engagement projects in a professional services firm, or internal projects by IT departments. Because these are high-profile projects involving core aspects of the business and large budgets, they are almost always the first targets of a PMO. The focus is on the professional project managers and team members. When things are done right the introduction includes managers of team members and upper managers who sponsor projects and serve on project review boards. People in these roles are taught the basic tool kit and best practices in PM and supported in using it.

In one financial services firm, major projects received all the attention. A PMO brought in consultants and training companies to help develop policy, process, and procedures as well as to train everyone involved in large strategic projects. They ignored the plethora of projects taking place throughout the organization in other areas because each one was much smaller than any of the strategic projects. However, in total this tier of work probably had as much if not more impact on the business of the company.

The PMO did not even officially acknowledge that these projects existed. During interviews with people who were struggling to implement projects outside the purview of the PMO, it became obvious that the most elementary project management best practices were being ignored. People confided that they went to kickoff meetings assuming that they were playing the role of project manager and finding that everyone else at the meeting had the same idea. In essence there were no project managers because the whole team was the project manager. The accidental project managers, team members, and project sponsors were simply going about their business as usual untouched by the PMO and all its efforts in the IT area. Since many of these smaller projects were essential for supporting the larger strategic projects, the business improvement potential of the larger strategic projects was squandered because PM as a core business process was not spread throughout the organization.

Solving this breadth problem requires that PMOs established at division or departmental levels are multiplied across the organization. One approach is to establish a corporate PMO to support the spread, as suggested in Chapter Four. Eventually, as the concept of the corporate office becomes more business process oriented, individual project offices should lose their ties to structural boundaries in the organization. They should be associated with related business processes to promote venture project management (Cohen and Graham, 2001), which was discussed in Chapter Two. This approach links project triple constraints to longer-term business outcomes and helps to embed project management into core business processes. For instance, instead of a project office focused only on R&D, the new perspective would include product management from concept generation through development to manufacturing and on through to sales. This way the organization begins to rely on project management as the primary driver of the cash flow associated with the whole value chain.

Changing the Project System

For projects to proceed more successfully, something like the *Project Management Body of Knowledge (PMBOK™)* and its associated best practices must be carried out, but individuals cannot carry them out alone. An individual certified project manager is not enough to make a successful project. It takes an organization. The project manager is only part of the equation. The project team, the system of project stakeholders who influence the project, and the rest of the organization who constitute the project's environment must support the project manager for projects to be successful. The first step is not to educate just the PM but rather to educate and change the behavior of all actors in the environment. By doing this the organization can begin to change the set of reciprocal roles and relationships that constitute the project management system.

One example is the issue of project planning. In general an important contributor to project success is that sufficient time was devoted to planning by the project manager and the project team. The time needed to plan and when it will be needed will vary from project type to project type. Projects that do not devote the proper amount of time to the planning process suffer from problems that lead to rework. This extends the time of the project beyond what was saved by not planning enough in the first place. The solution to this problem looks simple. Teach project managers how to plan and make sure they understand that it is important to plan. This is often not enough, however. Upper managers, impatient to move up the project deadline, often demand that the team stop meeting so much (to plan) and get to work. Team members often resist the planning because they do not appreciate its importance, or their bosses do not support their wasting all that time in meetings when there is departmental work to be done. Not until all relevant actors learn their reciprocal roles in the planning process and play them well will planning proceed as needed to produce successful projects. This means that project management is not just for project managers anymore. It is for everyone as it becomes recognized as a core business process.

The importance of the project environment was demonstrated by Graham and Englund (1997). As mentioned in Chapters Two and Three, the Strategic Management Group (SMG), a performance-consulting firm based in Philadelphia, worked with Graham to develop the Project Environment Assessment Tool (PEAT)—a tool designed to diagnose the areas of strength and weakness in the system (see discussion of success factors later in this chapter).

SMG and Graham also developed an organizationally based performance consulting approach to providing solutions for poor project system performance as diagnosed by PEAT. At the core of this performance consulting approach is an online training and performance support program aimed at all important reciprocal roles and relationships in the project management system. This program, called Maximizing Project Performance (MPP), targets the system as a whole in order to align and mobilize its actors to provide a foundation of shared knowledge, assumptions, and reciprocal role-based best practices to anchor improvement. Because it is Internet based, the program can influence large numbers of people quickly. This, along with other supporting tactics, helps to accelerate and then deepen the change. The way this works is based on both the dynamics of individual learning in support of behavior change and the way that these dynamics roll up into a system of cultural change. An analysis of the process can suggest methods for supporting the change over the long run.

At the individual level, social learning is the basis for behavior. Every behavior that we engage in is learned behavior of one kind or another. However, just because we learn it does not automatically mean that we do it. Any kind of changed behavior in an organization needs to be supported by four factors in a framework called L^2M^2—Leadership, Learning, Means, and Motivation.

Leadership is a well-articulated communication from the organization of what kind of new behavior is required and why it is required, along with a road map of the change that will take place over time.

Learning is the process of supplying the knowledge and skill necessary for individuals to carry out the new behaviors. In the case of enterprise project management it includes role-based knowledge and skill for all aspects of the project management process. This starts with project selection and proceeds to the end of the project outcome life cycle (Cohen and Graham, 2001, p. 9 for definition of POL). It includes learning support from the *PMBOK*, project leadership, and business skills, among other areas.

Means are all the resources necessary to carry out the behaviors, including tools, organizational policies and structures, and time. For enterprise project management this includes but is not limited to a project selection process, a project management process, a venture project management process, a supportive organization design, software-based planning tools, and information systems.

Motivation is the formal and informal system of incentives and consequences that reinforce the new behaviors. These again are differentiated by role so that the required role-based behaviors are supported in all parts of the organization.

Only when all four of these factors are working in concert will behavior begin to change. Without Leadership, organization actors will not know how to apply their new knowledge and skill in concert with business strategic and tactical objectives. Without Learning, actors may know what they are supposed to do from Leadership, but not know how to do it. Without Means, actors may know what to do and how to do it, but not have the tools and resources to carry it out. Without Motivation, actors may know what leaders want and how to do it, and have the resources to carry it out, but simply not bother to do it.

It is not easy to coordinate all four of these factors for all reciprocal roles and relationships in the project management system. The process is long and arduous. At the same time that the project managers are learning their craft, the team members must learn their role to participate effectively in the system. Without team training, members are resistant to such PM practices as participative planning and regularly scheduled core team meetings. They may lack the knowledge and skill to engage in effective estimating or contribute to risk management processes. Individual contributors are often unprepared for working in the cross-functional team environment of a project. Upper managers need to learn effective project portfolio management to establish the system in the first place, and must also learn how to support project management best practices such as stable core teams and triple constraint trade-offs. Managers who supply team members to the project need to learn to support stable teams and the priority of project work.

A specific example of how to coordinate these factors comes from the MPP online program. It is keyed to five factors that are most likely to block the alignment and mobilization of the project system:

- Upper management does not often support project management best practices.
- Project planning is not done effectively.
- Project teams are not developed effectively.
- Project managers do not use a consistent project management process.
- Customers and end users are not involved enough in the project process.

The MPP program helps to support a successful intervention because it supports the factors of L^2M^2. In a successful intervention, everybody will be informed about what changes in their behavior will have to take place. MPP does this as an online program that is delivered to the desktops of everyone in the organization. Each actor learns the knowledge and skill necessary to engage in the changed behavior. MPP does this through simulation and tutorials. Everyone receives the resources necessary to carry out the change. MPP supplies performance support tools for project management. Participants experience positive reinforcement for changing and consequences for not changing. MPP provides the opportunity to provide this reinforcement through custom messages.

MPP provides a quick start and solid foundation for change by aligning large numbers of people quickly around the five major issues. It also supports the process over the long run by serving as a resource center throughout the change. Dennis Cohen, vice president for the Project Management Practice area at SMG, says, "When everyone is engaged in this process together, we say that the system is aligned and individuals in the system are mobilized. MPP has a community function to help promote alignment and mobilization. All of this increases the probability that the change will take place, and that the company will realize the value of improved project management." Will this be enough to guarantee that the change will last? No. For lasting results, the change must become part of the culture of the organization.

Why is it not enough to get the project management system aligned and mobilized? One would assume that once this is done the system would develop a positive inertia that would favor the change. With each role reinforcing the other roles this would seem to be the case. And it is an important first step—and one that many organizations never even get to—but unfortunately it is not enough. Built-in forces left over from the past constantly pull the organization away from the direction of the desired end state and back toward the starting state, simply because of the dynamics of organization culture. Past behaviors always lurk beneath the surface of an organization, waiting to reemerge. Why? Because most people in the organization remember the way things used to be. In many cases things used to be that way because there were advantages for people having them that way. The good old days often bring back fond memories. Even when memories are not so fond, they are still familiar. During the stress of the change process, familiar is often attractive.

Take the case of AT&T at the beginning of divestiture almost twenty years ago. A major benefit that AT&T sought to achieve with divestiture was to enable it to compete with IBM in the computer industry. A key role in this strategy was the new branch managers for AT&T Information Systems. These people were in charge of sales branches in the midst of the very competitive beginnings of the personal computer industry. Many had started their careers by taking orders as Yellow Pages salespeople. They were ill prepared for the changes awaiting them.

As they discussed their present state, the major topic of their conversation went something like this, "Wow, last year was incredibly chaotic and this year is turbulent as hell, but I am sure that next year will calm down and be much more like the environment we're used to." During their first year many of them refused to believe that the future was never going to be like what they were used to. This was because what they were used to was a noncompetitive, monopolistic regulated environment and an organizational culture formed in that environment. Their present situation was a very competitive nonregulated and turbulent environment—but no one wanted to see that. They found it easier to succumb to the seductive power of their collective memory of the "good old days." This is organizational culture at its strongest. It conjures up the feeling that this is the way that things have always been around here and that anything new will soon pass, reverting to the old familiar pattern.

The Dynamics of Organizational Culture

As presented in Chapter One, organizational change typically goes through three phases—unfreezing, change, and refreezing. The change phase at the organizational level involves new structures and processes. At the individual level it is a process of cognitive restructuring (learning new things) and changing behavior. The refreezing phase at the organizational level is a process of changing the organizational culture. This means that the shared basic assumptions about reality change. At the individual level what has been learned turns into what is known, and the new behaviors become habits that occur without thinking about them. The transition from change to refreezing is difficult because organizational culture is a system with its own dynamic that produces a shared point of view based on the habits of the past. This is called a *social construction of reality*. How does culture as a process create a social construction of reality? To understand how this occurs helps to develop insights on how difficult refreezing can be and point toward methods to make it happen.

Think of culture as a process that occurs in groups to socially construct the reality in which the group functions. Dennis Cohen offers the following discussion of the social construction of reality as his interpretation of Berger and Luckmann's work (1966). He uses some of their concepts to describe one aspect of culture, whereas their original intention was to develop a sociology of knowledge. The process consists of three interacting subprocesses.

Externalization. The first subprocess is externalization. People in the group express their beliefs, thoughts, and values through action. Every time someone in the organization does anything, it is a result of externalizing a mental process and converting it into behavior. Everyone with whom the actor comes into contact experiences this action.

Socialization. The second subprocess is socialization. Everyone in the organization is subject to social learning reinforced by the behaviors of others. They are told to learn policies and procedures when they enter the organization. They are subjected to positive reinforcement and negative consequences when they follow or break formal and informal rules. This helps them to learn what everyone in the cultural system believes is right and real.

Objectivation. The third subprocess is objectivation. Because of the reinforcing nature over time of the first two subprocesses, everyone experiences the implied rules of behavior and underlying basic assumption as a concrete, objective reality (Berger and Luckmann, 1966, p. 61). This is why organizational culture is often defined simply as "The way we do things around here."

In the beginning of any organization the founders start the process with beliefs about how the organization should function and externalize them through their behaviors. Others who enter the new organization learn these beliefs through socialization and the process of objectivation begins. Soon everyone is engaged in experiencing the underlying beliefs as a concrete reality. People forget that the rules of the game were actually invented by human beings. Instead, the rules are experienced as something that has always been, and will always be.

A simple example might be a family enterprise formed in an empty territory. Say a man and his wife find a plot of land in the wilderness that is suitable for farming, but first it must be cleared. They lack any modern tools, so they begin to work together to move large objects such as boulders and tree limbs off the plot to clear it. As they work they begin to develop habits simply because it is easier and more efficient to always approach the objects and lift them in the same manner. So the man always stands on the right side and the woman always on the left. They pick up the object on the count of three, walk it over to the edge of the property and on the count of three again throw it into the brush bordering the plot. Soon, out of habit this becomes their work process.

As time goes by they have children who first watch their parents work and then begin to help them. Always they see that the man is on the right and the woman is on the left as well as the rest of the process. When they try to do something different such as count to four instead of three, the object gets dropped and their parents administer negative reinforcement. The parents, of course, praise the children when they get it right. The children were not around when the parents developed the process. As far as they are concerned, this is the way it has always been. It is something to be learned. It is reality, not something that was invented by a human being.

Organizational culture develops according to the same dynamic. Changing this dynamic to achieve true cultural change means that organizations must deal with all three subprocesses at the same time until they all change. If this does not happen, the unchanged subprocess will bring the system back to equilibrium, the initial state that the change began with. Using the L^2M^2 framework helps get a grip on the subprocesses. Leadership is the process of declaring that the existing reality must change; it begins to change the objectivation process as it starts the cognitive restructuring that is the change process. This is intensified and reinforced by Learning. This process helps to complete the cognitive restructuring and provide a common map for everyone to follow. It is important that all parties to the change are subject to the learning, or the process will not be complete. Means provides the artifacts necessary to consolidate and implement the changed behavior. Motivation issues ensure that the changed behavior prevails over time due to positive reinforcement and negative consequences. It is an important part of the socialization process that turns cognitive learning into social learning with longer-term consequences.

If all these changes prevail over time, the new behaviors become habitual, eventually becoming embedded in the culture. The final definitive end to the process is when people do not remember a time when things were done differently. This may not occur until everyone who was there at the beginning of the change has left the organization or retired. At the very least it will not be consolidated until those who are fundamentally opposed to the change have left the organization and everyone has become totally habituated to the new way of doing things.

Steps to a Project-Friendly Culture

To sustain the change necessary to fundamentally improve project management as a core business process, the project management office (PMO) can engage in the steps outlined in this section. In some cases the PMO may be able to take the steps directly, and in other cases it may simply become the catalyst to influence other forces in the organization to engage. The steps are based on nine success factors defined in PEAT, which in turn are based on the research and writing of Graham and Englund (1997) and Cohen and Graham (2001). For each success factor we list actions and describe what success looks like to sustain the change. These are grouped by L^2M^2 categories. In addition, for each success factor there is a discussion of the cultural implications of organizational change. We point out existing cultural values that may enable the change to a project-friendly culture and those existing cultural traits that may inhibit such a change.

Strategic Emphasis

Strategic emphasis, the first success factor from PEAT, is an indicator of how well the company aligns projects with its business strategy. To do this there should be a sound project selection process in place supported by the upper management team. Business strategy should be developed, well articulated, and understood by the project manager and team members. There are a number of enablers associated with each of the four categories of L^2M^2 to promote the needed change in this area and consolidate it into the organizational culture.

In the Leadership area the PMO can emphasize the following enablers. Communicating strategy to project managers and team members and framing the strategy so project trade-offs are clearly connected to strategy implementation will begin to equip people to incorporate strategy in their decision making and project implementation. Developing a policy and process for incorporating strategic priorities in the project selection process will help each project begin with strategy in mind. If leaders communicate the big picture to project managers and team members through formal and informal communication channels such as meetings, e-mail, and newsletters, this reinforces the strategic direction.

Develop a standard policy that mandates a process for each project in the portfolio to define the final goal statement. Include heavy project team involvement along with final approval by upper management. Also develop an interactive process between directed strategy as articulated by upper management and emergent strategy as implemented by project personnel, producing a realized strategy that is realistic and adds value to the company (Cohen and Graham, 2001, pp. 64–68). Management can also specify functional manager roles in supporting team members' project work, along with ways for projects to develop measures of success that facilitate agreement with functional managers. This will also help to align and strengthen strategy implementation.

In the Learning area the PMO can train project managers and team members so they are proficient in applying company strategic priorities to their project work. They can also train project managers to work with Finance and Marketing to develop a business case or to understand the business case that Finance and Marketing develop. Training project sponsors and selection board members to use strategic priorities in their selection process supports a strategic project portfolio. When project managers and team members learn strategic business acumen for project success, they are better able to apply sound business decision making in their projects. Training project managers and team members to construct goal statements that include both the individual project goal and the link to strategy also reinforces strategic alignment. Training upper managers to engage the team in an interactive process to develop the final goal statement further supports strategy implementation. Also train functional managers on project management best practices to support the project, and train project managers on how to develop realistic and relevant measures of success at the beginning of the project.

For Means, a PMO can include the development of a checklist or process to help project managers and team members think through the strategic priorities of each project and determine alignment with corporate strategy. Supply templates, procedures, and standard criteria to help in the selection process. Actors also need time for training as well as follow-up reference materials, decision aids, and other performance support resources. Management needs to provide both the time needed by the team to develop goal statements and a process template or support tool for the team to use. Finally, management systems can allocate time needed for functional personnel to support project work and provide processes to include functional support. Progress becomes evident when there are measures of success and a process for tracking project outcome life cycles to collect the data needed to measure success over the long run.

Motivation reinforcement can include project sponsors and review board members asking about how the project supports strategy, offering recognition for good work in this area, and suggesting remedial work to correct deficiencies. Strategic alignment should be identified for any project before moving from initiating to planning. The PMO makes the selection board members and project managers accountable for the business success of their projects through a performance management system. Reinforcing desired behaviors through informal rewards and recognition helps to motivate everyone to manage the project portfolio and individual projects with strategy in mind.

Project sponsors and review board members can engage project managers and team members in a dialogue about the big picture. Make this an agenda item during periodic reviews. It is motivating to recognize and reward good goal statements in the review process. Functional managers' performance management evaluations can include an evaluation of how well they support their direct reports' project work. Recognize and reward project managers and teams based on short- and long-term measures of success that are linked to strategic alignment.

Basic cultural assumptions that would block this success factor include believing that strategy does not matter because companies cannot influence their own destiny by developing a strategy. Another inhibiting basic assumption would be that strategy is a top secret plan that only upper management should be exposed to. If upper management believes that they should be the font of all truth and simply direct those below them in what to do, this, too, would get in the way of success.

Enabling the strategic emphasis success factor would be basic assumptions that important decisions can be made at the project level as emerging strategy to align project decisions with directed strategy. Another would be that strategy is important and that it should be communicated throughout the organization. In an organizational culture where upper management assumes that strategy is implemented simply by being articulated, this success factor will have a low probability of success. In a culture that explicitly focuses on the execution of strategy after it has been articulated and emphasizes the interaction of directed strategy with emerging strategy to create realized strategy, it has a greater chance for success.

Upper Management Support

Upper management support is the second PEAT success factor. This factor is based on the fact that projects are not really separate from the management structure of the organization. They are embedded in it. Without support by management for projects and for the process that ensures successful projects, the organization suffers. Upper management needs to support each project in the first place and to continue to support project managers even when they stumble. Upper managers need to refrain from interfering in day-to-day project management. Most important, they should fully support project management best practices in the organization.

For Leadership, the PMO can specify the project management process including the roles and responsibilities of project sponsors, review board members, and functional managers to support the project and process. It can specify the role of project sponsor as a formal part of the project management process and define the sponsor's proper planning role in the project process. Another important supporting factor is for leaders to emphasize how important planning is for ulti-mate project success and how upper management should support the planning process. Leaders can communicate reciprocal roles and responsibilities between upper management and project managers in the project management process. They can stipulate how negotiations should occur on issues of project goals, pri-ority of constraints, and major milestones as well as the stage-gate project review process. Designating the team's important processes as a formal part of project management helps to support teamwork. Communicating how important it is for everyone to follow and support project management best practices helps build the legitimacy of these practices in the organization.

For Learning, the PMO can train upper managers about the project manage-ment process, their roles and responsibilities, and how they can support an envi-ronment that enables projects for business results. In such training sessions, upper managers often say that they did not realize that project management is often coun-terintuitive from a standard department manager's point of view. Training sponsors and project managers in their reciprocal roles and responsibilities for managing projects also provides further support for projects. Convince and train upper man-agers to support the planning process. Help them understand why planning is so important and how it supports their goals for reducing project cycle time. Give upper managers and project managers learning opportunities to work together. Develop a roles and responsibilities matrix that specifies responsibilities of each role at the beginning of the project; this helps to avoid upper management interference.

To provide the Means necessary for the change, the PMO can develop guides, templates, Web sites, and job aids to help upper managers remember and execute their roles and responsibilities. Reinforce learning. Recognize the sponsor role as formal work and provide the time needed to carry out the responsibilities, or the work will always become "my other work" that never gets done. Provide guide-lines, coaching, job aids, and performance support tools to support the roles. Spec-ify responsibilities in relation to other organizational roles so that the sponsor has enough authority to prevail in conflicts with other managers. Furnish guidelines and other reminders to help upper management remember their role in support-ing the planning process. Specify the project team's requirements for time to plan, and provide performance support tools based on the specified process and guide-lines. Developing a roles and responsibilities matrix to illustrate the suggested re-lationships between upper management and the project manager and team will facilitate negotiations on how they work together. This means that the process also allows for flexibility to adjust for circumstances and style. Everyone needs time al-located to follow these core processes.

For Motivation, executives need to recognize and reward upper management behavior that supports the project management process and discourages behavior that does not. Sponsors and review board members should be held accountable not only for project results but for following project processes as well. Functional managers also need to be accountable for their work on projects. Provide informal rewards and recognition for good processes and remedial actions for poor processes. Hold sponsors and review board members accountable for supporting sufficient planning. All players—upper managers with project responsibilities, project managers, and team members—should be accountable for short- and long-term project success. Provide informal recognition for those who engage in the preferred process. Hold formal project reviews that include process reviews.

Basic cultural assumptions that may inhibit the change include any that contradict project management best practices. For instance, in a culture that does not regard planning as a productive activity, it will be difficult to encourage upper management to support project-planning processes. Basic assumptions of hierarchy as micromanagement with a tight chain of command may inhibit the change. Another inhibitor is a basic assumption that there is never enough time to really engage in process.

Assumptions that would enable the process include those that value process in general. An assumption that there is always enough time to do something the right way is extremely helpful. A basic assumption that it is acceptable, useful, and expected for subordinates and bosses to negotiate over deadlines, budgets, and specifications also enables this success factor.

Project Planning Support

Project planning support, the third PEAT success factor, emphasizes the importance to project success of having the team participate in an extensive planning process to align everyone on the triple constraints and business goals of the project. The planning process should specify deliverables, lay out milestones, and use historical data from past projects. Include a budget, business plan, and risk plan. The deadline specified in the project should be realistic in the eyes of the team. The project manager cannot do this alone. Without the support of the project team and other major stakeholders, it will not happen. All roles must be supported by L^2M^2.

To provide Leadership, the PMO should specify the planning process as part of the project management process. It must emphasize that the participative process is more important than the plan itself and explain why it is important for project success, so as to support the process of planning over pro forma, formalistic project plans. Stipulating the use of historical data as part of the project planning process will help everyone learn from experience. The process can be further supported by defining ways to finalize the deliverables and milestones on which all stakeholders agree, and communicating a procedure in which these are written down in detail with all parties signing off, showing their understanding and agreement. When the project is not allowed to progress to the next stage without these signatures, the process begins to have teeth. When the PMO articulates a risk management process and explains the importance of following that process, risk management begins to take form. The project deadline can be changed from a fixed point set by fiat to an array of probabilistic negotiated dates by articulating a process for determining and changing a project deadline, and then communicating it to all involved parties.

For Learning, upper management, project managers, and team members can all be trained how to perform their specified reciprocal roles and to carry out their responsibilities in the planning process. Project managers and team members should learn to access and properly use historical data in planning. Include training on how to avoid misuse of historical data and how to learn from past mistakes. Further develop the process by training all parties to develop clear specifications of deliverables and milestones, and to communicate these specifications to each other. Coming to a mutual understanding that is more consensual than imposed from above leads to greater probability of project success. Risk management training includes training on how to communicate potential risks throughout the organization: project risks in general for projects, how to deal with risks for upper managers, and how to share risks between project and upper managers.

To furnish Means, the PMO can supply the tools needed to engage in proper planning, making sure to support participative planning and collaborative work such as Web-based planning tools and team rooms. Develop a process and tools to collect, store, and retrieve needed historical data for projects, and provide templates and support tools to guide development of deliverables and guidelines. Authorize and communicate the time needed for negotiations and final agreement. Supply forms for the formal document that appropriate parties must sign. Provide tools to estimate and analyze risks as well as collect historical data that can help determine probabilities of common risk factors. Provide lists of common risks and their usual mitigation and standard contingency plans when applicable as well as a process for documenting and communicating final deadlines.

For Motivation, the PMO can ask everyone to accept accountability for the planning process as well as the plan. Include a process review at the beginning of each project's planning phase. Engaging in informal recognition and rewards for following and supporting the process goes a long way to get it started and to sustain it. Review the use of historical data for planning, as part of the project review process, to reinforce its use. Hold the project manager and team accountable for accessing and using all available data. Hold everyone accountable for producing final documents, and review the process that led to it. Review risk plans. Reward project managers and teams who practice good risk planning, even if a problem occurs in spite of all the planning. Point out possible consequences for teams that do not develop a risk plan, even if everything turns out OK. Finally, function as a gatekeeper and question project teams that try to move ahead without specified, communicated, and negotiated deadlines. These steps position the PMO to support planning as a process rather than a product.

Cultural assumptions that may inhibit this change include the idea that planning is not necessary for business success. Another is that planning should be a top-down process with those in the upper part of the organization doing the planning and those in subordinate positions carrying out the plan. This interferes with the participative planning process. In a culture that treats everything as controllable, risk planning will be difficult. By contrast, participative and collaborative cultures help to support participative planning. Cultures that have dealt with risk in other areas such as financial services firms or energy exploration companies may hold basic assumptions that make it easier for them to support risk management in other types of projects or in other areas of the process.

Customer and End-User Input

Customer and end-user input is the fourth success factor. This emphasizes the importance of bringing customer and end-user needs into projects early and often. It is supported by practices such as including end users in the planning process and allowing customers on the core team. It also requires the development of a quality plan. Organizations that are technically driven or internally oriented often have a difficult time doing this. Without successfully translating this input into project outcomes, projects usually fail to meet end users' needs and thus fail to produce value.

For Leadership, the PMO can specify a course of action for including customers and end users in the planning process. Explain why it is important and how it will support project success. Define a process that deeply involves team members in learning about the problems that customers and end users are trying to solve. Require that project teams use an appropriate prototyping technique or an equivalent process to determine end-user expectations. The PMO can also mandate a quality planning and management process to formalize aspects of improving customer and end-user satisfaction.

For Learning, the training of project personnel in methods for observing, interviewing, using prototypes, and other methods for understanding customer and end user needs and expectations go a long way to support this success factor. Train team members in methods that help them to observe, communicate with, and empathize with customers and end users to fully understand the problems they are trying to solve. Also train the team to understand user expectations.

The PMO can supply the Means necessary to support customer and end-user input by providing tools and methods to enable the inclusion of customers and end users in the project planning process and throughout project implementation. Develop methods to make it easy for project teams to access customers and end users. Enlist upper management support for customer visits. Provide tools to help collect data from customers and end users as well as guidelines for relevant processes and other support tools and job aids to carry out these processes. Ensure that time and resources are allocated to carry out customer contact.

For Motivation, use project reviews to hold the team accountable for including customers and end users during the planning process and throughout the rest of the project. Continuously inquire about each team's understanding of customer and end user problems. These questions convey a sense of importance. Make project managers and teams accountable for ultimate success of the project outcome life cycle. Designing the quality process so it is user-friendly encourages usage. During project reviews, hold teams accountable for using a quality planning and review process.

Basic cultural assumptions that might inhibit the change toward including more customer and end user input include the idea that all important knowledge comes from technical experts and that they can say what the customer and end user should have. A basic assumption that the customer and end user really do not know what they want (which is sometimes true) and that they will never know what they want until they see the technically superior product produced by the experts will also get in the way. In companies that assume that wisdom comes from the hierarchy, it will be difficult to shift orientation from the expectations of the project sponsor or upper management to end user needs unless they are the same. Companies that hold a basic assumption that the customer should be the center of attention will have an easier time improving on this success factor. Acceptance of the principles and values of Total Quality Management or Six Sigma programs help to prime the pump for this factor.

One computer and server manufacturing company holds project managers accountable for projected sales of the products they develop. The business case that the project manager develops with Marketing becomes a contract for the project manager and team. This is a very effective way to motivate the project manager and team to craft the project outcome to meet customer and end user needs because only then will it sell at the level guaranteed by the business case contract.

Project Team Support

Project team support is the fifth success factor. Good project management requires cross-functional core teams for an integrated quality outcome. Manage and support them as a team rather than a group of individuals who simply represent the interests of their functions. Team members need to understand the benefits of working on their projects and feel they will be rewarded for this work. They need to focus on one or two projects at a time rather than many and have their skills matched to the appropriate project to be effective team members. For many companies, this requires a radically new approach to work that requires the support of all important project management stakeholders.

For Leadership, the best way to support teams is to specify the use of cross-functional core teams for all projects. Explain why they are important and how stakeholders promote project success. Implement a core team selection process that aligns the benefits for team members who work on the project with the benefits for the project and company. Design a process to match member skills to project needs. It helps to limit people to a maximum of two projects at a time so that they will be able to fully contribute to each team. Communicate the importance of following best practices in project selection to keep the project system from becoming overloaded.

For Learning, train project managers in core team design and selection techniques. Upper management training can include ways to support the selection process, as well as understanding how to facilitate the core team concept and process. Train core team members how to work as a team and what to expect to happen during the team development process. Train project managers in leadership, team development skills, and performance management competencies. Upper managers often need training on the project portfolio management process so that the project system does not become overloaded. Project and functional managers may also need to be trained on how to participate in the project portfolio management process.

For the Means necessary to promote project team support, the PMO can provide a process for core team selection. The process should specify that core team members will be full time for the life of the project. Provide tools and templates to support the process to align team member skills and needs with project requirements. This may include a project human resource tracking system and a performance management process that supports project work. Implement a project portfolio management process and the tools necessary to support it, including a resource management system, project pipeline tracking system, and project tracking system. Developing the tools necessary to implement the process, including a data bank on potential project personnel with their preferences for project work, will support the team building process to an even greater extent.

For Motivation, the PMO can provide positive reinforcement for project managers who select and maintain their core teams. Hold the project manager and core members accountable for forming and maintaining the team. Hold upper management accountable for supporting core teams. Holding project managers accountable for team member satisfaction helps to align their goals with team goals. Include project work as an important part of the performance appraisal

process. Holding upper management accountable for managing the project portfolio so that project managers and team members are not overloaded will also reinforce this success factor. To further align functional managers' support of project
team needs, the PMO can supply project member satisfaction scores (how well
members think they have been matched to projects) as well as project manager
satisfaction scores (how well they think that the project requirements for personnel have been met).

Basic cultural assumptions have a lot of impact on this success factor. Particularly in Anglo-American cultures, teamwork itself is problematic. These cultures
are the most individualistic in the world. A sense of team identity is not natural.
It must be practiced and learned. Almost all companies talk teamwork but reward
individuals and reveal the true basic assumption that it is somehow not fair to reward a team member who did not stand out as a star individual performer. The
past fifteen years show a growing acceptance of the team concept, but it is still
not universal. Tension remains in many organizations. However, in those organizations that accept and reward teamwork, this success factor is easier to promote.

Project Performance Support

Project performance support is the sixth success factor. The company environment needs to support performance in projects for them to be successful. Assign
sufficient resources, give team members sufficient time to work on projects, and
assign sufficient space for project work. Trust between management and project
participants is a necessary condition for open communications. The existence of a
group such as the project office assigned to focus on improving project management leads to greater performance on this success factor.

For Leadership, the PMO can drive to implement a process that matches
needed resources to project needs, or postpones projects until necessary resources
are available. Advocating full-time membership for project team members whenever practical goes a long way toward increasing probability of project success.
When full-time team membership is not possible, the PMO can lead negotiations
between project managers and functional managers on time allocations for each
team member. On a larger scale, the organization needs to emphasize the importance of an open learning organization and support the formation of a project
office, internal project consulting, or a support staff group to further provide a
nurturing environment for successful projects.

For Learning, training managers to recognize the need to supply adequate resources helps to ensure realistic staffing. Training project managers and functional
managers how to work out the time allocation of project team members (when
they are on the project part time) helps to support projects when full-time team

membership is not possible. Training upper management to use authentic communication techniques promotes open, risk-free communication about problems that may arise. PMO personnel can constantly be training in the latest project management best practices, data-gathering procedures, and consulting techniques.

For Means, the PMO can supply all tools necessary to implement the project process from project selection to the end of the project outcome life cycle. Provide a way for managers and project managers to put a project on hold if it does not have sufficient resources. Provide planning tools to project managers and functional managers to help them determine the work they require of team members, and how they might adjust that to meet the needs of each member's functional manager. Develop a process to enable communication about projects throughout the organization; the PMO can serve as the hub. The support group can acquire diagnostic tools such as PEAT to help them develop methods for closing gaps between the present state of project management and a more desired future state.

For Motivation, the PMO can point out the dangers of proceeding if projects do not have adequate resources. Holding both project managers and functional managers accountable for the utilization and satisfaction of team members helps to focus them on optimizing human resources. Rewarding the communication of bad news is one important way to reinforce this behavior. Provide feedback and coaching to upper managers on open, honest communication actions that support authenticity and integrity about project work. When possible, the PMO can run as an internal business, dependent on charging for its services. This structure supports and motivates an achievement focus, instead of projecting a controlling atmosphere.

Basic cultural assumptions derive from the status of project management in the organization. In organizations that recognize project management as a core business process, issues of performance support are actively under debate and consideration, even if they may be undecided. In organizations in which project management is seen as a cluster of competencies for people who happen to manage projects, there are more likely to be blind spots about most of these issues.

Communication and Information Systems Support

Communication and information systems support, the seventh success factor, is supported by an updated project plan that allows all stakeholders to easily obtain project information. This factor signifies an environment in which it is easy for team members to communicate with all other project stakeholders. It depends on a management information system developed specifically to support project management. The most important source of project information comes from project reviews, which need to be held regularly, and the findings need to be shared across the organization.

For Leadership, the PMO can specify formats for project documents designed for easy understanding by everyone, as well as methods of distribution and posting so they are easily accessible to all stakeholders. Specifying a liberal policy for open access to stakeholders by project team members helps support this success factor. To help the organization make the best use of project management knowledge, the PMO can aid in the implementation of a project information system, and facilitate project reviews at each major milestone and a final review at the end. In addition, it can evangelize and institutionalize knowledge management processes for project review data and lessons learned. The PMO can sponsor conferences or forums where interested and informed people gather to interact and share their insights.

For Learning, train project managers and team members how to write clear documents and how to post them. Train project team members in communications and how to optimize their contacts with stakeholders—competencies often lacking in technically trained project managers and team members. Reciprocally, also train stakeholders how to respond appropriately when approached by project members. Everyone should be trained to input data into any knowledge management system, run the system, and use the output of the system. Project managers, team members, and upper management can benefit from training on how to conduct a project review and why it is important to prevent reviews from being formalistic and without real substance—or worse, a search for scapegoats. To support a knowledge management system, the PMO can train project managers and team members how to input data from their project reviews and how to access data at the beginning of their projects to learn from other projects' experience.

For Means, the provision of templates for project documents and communications supports this success factor, as does supplying an electronic system for posting documents, making them easily accessible to all stakeholders while maintaining security and version control. Providing guidelines, e-mail addresses, phone numbers, and other appropriate access information is important to supplement the electronic database. In some cases personal contact may be more frequent than database access. Inform stakeholders who are on the list and request that they respond when contacted. The PMO can support the use of the formal system by providing reminders, training aids, and help screens. Providing a project review process and tools to support it, designing the process carefully, and installing an electronic storage and retrieval system are all important supports for this success factor. Providing an informal community chat bulletin board for project managers and team members will be a first step in helping to develop a community of practice.

For Motivation, the PMO can follow through to ensure all managers and stakeholders use the system, reward and recognize those who use it, and highlight consequences for those who do not. Reinforce proper contact behavior for team members by sharing observations and supplying personal feedback. Devise metrics that make stakeholders accountable for responding to team member requests (and make sure those metrics lead to consequences when people do not respond to requests). Positively reinforcing proper use of the system will probably not be enough. Making it user friendly to promote use will go a long way toward supporting its use. Get explicit commitments that project managers, sponsors, and review board members will conduct project reviews and take action on their findings. If a knowledge management system is set up and its use is ignored, it will probably languish. There is no better way to extinguish desired behavior than to ignore it.

Basic cultural assumptions that support this factor are espoused acknowledgment that information and knowledge management are important open processes for the success of the company. An inhibiting assumption would be that knowledge is power and everyone should closely guard their knowledge rather than share it. Another inhibiting assumption would link a need-to-know norm to knowledge based on position or status. Times of great changes place a huge burden on communication systems, which can either support or hurt the change initiative, depending on the values of its leaders and how well good communications are supported by the project office.

Organization Support

Organization support is the eighth success factor. This depends on how well the organization supports project management best practices. It includes supporting teamwork, applying a consistent project management process, and defining the role of project manager as a professional position with specific selection criteria and career path. This factor is a measure of important aspects of the organization's culture necessary to support project management over the long term.

For Leadership, the PMO can specify that rewards and recognition will consider teamwork as a crucial factor. Encouraging the use of one adaptable process across the organization, with variations based on project size, complexity, and type, helps to achieve common terminology and consistent expectations through project life cycles. Designating *project manager* as an official job title with a recognized career path is crucial. Project management as a professional position is supported by establishing a standard selection process, as is emphasizing that project management is a core business process essential for business success.

For Learning, the PMO can train managers to set goals for performance in terms of contribution to the project team rather than in terms of individual behavior. It can provide training so everyone understands how to use the adopted project management process. The process can be further supported by training project managers in a curriculum that meets the needs of the type, size, and complexity of projects they will work on. A certification process can qualify them for progressive levels of size and complexity as they gain training and learning on the job. All training can include technical process and techniques, leadership, and business skills. The PMO can provide learning resources to reinforce these factors over time.

For Means, the PMO can develop a formal process that rewards teamwork appropriately. Design a process that can be modified depending on the size and complexity of projects. Develop a tailored curriculum for project managers to meet specific needs. Specifying or adopting a certification process based on practice as well as formal education helps ensure that project managers apply their knowledge to create successful projects rather than just pass certification exams. Supply performance support tools to support a common and consistent use of the project management process throughout the organization.

For Motivation, the PMO can hold everyone involved in the project accountable for the outcome, process used, and the work of the team as a whole. Enlist support from project sponsors and review board members to support proper use of accepted processes. Push for established career paths specifically for project managers. Rewarding project managers appropriately with competitive compensation and tying that compensation to certification as well as performance helps tremendously to support this success factor.

Basic cultural assumptions related to this success factor are associated with the status and prestige of project management and of project managers in the organization. If project management is considered a core business process, the organization is much more likely to support professional education for project managers as well as a career path for them. If project management is viewed as a set of competencies to use tools and techniques rather than as an organizational process, you may still see support of project management education and career paths. What remains missing would be everything else that we have laid out here.

Economic Value Support

Economic value support is the ninth success factor. This is based on how well the environment supports entrepreneurial or business-focused behavior for the project manager and team. The includes projects' being based in part on a business case that includes market analysis, cash flow, investment analysis, and a listing of all assumptions. When this factor is strong, project managers are fully involved in developing the business case with the support of Marketing and Finance rather than just handed a final business case after the project is approved. The team reviews the business case as part of project start-up. The business case is developed into a business plan as part of the overall project strategy and planning process. The core project team includes key members who will have primary responsibility for managing operations to achieve the project outcome. Information is collected regarding the success of the project outcome, then it is compared to the business case as part of the lessons learned by the organization. This factor is a measure of how much the organization emphasizes return on investment and shareholder value as important requirements for project success.

For Leadership, the PMO can specify a standard for developing a business case as part of the project selection process and require the involvement of Finance and Marketing with project managers to make sure the cases are sound. Identify the role of the project manager in developing the business case and the project team in reviewing the case as part of the project start-up. The PMO can strongly mandate that members of the core team include a key representative of those responsible for operating the project outcome to promote a more holistic development of the total project venture. Developing a review system for an operate-and-evaluate outcome phase of the project and incorporate learning into the project review system will go a long way to broaden the perspective from project-centric to venture-oriented for creating shareholder value.

For Learning, the PMO can develop business acumen among project managers and upper managers involved in project selection. Consider simulations and what-if analysis case exercises to develop the business acumen of all project managers and team members. This training encourages all team members to develop a commercial mind-set and make decisions with the commercial success of the project outcome in mind.

For Means, providing templates and tools to carry out business case analysis helps to support it, as does authorizing the time needed to do the job. Further support comes from providing performance support tools to promote translating business cases into project goals and specifications, and incorporating them into project plans. Use these tools to supply inputs to decision support systems during project execution.

For Motivation, the PMO can hold the relevant actors responsible for their roles in developing proper business cases. Engaging the team in a discussion about the business goals for the project helps incorporate these goals into the team's behavior. Holding the team responsible (along with other organizational associates) for the business success of the project provides the natural consequences to reinforce venture-oriented behavior. Holding the project manager and team accountable for creating a project outcome that meets the commercial goals set out in the business case helps to promote the development of more realistic business cases.

A basic cultural assumption supporting this factor is that everyone can and should influence the economic profit of the organization. Another is that project management is connected to the process of asset utilization that is important for business success. This connection is very evident in a company like Chevron (now ChevronTexaco) where capital expenditures are so large that efficient deployment of capital is crucial and tightly connected to a strong project management process (Cohen and Kuehn, 1996, 1997). This success factor may be inhibited by professional values that favor technical definitions of success rather than business definitions. It may also be inhibited by an internally focused process culture in which economic profit is guaranteed through regulation or some other monopolistic mechanism.

ChevronTexaco represents a good example of what to expect when a PMO sets out on the long journey of embedding project management success factors into the organizational culture. The Chevron side of the company has long been a champion of promoting a project management process. The Chevron Project Development and Execution Process (CPDEP) is acknowledged in the industry and widely used and respected within the company. Chevron contributed to the best practice database for PEAT. Yet it took a long time for the company to get where it is today and it continues to develop and evolve as a project-based organization. CPDEP was developed in 1993 as a response to benchmark data collected between 1989 and 1992 that showed Chevron ranking very low compared to its competitors in the efficient and successful utilization of capital (Cohen and Kuehn, 1996). In an industry that is as capital intensive as big oil this was a serious problem. CPDEP emphasized proper project selection as well as implementation and evaluation—pick the right projects plus execute projects right (Cohen and Kuehn, 1997).

As the process was developed and refined, managers responsible for sponsoring and reviewing projects as well as project managers were trained in the process. The introduction met the usual resistance in the organization and a group was developed to train, consult, and support the process organizationally. This group, the Project Resources Company (PRC), focused on the larger more strategic projects. By the late 1990s it was evident that CPDEP was taking hold for larger projects, but was not widespread in the rest of the organization. The PRC developed a CD-ROM training program to introduce CPDEP training to a wider audience. Live CPDEP training was expanded through the Human Resources organization to include both formal and accidental project managers—people with the title and those who had just found themselves responsible for projects— throughout the organization.

Today there are still parts of the former Chevron organization that are in the process of adapting CPDEP to fit their needs. Now that Chevron has merged with Texaco, the company has a whole new group that will need to incorporate this process and the supporting success factors into their organizational culture. It seems that the process never ends, or at least everyone involved needs to realize that it will take a long time. This started at Chevron in 1989. It has been going on for over twelve years. It is not complete, nor will it ever be. Evolving circumstances and the changing environment mean that the cultural transformation will be an ongoing process of aligning and mobilizing the organization around best practices and the success factors as they evolve to fit the business needs of the organization.

Conclusion: Leading Strategy into Action Through Project Management

This chapter explains the structure and dynamics of organization behavior and cultural change necessary to consolidate a PMO in any organization to accomplish its potential for adding value to the business. It suggests a concrete, coordinated set of actions based on PEAT and L^2M^2 that will help to reinforce behaviors necessary to create an environment for successful projects. These actions increase the potential for environmental changes to become embedded in the organizational culture. These suggestions are not meant to be exhaustive, they simply demonstrate the importance of recognizing the systemic character of organizational change at the technical, behavioral, and cultural levels.

This complicates the role of a PMO in any organization if it is to be truly successful. While the PMO can provide Leadership, it also influences leaders throughout the organization to support the project environment. Training to provide Learning, a classic function of the PMO, is not just for project managers anymore. It has to include team members and all influential stakeholders and suppliers of projects so as to treat the whole project system and promote behavior change and development toward organizational culture change. A successful PMO has the status, influence, and authority to make sure that the Means and Motivation exist to support all aspects of desired change toward a more successful project system. This includes many areas that are outside the traditional sphere of a PMO, such as changing reporting relationships, budgeting resources, and influencing the performance management system. True success will be quite a challenge!

To invest in this challenge effectively will bring impressive returns because project management is much more than a set of competencies, tools, and techniques to organize discrete packages of work. Project management is a core business process essential for implementing the strategy of any company. Through its project portfolio, any organization is creating its future just as its present success is based largely on the project portfolio of its past. Thus creating an environment for successful projects is essential for improving business results. Embedding these PEAT success factors in the organizational culture will create a culture that supports leading strategy into action for business success.

Summary

This chapter lays out suggestions for how to drive the process of transforming the organization's enterprise project management to its ideal state. It demonstrates ways to make the change stick and embed enterprise project management into the culture of the organization. We suggest that the principles of enterprise project management must become habits for everyone in the company to reach final success. A framework is presented that focuses on a combination of action areas. These include Leadership to define the change, Learning to provide the knowledge and skill necessary to support the change, Means to supply the resources for the change, and Motivation to reinforce the change. These are then applied to the important success factors necessary to support enterprise project management:

Strategic emphasis

Upper management support

Project planning support

Customer and end-user support

Project team support

Project performance support

Communication and information systems support

Organization support

Economic value support

The complete successful change agent

- Invokes a project office to take on the role of leading the change
- Provides the learning to support the new ways
- Ensures the resources and all necessary means are in place to carry it out
- Provides motivation
- Uses a framework that supports action toward the ideal vision of enterprise project management
- Realizes that making change stick requires concerted attention and continuous efforts applied systemically across the organization

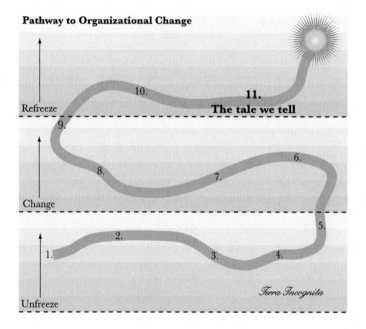

Pathway to Organizational Change

Refreeze

10.

**11.
The tale we tell**

9.

8.

7.

6.

Change

2.

1.

3.

4.

5.

Terra Incognita

Unfreeze

This chapter adds a few concepts and metaphors aimed at cinching the creation of a successful project office. The objective is to reach "the tipping point." We describe templates from workshops that serve a convenient means to plan your approach and record your thoughts. The tale we tell is completed but yours may be just beginning.

CHAPTER ELEVEN

THE TALE WE TELL

It was a dark and stormy night. The cell phone rang. The boss wanted to know "Where is that . . . ?" The program manager didn't have a clue.

The surprise was, this was the first time he heard of this request from the manager. So the dream was really a nightmare.

Many dreams exist for what should be in a final chapter to pull everything together for a book's readers. Fulfilling that dream is especially difficult for such a complex undertaking as changing an organizational culture to realize the potential of a project-based organization. We would love to try to put on one page, in a large font, the secret answer to creating a project office and leading organizational change—but our publisher would not let us take up a page and a half of blank space to make the point, and that is as close as we could come.

The truth is that there is no simple or secret answer. The journey is long and arduous, but for those armed with the drive and support and guidelines herein, well worth the effort. Nonetheless, sometimes you may find that modifying or cutting short the journey may be the right thing to do under the circumstances. Greater value may be obtained by moving on to something else rather than spending valuable resources on something that the culture may never support or reap benefit from.

Taming your chaos starts with naming the resistance. So give real names to the obstacles—lions, tigers, and bears—the upper manager who doesn't get it, the

HR or Training department that insists on reducing project management training to a brown bag "lunch and learn" session, or the Finance department that will not change antiquated accounting procedures. And do not lose hope. Even if all you can do are little things, little things add up.

Reaching for the "Tipping Point"

Malcolm Gladwell (2002) writes about that "magic moment when an idea, trend, or social behavior crosses a threshold, tips, and spreads like wildfire" (back cover). Small changes can make a big difference, just as in chaos theory when small initial conditions can have enormous consequences, however unpredictable.

The ebb and flow or transformation of unknowns into widespread applications may be thought of as resembling epidemics. "Ideas and products and messages and behaviors spread just like viruses do. . . . Epidemics are a function of the people who transmit infectious agents, the infectious agent itself, and the environment in which the infectious agent is operating" (p. 18). The three agents of change, according to Gladwell, are the Law of the Few, the Stickiness Factor, and the Power of Context. We call these the people, the process, and the environment.

People. "In a given process or system some people matter more than others . . . a tiny percentage of people do the majority of the work. . . . Social epidemics are driven by the efforts of a handful of exceptional people" who have social connections, energy, enthusiasm, and personality (pp. 19-21). Gladwell calls them Connectors—people with a special gift for bringing the world together, of making friends and acquaintances; Mavens—people who accumulate knowledge and want to tell others about it; and Salesmen—people who persuade others not only with words but through movement and speech as well.

Process. Some epidemics tip because the message or the agent has changed in a way that makes it more contagious. The question is "how to make messages more contagious?" (p. 20). The Stickiness Factor says small but critical adjustments in the presentation and structuring of information can make a big difference in how much of an impact the message makes. "There is a simple way to package information that, under the right circumstances, can make it irresistible. All you have to do is find it" (p.132).

Environment. "The key to getting people to change their behavior . . . sometimes lies with the smallest details of their immediate situation. The Power of Context says that human beings are a lot more sensitive to their environment than they may seem" (p. 29). "Epidemics are sensitive to the conditions and circumstances of the times and places in which they occur" (p. 139). They "can be reversed, can be tipped, by tinkering with the smallest details of the immediate environment" (p. 146).

Studies show the impact of the Law of the Few and the Power of Context can be enormous: our "inner states—preferences and emotions—are actually powerfully and imperceptibly influenced by seemingly inconsequential personal influences [and] our inner states are the result of our outer circumstances" (p. 152). "We are a lot more attuned to personal cues than contextual cues" (p. 162). Context does matter, however, and environmental tipping points are things we can more easily change.

Gladwell would doubtless concur with the basic premises we propose in Chapter Ten. He writes, "If you want to bring about a fundamental change in people's belief and behavior, a change that would persist and serve as an example to others, you need to create a community around them, where those new beliefs could be practiced and expressed and nurtured. . . . Small close-knit groups have the power to magnify the epidemic potential of a message or idea" (pp. 173–174).

He summarizes by saying that Contagiousness is a function of the messenger while Stickiness is primarily a property of the message. A successful change agent has changed the context of the message, changed the messenger, changed the message itself, and focused the change efforts. Starting epidemics requires:

- Concentrating resources on a few key areas
- Conducting tightly focused, targeted interventions
- Solving problems with the minimum amount of effort and time and cost
- Reframing the way we think about the world
- Believing that change is possible, that people can radically transform their behavior or beliefs in the face of the right kind of impetus
- Knowing it is the nature of people and events to be volatile and inexplicable
- Reaffirming the power of intelligent action

On the other hand. Epidemics grind to a halt when people develop an immunity to the infectious agent. Too much e-mail, too many telemarketing calls and people turn away from the message or the technology. "When people are overwhelmed with information and develop immunity to traditional forms of communications, they turn instead for advice and information to the people in their lives whom they respect, admire, and trust. The cure for immunity is finding Mavens, Connectors, and Salesmen" (p. 175). We come to increasingly value face-to-face communications and word of mouth.

These factors help to explain why the players in the case studies described in this book are so successful. They connect with the right people and create guiding coalitions; they develop streamlined methodologies (processes) and package them to fit the needs of the people and the organization; and they unceasingly work the environment through constant and thorough communications and coaching. There is no one right way to do all this. Both Gladwell's and our case studies show it takes continuous experimentation, sometimes with many little things, to find the combination that works. Perseverance combined with focused efforts on people, process, and environment is what it takes.

Focus on Your Core

Management consultant Geoffrey Moore, in *Living on the Fault Line* (2000), says the new resource scarcity in managing for shareholder value is time, talent, and management attention. Old systems of saving money (cost) are out of synch with a new world that wants us to save a lot of time. He believes too much time is being spent on tasks that are *context*, too little on tasks that are *core*. He passionately argues that *"Any behavior that can raise your stock price is core—everything else is context"* (p. 27). Core tasks differentiate companies in their targeted markets. Context tasks certainly add value but do not contribute to competitive advantage. He recommends outsourcing as distancing the company from context, and "doing it can raise your stock price because it communicates to investors that you are putting your time, your talent, and your management attention to work on core issues" (p. 39).

These issues can help position a project office. One role is to take over context tasks so other people can focus on core tasks, much as Bucero did with HP Consulting. Another role is to take on management of outsourcing, which creates a double benefit. Context tasks are shifted outside the organization, and scarce management attention does not have to spend much time on the outsourcing relationship because the PO takes care of it. An even more powerful role, the strategic project office, greatly facilitates the selection process and execution of core tasks that lead to competitive advantage.

Another way to position a project office is to set it up jointly with the customer. Debra Henrichs of HP's global program management office did this with a large insurance company. The joint office reinforced the intercompany partnership and gave HP greater insights into the customer environment. It was useful to both companies to have a consultative situation for project management, and HP management recognized that their success often depends on customer success. Working sessions whose purpose was to identify project relationships and responsibilities surfaced issues such as these:

- Too many sponsors
- Overlapping resource needs
- Dependencies known but not documented
- Priority-driven requirements and changes were lacking

Joint project office successes included a change control process that turned into a key communication device. The cooperation provided visibility into the "real" project and customer issues and made the escalation path clear. It had a positive impact on financial services performance, allowed customer executives to leverage the experience in a reorganization, and eventually turned it its final deliverables two weeks early. HP and the customer shared project management and software development best practices, and both sides profited. When it comes to increasing the customer and end-user success factor and to focusing on core issues, the joint project office concept is a winner.

Making It Work

We offer a few more obstacles and suggestions for making change stick that might help answer frequently asked questions:

1. A PO was originally aimed at resolving the issues of a specific department. Before implementation, the scope was broadened to include an entire organization. This set off a political feud early on. *Proposed solution: Clarify matters in an executive briefing to top management, in an introductory talk to a larger audience and through one-on-one coaching. Also the PMO should try to meet the needs of all stakeholders.*

2. During the development of a PO, the internal client's expectation of the PO was slanted toward a technological, methodological, software-type solution— a black box that would resolve the ills of project management in the company. The head of the new PO, who was supported by an outside consulting company, was faced with the issue of convincing upper management and other stakeholders that basic PM concepts, training, and processes are necessary before implementing

tools. *Proposed solution: Use literature and opinions from outside experts to influence stakehold-*
ers. Also hold workshops in which the basic issues of project management are discussed.

3. Ten months of work by outside consultants were spent developing procedures for a PMO in the IT department of a telecommunications carrier. Due to a
budget cutback, the implementation stage of the project was canceled. Subsequently, there was a downturn in the market and the IT group was downsized
substantially. *Proposed solution: Wait for better times.*

4. I am a project manager and the organization that I work for does not have
a project office nor intend to establish one. What is it that I can do within my organization? *Proposed solution: Become a Project Office of One. Individuals can embody all the*
traits, skills, and knowledge that we cover in this book. Individuals learning to unfreeze, change,
and refreeze the people around them offer tremendous value.

Organic Metaphors

The California-based authors especially enjoy the beauty of the state's giant redwood forests, containing some of the tallest and oldest trees on the Pacific coast.
The redwood forest, through its root system, is completely interconnected. An interesting thing about redwoods is that they have very shallow roots which make it
difficult for them to survive. Growing along the coastal fog belt in California and
up into southern Oregon, they need the fog to get through dry summers. Shaded
canyons also supply water for their very shallow roots. The root system goes out
as far as a mile; the roots interlock and grow together in a way that allows those
trees closer to the water source to send roots up the hillside and supply water to
trees that are further away. The trees depend upon active teamwork for survival.
Effective teamwork on projects also needs a solid base of interlocking roots.

The project office is a primal means to provide systemic interconnectivity.
Many projects may not survive on their own but are important as part of the organization's ability to offer a total solution to customers. An important role for the
project office is to deliver sustenance across the organization—information, motivation, and resources—so that team members and management alike do the
right projects and do projects right.

A fruit tree is a powerful metaphor for organizational dynamics. Peter Senge
and Daniel Kim (*The Systems Thinker,* Pegasus Communications, May 1997) describe *The Cycle of Knowledge-Creation:* "Like theories, the tree's roots are invisible,
and yet the health of the root system determines the health of the tree. The
branches are the methods and tools, which enable translation of theories into new
capabilities and practical results. The fruit is that practical knowledge. The tree
as a whole is a system."

A gardener has to create an environment for the tree to flourish—he or she cannot command it to grow. Managers in organizations may be tempted or desire to command others to perform, but this approach is like a gardener yelling at a tree and commanding, "Grow!" The tree does not understand the language and pays no heed (this is also true with people!); it performs when soil, fertilizer, sun, and air are in correct balance. The successful gardener does what he or she can to supply these elements in the right quantity at the right time. The tree responds by doing what it innately knows what and how to do—create a bountiful harvest. If managers in organizations want to create an environment for project success, apply a similar approach to empowering project teams.

As a tree's root system absorbs nutrients from the soil, people in organizations develop theories from research (see Figure 11.1). Nutrients flow through the trunk and into the branches and leaves and fruit. Best practice organizations turn theories into methods and tools that they use to create results—project deliverables. These activities are repeatable because they derive from a solid (known)

FIGURE 11.1. CYCLE OF KNOWLEDGE.

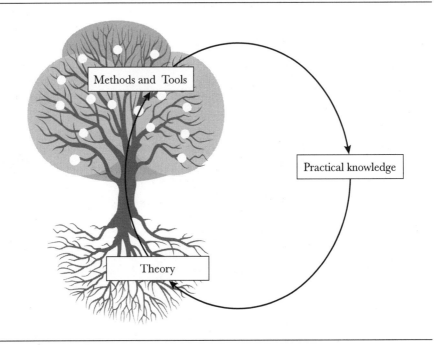

foundation (roots and theories). Pollination is also required for fruit to develop. External sources (such as bees) provide cross-dissemination, a requirement that cannot be satisfied within the organism itself.

Success requires investment in an innovative infrastructure (theories, methods, and tools) and the practical application of knowledge into results (fruit). Knowledge brokers and facilitators provide pollination. The low hanging fruit is easy to harvest. Greater, sustainable results take more effort to climb higher up the tree and gather the rest of the harvest.

The whole process begins with seeds and seed distribution. Seeds represent the potential for an organization. All growth starts small. It then builds linkages and grows organically. Additional growth comes from new branches on old trees. Success creates seeds that seek fertile ground to grow into new opportunities. Many seasons pass before the orchard reaches its full potential.

Change agents in organizations can take solace and inspiration from this natural progression when beginning their journeys. Failing to build a solid root system causes programs (or start-up businesses) to fail. Focus on core, uniting competencies provides the interconnectivity that, in turn, supports business goals to grow sustained performance.

Beginning the process involves discovery of good new problems to solve. Christopher W. Miller, founder of Innovation Focus Inc., says this requires a lot of observing, climbing, and digging (2001, p. 13). "In the early stages, one should stand at the base of your research tree and look up. If you've done your job well, you should see a full, rich canopy of branches and leaves. The implication here is that if there aren't enough branches (patterns and themes) or leaves (implications and needs) you're apt to get all wet when bad weather comes along. Once the canopy is full, it's time to dig down to the roots and find the primary causes of these opportunities (being careful not to kill the tree)."

Ironically, impatient manager-gardeners often yank trees out of the soil. One reason is to determine if the roots are growing—"Is anything happening?" Another is to replace it with another "more appropriate" tree. This practice occurs when interchanging core project team members. These actions, while ostensibly justified as getting status reports or solving short term problems, at the very least seriously impede if not totally stop progress. Knowledge workers are not interchangeable parts. The visioning, commitment-building, and decision-making processes that develop as a team moves from forming through to performing are intangibles that cannot be easily replicated by replacements. A single addition can change the fortunes of a team, and any subtraction from the core has momentous negative effect. Avoid or minimize these distractions as much as possible.

Aligning Projects with Strategic Goals through Project Portfolio Management

One of the most vocal complaints of project managers is that projects appear almost randomly, like weeds in an untamed garden. Projects seem unlinked to a coherent strategy, and upper managers appear to be unaware of the total number and scope of projects undertaken. As a result, people feel they are working at cross-purposes, on too many unneeded projects, and on too many projects generally. Team members struggle to understand how their projects fit into core business competencies. Giving projects a strategic emphasis helps resolve such feelings and is the first move toward creating an environment for successful projects.

Engage in a holistic approach to the problem. Draw from experienced project and program managers and consultants to address:

- A project portfolio management process.
- The role of management teams—any dissension in the ranks of upper management will be reflected in the behavior of project teams.
- Organizational capacity for doing projects—resource utilization has its own tipping point; once over that point, capability rapidly declines.
- Whether you want control or results (pick one or the other).
- Developing accountability for the success of the whole.
- Gaining portfolio buy-in.

Training is not enough. The environment where project managers operate has more to do with their success than their training, skills, or aptitude. Good people always seem to get things done. A great environment enables even average people to achieve extraordinary results. The role and impact of upper managers need to be addressed in any intervention aimed at improving project success.

A key measure for the *value* of project office services may be enduring improvement in your project management practices as a result of its involvement. Get the concepts and practices into the heads and hearts of people so they improve their performance. Clearly link project results with business performance.

Training and presentations need to include *what* to do (and it is hard to find something truly new) as well as *why* and *how* (these are often unique and conjure up fascinating possibilities). Relate experiences from real case studies, and show pictures of people in teams clearly engaged in discussions. Get management teams to simulate what they would do in various scenarios. Through judicious use of video, audio, and stories, create experiences that people remember because more senses are activated and their preferred processing style is engaged.

Project office consulting engagements need to be client-centered. That is, the client sets the objectives and agenda. The consultant brings a disciplined development process and facilitation skills to help make it happen.

Encourage cross-industry fertility. Organizations like the Product Development and Management Association bring a cross-industry focus to new product development. A key principle is that core issues are very similar across industries; the main difference is in the stories they tell.

Implementing the Project Office Review

The Appendix presents two templates from workshops that can serve as convenient means to plan your approach and record your thoughts: "Creating an Environment for Successful Projects" and "Implementing a Project Office for Organizational Change."

The template on Creating an Environment for Successful Projects provides room for individuals or teams to record their PEAT questionnaire scores and action plans. PEAT has nine questions in each category. Here are sample statements to score:

Strategic Emphasis

The project goal is clearly linked to business strategy.

Upper Management Support

Managers of all team members fully support this project.

Project Planning Support

There is a detailed plan developed by the core team.

Customer and End User Input

End users consult with the team on a regular basis.

Project Team Support

All team members feel responsible for the success of the project.

Project Performance Support

The project is staffed with all necessary resources.

Communication and Information Systems

Project team members communicate easily with each other.

Organization Support

A consistent project management process is used.

Economic Value Support

Project decisions link to the project outcome life cycle

Open-Ended Question

What do you think is the most important thing that can be done to improve project management in your organization?

Scoring

1 Never or not at all
2 Extremely small extent
3 Sometimes
4 Average degree or frequency
5 Majority of times
6 Most of the time
7 Always or without fail

Workshop or Web survey participants get data from the benchmark database to compare against. The next step is to decide if your organization excels, is OK, or needs improvement. Then outline necessary action steps that are appropriate for the culture.

Use the following outline in preparation to complete the template on Implementing a Project Office:

Develop a project office vision. What is it that this overall movement toward project offices is meant to achieve? Most organizations are changing (or will change) to become project-based, that is, projects will represent the bulk of business activity. For many organizations this will represent a radical change in management approach. The implementation of a project office (or several offices) will be the vehicle for changing the management practices necessary to transform the organization. Thus the project office movement is the spearhead for the radical organizational change necessary in the next decade. It will totally change the way future organizations are managed.

Define an implementation approach. In many ways the project office has a mission to reeducate the culture of the organization and help its denizens change their ways. History tells us that the approach taken will influence success so that the approach must match the culture of the organization. Guidelines to consider:

• In some organizations what we call the "Quaker" approach is the only way that will work. For example, in organizations with a heavy research component, those run more like universities, the command approach—trying to force change or threaten doom—would be scoffed at and it would fail.

- In other organizations run more along a military model, where members are accustomed to forced change, the Quaker approach would be perceived as weak, so a full-scale, top-down, Attila, CEO-directed change effort would be more successful.
- In either case it is obviously important to consider the organizational culture before forming an implementation plan.
- In all cases it is important to have a sponsor who is influential in the organization. For the Attila approach, a higher-level person is needed. For the Quaker approach, the level may not be as important as the sponsor's stature and breadth of influence.
- The Quaker approach takes time and patience, values notoriously absent in many organizations.

A hybrid approach begins in the indirect Quaker style and moves toward the Attila model if necessary. Organization members can be triaged into one-third "true believers" in project management who can't wait to change, one-third "show me" skeptics who may change if they see the benefit, and one-third "die-hard" grizzled veterans who have seen it all before and will resist to the bitter end. The hybrid approach starts with the true believers who demonstrate, through small wins, the benefits of a project office. This approach helps develop credibility and offers something to show the "show me" gang. When they are converted and you achieve critical mass of two-thirds of the organization, it may be necessary to apply a little top-down command to convince the die-hards. This is a practical and realistic approach for most organizations.

Refine the concept of a project office. What is a project office and where did it come from? Project management began as a countercultural movement. Early project managers worked outside the organization. In fact they were often literally outside—in a trailer at a construction site, where decisions were made regarding the project. The original project office referred to a place for the control of a specific project, what we would now call a project control office. As projects moved inside the organization, the role of the project office has expanded. Guidelines:

- Aim at a particular goal, call it Level 3, to use the terminology introduced in Chapter One, but remember that it may be best to start small, say Level 1, and document benefits of a project office for a few projects. This idea is in concert with the hybrid approach mentioned earlier.
- You need an organizational group, like a council or project management initiative, to give legitimacy in different divisions and to help cross organizational boundaries.
- A physical space is important. It helps the work and also provides group identification.
- Treat the implementation plan itself as a project.

Now document the plan on the "Implementing a Project Office" template provided in the Appendix.

Develop an implementation goal. Specify an important and measurable goal for the endeavor. For example, implement a Level 3 project office to cut cycle time 20 percent and produce 30 percent more new products while maintaining current headcount.

Determine the value to the organization. Why should the organization do this? Will it help implement strategy? Fight competition? Are similar companies doing this? How will life be better when this is done? The value should be stated in business terms best understood by upper managers, such as the ROI of the project office. For example, determine the increase in shareholder value that will result when the stated goal is reached. Calculate the benefits if you had reduced cycle time by 20 percent in the past and how that would have increased value on the last five projects. Then determine how many projects you will do per year to get an estimate of the value of reducing cycle time. Also determine how much the implementation of the project office will cost. From these figures you can determine the project office ROI, a figure that is near to the heart of most upper managers.

Develop a set of metrics to show progress. Be careful here—you will get what you measure, which may not be what you want. For example, you might determine that your staff should attend more stakeholder meetings to help reduce cycle time. However, if you then measure meeting attendance, people will attend plenty of meetings, but cycle time may not be reduced. Ensure that office members and all project managers are well versed in those actions that actually lead to shareholder value in the organization, and then measure those actions.

Determine project office content. What will be in the office? This depends on the goal of the office. Typical functions to be included are project selection and prioritization procedures; mentoring and coaching help for project managers; developing and coaching upper management sponsors for projects; a common set of project management tools, techniques, and methodologies; consulting for ongoing projects; training and project manager development programs; and possibly an administrative home for the project managers themselves.

Develop an implementation plan. With answers to the questions raised thus far, determine how you are going to proceed, what to do first, second, and so on. Then put a detailed action plan together.

A Rewrite

Our greatest challenge is to rewrite the myth of Sisyphus (from Chapter Six). Modern organizations cannot afford futile and hopeless efforts. The new hero sees the value of getting the rock up over the mountain. The rewards, of both the destination and the journey, are clear, convincing, and compelling. They got that way by passionate visionaries sharing their dreams and enlisting a guiding coalition of supporters. The dangers of the rock slipping back impact not just one person but the prosperity of the whole organization—the interconnected community. The rock is carefully chosen while other pebbles are left as is; capabilities are limited to the critical few projects. Resources are aligned on tasks that help to pull the rock up, brace it from falling back, and remove uphill obstacles. Other players keep the lions, tigers, and bears from sidetracking progress.

The tipping point that allows the rock to reach the top and stay there is the right people employing efficient processes in an effective environment. The program is carefully planned, excellently executed, and nurtured once it reaches the top. Because more mountains or opportunities can be seen from the new vantage point achieved by successful programs, the community realizes that the leadership, learning, means, and motivation it developed are the best means to tackle new challenges and expand its prosperity. Ever present is a core team of project officers who gird, goad, and guide.

Summary

The complete successful change agent

- Identifies a sense of urgency
- Lines up a guiding coalition of powerful forces
- Develops a clear, concise, compelling description of how the project office is chartered, structured, and staffed to meet organizational goals
- Communicates this vision across the organization to develop support
- Implements the strategy
- Thrives in the environmental chaos that surrounds any effort to create a new order of things
- Gets the right people on board; trains and supports them to be effective
- Lines up leadership, learning, means, and motivation
- Starts small but leads the drive toward large-scale positive impact on the organization as a result of a strategic project office
- Perseveres and draws upon a wide variety of sociological mechanisms to maintain the organizational change

TEMPLATES FOR
PROJECT OFFICE PLANNING

TEMPLATE 1: IMPLEMENTING A
PROJECT OFFICE FOR ORGANIZATIONAL CHANGE.

Name: _____

Organization: _____

Date: _____

Implementation Goal:

Value Argument:

**TEMPLATE 1: IMPLEMENTING A
PROJECT OFFICE FOR ORGANIZATIONAL CHANGE, Cont'd.**

Metrics:

Content:

TEMPLATE 1: IMPLEMENTING A
PROJECT OFFICE FOR ORGANIZATIONAL CHANGE, Cont'd.

Implementation Plan/Approach:

Procedure/Other:

TEMPLATE 2: CREATING AN
ENVIRONMENT FOR SUCCESSFUL PROJECTS.

Name: _____

Organization: _____

Date: _____

Strategic Emphasis   score _____   benchmark _____

- Emphasis: ☐ more   ☐ less   ☐ OK
- Steps:

Upper Management Support   score _____   benchmark _____

- Emphasis: ☐ more   ☐ less   ☐ OK
- Steps:

Project Planning Support   score _____   benchmark _____

- Emphasis: ☐ more   ☐ less   ☐ OK
- Steps:

TEMPLATE 2: CREATING AN
ENVIRONMENT FOR SUCCESSFUL PROJECTS, Cont'd.

Customer/End User Input   score _____   benchmark _____

- Emphasis: ☐ more   ☐ less   ☐ OK
- Steps:

Project Team Support   score _____   benchmark _____

- Emphasis   ☐ more   ☐ less   ☐ OK
- Steps:

Project Performance Support   score _____   benchmark _____

- Emphasis: ☐ more   ☐ less   ☐ OK
- Steps:

TEMPLATE 2: CREATING AN
ENVIRONMENT FOR SUCCESSFUL PROJECTS, Cont'd.

Communications/Information Systems   score _____   benchmark _____

- Emphasis: ☐ more   ☐ less   ☐ OK
- Steps:

Organization Support   score _____   benchmark _____

- Emphasis   ☐ more   ☐ less   ☐ OK
- Steps:

Economic Value Support   score _____   benchmark _____

- Emphasis: ☐ more   ☐ less   ☐ OK
- Steps:

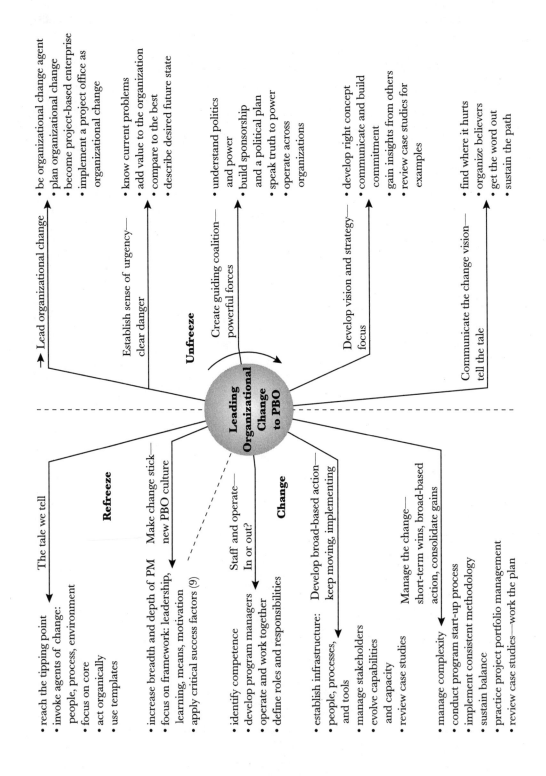

Leading Organizational Change to PBO

Lead organizational change
- be organizational change agent
- plan organizational change
- become project-based enterprise
- implement a project office as organizational change

Unfreeze

Establish sense of urgency— clear danger
- know current problems
- add value to the organization
- compare to the best
- describe desired future state

Create guiding coalition— powerful forces
- understand politics and power
- build sponsorship and a political plan
- speak truth to power
- operate across organizations

Develop vision and strategy— focus
- develop right concept
- communicate and build commitment
- gain insights from others
- review case studies for examples

Communicate the change vision— tell the tale
- find where it hurts
- organize believers
- get the word out
- sustain the path

Refreeze

The tale we tell
- reach the tipping point
- invoke agents of change: people, process, environment
- focus on core
- act organically
- use templates

Make change stick— new PBO culture
- increase breadth and depth of PM
- focus on framework: leadership, learning, means, motivation
- apply critical success factors (9)

Change

Staff and operate— In or out?
- identify competence
- develop program managers
- operate and work together
- define roles and responsibilities

Develop broad-based action— keep moving, implementing
- establish infrastructure: people, processes, and tools
- manage stakeholders
- evolve capabilities and capacity
- review case studies

Manage the change— short-term wins, broad-based action, consolidate gains
- manage complexity
- conduct program start-up process
- implement consistent methodology
- sustain balance
- practice project portfolio management
- review case studies—work the plan

REFERENCES

Bailey, F. G. *Morality and Expediency: The Folklore of Academic Politics*. Chicago: Aldine, 1977.

Berger, L. A., and others. *The Change Management Handbook: A Road Map to Corporate Transformation*. New York: Irwin, 1994.

Berger, L. A., and others. *Deengineering the Corporation: Leading Growth from Within*. Pennsylvania: Haverford Business Press, 1998.

Berger, P. L., and Luckmann, T. *The Social Construction of Reality*. New York: Anchor Books, 1966.

Birkinshaw, J., and Hood, N. "Unleash Innovation in Foreign Subsidiaries." *Harvard Business Review*, Mar. 2001, pp. 131–137.

Block, P. *The Empowered Manager: Positive Political Skills at Work*. San Francisco: Jossey-Bass, 1991.

Block, T. R. "The Seven Secrets of a Successful PMO." *PM Network Magazine*, 2001.

Block, T. R., and Frame, J. D. "Today's Project Office: Changing Attitudes." *PM Network Magazine*, Aug. 2001, pp. 50–53.

Bucero, A. "Implementing the Project Office, a Real Case of Innovation." Paper presented at the IPMA Symposium, Stockholm, June 2001.

Bucero, A. "Seamless Transitions: Managing Change on Difficult Projects." *PM Network Magazine*, Mar. 2002.

Buckingham, M., and Clifton, D. O. *Now, Discover Your Strengths*. New York: Free Press, 2001.

Camus, A. "The Myth of Sisyphus." In *The Myth of Sisyphus and Other Essays*. New York: Vintage Books, 1991. (Original work published 1942.)

Cohen, D. J., and Graham, R. J. *The Project Manager's MBA: How to Translate Project Decisions into Business Success*. San Francisco: Jossey-Bass, 2001.

Cohen, D. J., and Kuehn, J. "Navigating Between a Rock and a Hard Place: Reconciling the Initiating and Planning Phases to Promote Project Success." Paper presented at PMI Symposium, New Orleans, 1996.

Cohen, D. J., and Kuehn, J. "Value-Added Project Management: Doing the Project Right Is Not Enough." Paper presented at PMI Symposium, 1997.

Cooper, R. *Portfolio Management for New Products.* Reading, Mass.: Addison-Wesley, 1998.

Crawford, J. K. (ed.). *The Strategic Project Office: A Guide to Improving Organizational Performance.* New York: Dekker, 2001.

Dai, X. C. "The Role Of Project Management Office In Achieving Project Success." Unpublished Ph.D. dissertation, Department of Management Science, School of Business and Public Management, George Washington University, 2001.

Dinsmore, P. C. "Cookbooks, Restaurants and Enterprise Project Management." In *Winning in Business with Enterprise Project Management.* New York: AMACOM, 1998.

Dinsmore, P. C. "Project Office: Does One Size Fit All?" *PM Network Magazine,* Apr. 2000, pp. 27–29.

Dinsmore, P. C. "It's All About Power." *PM Network Magazine,* May 2001, pp. 27–28.

Dinsmore, P. C. "Project Offices: Best Practices Help Ride Out the Storm." *PM Network Magazine,* May 2002a, p. 24.

Dinsmore, P. C. "Sixteen Reasons Not to Implement a Project Office." *PM Network Magazine,* Feb. 2002b.

Druskat, V. U., and Wolff, S. B. "Building the Emotional Intelligence of Groups." *Harvard Business Review,* Mar. 2001, pp. 80–90.

Englund, R. L. "Linking Strategy and Portfolio at Front End." PDMA *Visions,* July 2000, pp. 22–23.

Englund, R. L., and Graham, R. J. "Speaking Truth to Power" *Today's Engineer,* Summer 1998, pp. 16–20.

Englund, R. L., and Graham, R. J. "From Experience: Linking Projects to Strategy." *Journal of Product Innovation Management,* 1999, *16,* 52–64.

Englund, R. L., and Graham, R. J. "Implementing a Project Office for Organizational Change." *PM Network Magazine,* Feb. 2001, pp. 48–50.

Gallwey, W. T. *The Inner Game of Work.* New York: Random House, 2000.

Gladwell, M. *The Tipping Point: How Little Things Can Make a Big Difference.* Boston: Back Bay Books, 2002.

Graham, R. J., and Englund, R. L. *Creating an Environment for Successful Projects: The Quest to Manage Project Management.* San Francisco: Jossey-Bass, 1997.

Graham, R. J., Englund, R. L., and Cohen, D. J. "Are You Ready for World Class Project Management?" Paper presented at PMI Symposium, Houston, 2000.

Kennel, J., "Creating a Project Management Culture in a Global Corporation." Paper presented at Project World conference, Santa Clara, Calif., 1996.

Kerzner, H. *Strategic Planning for Project Management Using a Project Management Maturity Model.* New York: Wiley, 2001.

Kleiner, A. "The Dilemma Doctors." *Strategy & Business,* 2001, *23,* 74–85.

Kotter, J. P. *Leading Change.* Boston: Harvard Business School Press, 1996.

Kuhn, T. S. *The Structure of Scientific Revolutions.* Chicago: University of Chicago Press, 1996.

Larson, E. W., and King, J. B. "The Systematic Distortion of Information: An Ongoing Challenge to Management." *Organizational Dynamics,* 1996, *24*(3), 49.

Levy, P. F. "The Nut Island Effect: When Good Teams Go Wrong." *Harvard Business Review*, Mar. 2001, pp. 51–59.

Lewin, R., and Regine, B. *The Soul at Work: Listen, Respond, Let Go; Embracing Complexity Science for Business Success.* New York: Simon & Schuster, 2000.

McMahon, P., and Busse, E. "Surviving the Rise and Fall of a Project Management Office." Paper presented at the Project Management Institute Annual Seminars & Symposium, Nashville, Tenn., Nov. 1–10, 2001.

Miller, C. PMDA *Visions*, Apr. 2001, p. 13.

Moore, G. A. *Living on the Fault Line: Managing for Shareholder Value in the Age of the Internet.* New York: HarperBusiness, 2000.

Naisbitt, J. *High Tech High Touch: Technology and Our Search for Meaning.* New York: Broadway Books, 1999.

Pinto, J. K. *Power and Politics in Project Management.* Upper Darby, Penn.: Project Management Institute, 1996.

Project Management Institute Standards Committee. *A Guide to the Project Management Body of Knowledge (PMBOK® Guide).* Upper Darby, England: Project Management Institute, 2000.

Saint-Exupéry, A. de. *The Little Prince* (K. Woods, trans.). Orlando, Fla.: Harcourt Brace, 1971. (Original work published 1943.)

Sandberg, J. "Understanding Competence at Work." *Harvard Business Review*, Mar. 2001, pp. 24–28.

Schneidmuller, J., and Balaban, J., "From Project Management Council to Center of Excellence: The Journey Continues." Paper presented at PMI Symposium, Houston, 2000.

Senge, P. *The Dance of Change: The Challenge of Sustaining Momentum in Learning Organizations.* New York: Currency Doubleday, 1999.

Senge, P., and Kim, D. "The Cycle of Knowledge Creation." *Systems Thinker*, May 1997.

Spicer, E. H. *Human Problems in Technological Change, a Casebook.* New York: Russell Sage Foundation, 1952.

Storeygard, B. "Growing the Professional Project Leader." Paper presented at PMI Symposium, New Orleans, 1996.

Storeygard, R. "The Project Leader Competency Model." 3M internal document released at the PMI Symposium, New Orleans, 1996, as part of the white paper "Growing the Professional Project Leader."

Storeygard, R. "Organizational Deployment of Project Management: The Next Big Aha for Corporate Project Leaders." In J. Knutson (ed.), *Project Management for Business Professionals: A Comprehensive Guide.* New York: Wiley, 2001.

Toney, F. *The Superior Project Manager.* New York: Dekker, 2002.

Wheatley, M. J. *Leadership and the New Science: Learning About Organization from an Orderly Universe.* San Francisco: Berrett-Koehler, 1994.

Woldhek, S. "Zealot Profile." *Strategy & Business*, 2001, *23*, 61.

INDEX

This page is a continuation of the copyright page.